Key Concepts in the Practice of

SUFISM

Emerald Hills of the Heart

3

Key Concepts in the Practice of

SUFISM

Emerald Hills of the Heart

3

M. Fethullah Gülen

Translated by Ali Ünal

TUGHRA
BOOKS
New Jersey

12 11 10 09 1 2 3 4

Published by Tughra Books
26 Worlds Fair Dr. Unit C
Somerset, New Jersey, 08873, USA

www.tughrabooks.com

Library of Congress Cataloging-in-Publication Data for the first volume

Gulen, M. Fethullah
[Kalbin zümrüt tepelerinde. English]
Key concepts in the practice of Sufism / M. Fethullah Gulen.
[Virginia] : Fountain, 2000.
Includes index.
ISBN 1-932099-23-9 1. Sufism - - Doctrines. I. Title.
BP189.3 .G8413 2000
297.4 - - dc21

00-008011

ISBN-13 (paperback): 978-1-59784-204-4
ISBN-13 (hardcover): 978-1-59784-136-8

Printed by
Neşe Matbaacılık Istanbul - Turkey

TABLE OF CONTENTS

INTRODUCTION

The Emerald Hills of the Heart or Key Concepts in the Practice of Sufism

The aspect of Fethullah Gülen's "mission" or personality as a trainer of the human carnal soul may be seen most profoundly and comprehensively in *The Emerald Hills of the Heart*, a four-volume compilation of his writings that had been published over the years in the monthly periodical, *Sızıntı*. In this series, Gülen elucidates the principles of Sufism, or to be more exact, the spiritual and moral facets of Islam—in a sense, those facets which are essential. This is done via a conceptual framework. Those who follow the articles can immediately see that this enunciation or style of analysis of the subject is fundamentally different from the methods followed by others who have laid emphasis on Sufi concepts, such as Abu'l-Qasim Abdulkarim al-Kushayri[1] in *ar-Risala*, 'Ali ibn 'Uthman al-Hujwiri[2] in *Kashf al-Mahjub*, or Ibn Qayyim al-Jawziyya[3] in *Madarij as-Salikin*.

---

1 Abu'l-Qasim Abdulkarim al-Kushayri (d. 1077): A *muhaddith* (scholar of *Hadith*) and *mufassir* (interpreter of the Qur'an). He mostly lived in Naysabur, in eastern Iran. He was the student of the great Sufi shaykh Abu 'Ali ad-Daqqaq. Although he is the author of several important books, he is mostly famous for his *ar-Risala ila as-Sufiyya* ("An Epistle to the Sufis"), which is one of the early books on Sufism. (Tr.)

2 'Ali ibn 'Uthman al-Hujwiri (d. 1073): He was one of the great saints and early writers who wrote about Sufism and Sufi masters. He lived in Ghazni and Lahore in Afghanistan and Pakistan respectively. *Kashf al-Mahjub* ("Revelation of the Veiled") has received great respect from students of Sufism for nine centuries. It contains biographies of certain saints and advice on many subjects such as reflection, generosity, spiritual courtesy, prayer, and love. (Tr.)

3 Ibn Qayyim al-Jawziyya, Muhammad ibn Abi Bakr (d. 1350): A famous, all-round scholar, a disciple of Ibn Taymiyya (d. 1328), and considered among the best repre-

Fethullah Gülen evaluates the heart, which in Sufi terminology signifies the biological heart's spiritual aspect, and which the Qur'an refers to as a spiritual intellect and mind, as the center of all emotions and (intellectual and spiritual) faculties such as perception, consciousness, sensation, reasoning, and willpower. A person's real nature lies in the heart. It is through this intellectual and spiritual faculty that one is able to know, perceive, and understand. Spirit is the essence and inner dimension of this faculty; the biological spirit or the soul is its mount. It is one's heart that God addresses and that undertakes responsibilities, suffers punishment or is rewarded, is elevated through true guidance or debased through deviation, and is honored or humiliated. The heart is also the "polished mirror" in which Divine knowledge is reflected.

The heart both perceives and is perceived. The believer uses it to penetrate his or her soul, corporeal existence and mind, for it is like the eye of the spirit. Insight may be regarded as its faculty of sight, reason as its spirit, and will as its inner dynamics. Faith, knowledge, and love of God and the spiritual pleasure attained through Divine love are the cause of creation and the ultimate aim of the heart.

The heart is the center of the human existence which is considered by God in evaluating humans. God treats people according to the quality of their hearts, as the heart is the stronghold of many elements vital to the believer's spiritual life and humanity: reason, knowledge, knowledge of God, intention, belief, wisdom, and nearness to God Almighty. If the heart is alive, all of these elements and faculties are alive; if the heart is diseased, it is difficult for the elements and faculties mentioned to remain sound. To the same degree that the physical livelihood and existence of the body is dependent on the heart, the organ that is located on the left side of the chest, so too is the spiritual life or the actual existence of humans reliant on the celestial counterpart of that biological heart,

---

sentatives of his school of thought. *Madarij as-Salikin* is a three-volume commentary on Abdullah al-Ansari's *Manazil as-Sairin*, a guide to the *maqamat* or spiritual stations of the Sufi path. (Tr.)

and the two hearts represent two facets of the same reality, insofar as their mutual relationships are concerned.

The heart has another vital aspect or function. It has the points or faculties of "reliance" and "seeking help" ingrained in it and in human nature, by which it enables the individual to perceive God as the All-Helping and the All-Maintaining. That is, it always reminds one of God in the tongues of neediness and seeking help and protection. This is vividly expressed in a narrated Prophetic Tradition, which Ibrahim Haqqi of Erzurum[4] relates as follows:

> "I can be contained by neither the heavens nor the earth," God said.
> He is known by the heart as a Hidden Treasure in the heart.

Belief is the life of the heart; worship is the blood flowing in its veins; and reflection, self-supervision, and self-criticism are the foundations of its permanence. The heart of an unbeliever is dead; the heart of a believer who does not worship is dying; and the heart of a believer who worships but does not engage in reflection, self-supervision, and self-criticism is exposed to many spiritual dangers and diseases.[5] Thus, *The Emerald Hills of the Heart* expounds all the requirements for the existence and sustenance of the heart, its indicators of health, along with the states, degrees and virtues acquired through such vivacity. To be more explicit, this is an effort to articulate the spiritual life of Islam from within a conceptual framework which, rather than perceiving Sufism as an intangible science with peculiar concepts, envisages Sufism as the spiritual facet of Islam, or simply a spiritual life per se.

The Emerald Hills of the Heart, from one vantage point, erects a framework, while from another vantage point it abolishes all limits

---

4 Ibrahim Haqqi of Erzurum (1703–1780) was one of the most outstanding figures in the Ottoman Turkey of the eighteenth century. He lived in Erzurum and Siirt in eastern Turkey. He was a Sufi guide and a prolific writer, who wrote on many subjects such as theology, morality, mathematics, astronomy, and medicine. His *Ma'rifatname* ("The Book of Knowledge and Skills") is very famous and still being widely read. (Tr.)

5 M. Fethullah Gülen, *Emerald Hills of the Heart – Key Concepts in the Practice of Sufism*, (Trans.), The Light, NJ, 2004, Vol.I, p. 26.

and frames. As the spiritual life has more of an "esoteric" nature and as proceeding on the "esoteric" track is both difficult and extremely strenuous, such a journey must be undertaken within a specific framework. Bediüzzaman Said Nursi warns that all the factions that have digressed (on the Sufi path) have been led astray by leaders who have set out into the inner dimension of existence, who for a moment made progress, but because they did not comply with the Sunna, presumed that what they had received meant that they had reached the apex, and thus regressed, misleading both themselves and others.[6] Since journeying on the spiritual path is highly risky and this path contains many special characteristics, those who enter it must observe the principles of Islamic jurisprudence strictly and try to advance in the lights it provides in order to be able to avoid possible deviances. Throughout history, stemming from partial ignorance or neglect of these principles, or simply from dissociation with them due to some theoretical considerations, many Sufi sects, deceptive in their esoteric inclinations, have emerged, while many other deviant sects or factions have sought a safe haven under the protection of Sufism. Hence, for spiritual or Sufi life to advance on the basis of Islamic principles or along the guidelines of Islamic jurisprudence without causing or suffering any digressions, *The Emerald Hills of the Heart* delineates the limits of the spiritual path, illuminating it at the same time with floodlit projectors that it has placed at every stage and station.

While sketching such limits, *The Emerald Hills of the Heart*, as we have indicated, destroys all limits and borders imposed before the spiritual journeying. Such a spiritual progression is virtually infinite, and is comprised of as many stages and ranks as there are believers, from the most honorable of all creation, the Prophet Muhammad, upon him be peace and blessings, to the most ordinary Muslim. Furthermore, although on the one hand this path is accessible to all, from another perspective it has particular lanes,

---

6 Said Nursi, *al-Mathnawi al-Nuri* ("Seedbed of the Light"), The Light, NJ, 2007, p. 190.

along which only very few humans are able to walk. The school of Muhyi'd-Din ibn al-'Arabi,[7] or the doctrine of *Wahdat al-Wujud*, which literally means "the Transcendent Unity of Being," for instance, may be considered to be among the most particular of these lanes. The spiritual path also contains various distinguishing subtle characteristics or particularities that can only be comprehended by those with the ability to brave these rough terrains. Those characteristics or particularities are of such nature that since those that were found in Mansur al-Hallaj[8] (858–922) and Suhrawardi the Slain[9] (1155–1191) apparently opposed the jurisprudential limits of the path, they cost them their lives. *The Emerald Hills of the Heart,* however, is able to evaluate these characteristics both within the boundaries and limits of the Islamic measures and the enormous profundity and infinity of spiritual life.

The Emerald Hills of the Heart presents God through His Attributes and Names such as Uniqueness, Oneness, the First, the Last, the Outward and the Inward, thus profusely illuminating the way. This feature allows for the sciences of theology, Sufism and wisdom, or *Hikmah*, as it is termed in Islam, which is different from philosophy, to emerge from within *The Emerald Hills of the Heart* as a science of *Ma'rifah*, or knowledge of God. These sciences in unison expound a detailed synoptic map of the Divine manifestation and the relationship between the Creator and the created,

---

7 Muhyi'd-Din ibn al-'Arabi (1165–1240): One of the greatest and most famous Sufi masters. His doctrine of the Transcendental Unity of Being, which most have mistaken for monism and pantheism, made him the target of unending polemics. He wrote many books, the most famous of which are *Fusus al-Hikam* and *al-Futuhat al-Makkiyyah*.

8 Husayn ibn Mansur al-Hallaj (857–922) was one of the most famous of Muslim Sufis. He was born in Shushtar in western Iran and lived in Baghdad. He is famous for his utterance "I am the Truth." He is also famous for his austerities.

9 Shihabu'd-Din Yahya as-Suhrawardi (1155–1191) was a Muslim philosopher Sufi, and the founder of the School of Illumination. He was born in Suhraward in present-day northwest Iran. He mostly lived in Syria. *Kitab al-Maqamat* ("The Book of Stations"), *Kitab Hikmat al-Ishraq* ("The Book on the Wisdom of Illumination"), and *Hayakil an-Nur* ("Temples of Light") are among his most well-known books.

which are often alluded to in Islamic Sufism represented by certain particular persons such as Muhyi'd-Din ibn al-'Arabi in the shade of certain mysterious symbols and expressions that are incredibly difficult to comprehend. In addition, both through the concepts and subjects mentioned and certain other concepts and subjects it discusses such as "Heavenly Realms," "Archetypes and the World of Representations or Ideal Forms," *The Emerald Hills of the Heart* presents ontology and draws a metaphysical road map that can shed a light on physics and astrophysics. In addition to these, by way of utilizing such spiritual ranks as *Nujaba* (the Nobles), *Nukaba* (the Custodians), *Awtad* (the Pillars), *Qutb* (the Pole), *Qutb al-Aktab* (the Pole of Poles) and *Ghawth* (the Helper), *The Emerald Hills of the Heart* discusses the relationship between God and His human creation in the most unique and sensitive aspects of this relationship, while at the same time it focuses on the identity of humans as of the best stature and the perfect pattern of creation, and the vicegerent of God on earth by making use of the concept of the Perfect, Universal Human.

Another important attribute of *The Emerald Hills of the Heart,* at least as important as the other attributes mentioned above, if not more so, is that it presents the Islamic spiritual life that constitutes the core of Islam not as a theoretical subject but as lived by the Companions of the Prophet. It presents this life as a profound experience of the heart, mind, and body described and appointed by Islam. It also investigates how it has taken shape throughout history. *The Emerald Hills of the Heart* bequeaths to future ages—a time in which perhaps apparently different realms of religion and reason, science, technology, rhetoric and welfare will, in cooperation, make unprecedented and inconceivable progress—the legacy of Sufism, with all its dimensions, or the spiritual life of Islam in its immense entirety as a safe and sound road that has been protected against all manner of deviations.

***

A note to the reader: Throughout this book, the masculine pronoun may be used in reference to both guides and initiates. However, this should never be understood to be exclusive; it is simply the case that the repetitive use of "he or she" and "him or her" is cumbersome and adds unnecessary complexity to a text which is intended to be, first and foremost, a broad invitation to the understanding of the discipline of Sufism which is inclusive and embracing of all humankind.

Ali Ünal

IRSHAD AND *MURSHID* (GUIDANCE AND THE GUIDE)

Guidance is defined in different ways, among which are directing to the right path, awakening hearts to the Ultimate Truth, helping feelings and thoughts reach God by removing the obstacles between Him and people's minds and hearts, and serving as a means for the souls to have some acquaintance with God, and for the souls who have acquired acquaintance with Him to deepen in their relationships with Him. It consists of educating people individually or in communities and, thus, elevating those endowed with the required capability and merit from among them from being potentially human to being really human, or directing them to the horizon of being perfect humans.

We can also see guidance as a call which a perfect teacher, who has full knowledge of the outer and inner aspects of the Religion and who is able to combine them in theory and practice, makes to those endowed with the required capabilities to be human at a certain level of humanity. From this perspective, we can regard guidance as the special efforts of heroes of spirituality to convey to others whatever of spirituality they have particularly been favored with. In the hands of such heroes, coal has always been transformed into diamonds, and rocks and soil have been raised to the level of gold. The teachers of Sufism have dealt with the matter of guidance and guides in this respect and have considered it as the superhuman effort of those with transcendent qualities. They do not regard endeavors at a low level as guidance, nor do they consider as guides those who are unable to open the doors to the horizon of perfect humanity for souls with the required capabilities. For these, themselves, are in need of guidance and must certainly be trained. A famous Turkish proverb states:

> A guide who himself is in need of special favor
> Cannot know how he can impart favor to others!

It is truly as if this proverb has been coined in regard to such people. Salim Süleyman Üsküdari[10] voices the same consideration in a poetic way:

> Our teacher himself suffers from a lack of knowledge,
> So how can he know what guidance really is?

Ruhi of Baghdad[11] approached the matter a bit more humorously:

> Look at the ascetic: he aspires to be a guide;
> He started school yesterday, today he wishes to teach.

It is a fact that if there is one thing that is the most enduring in this world and the most meritorious in the Hereafter, it is guidance; and therefore a guide is the most valuable person. However, guides can only educate according to their own capacity. It is possible to talk of a wide range of guides, from the spiritual poles or axes to ordinary preachers.

As we have briefly mentioned, guides are, in a general sense, heralds of truth who possess whatever is necessary for guidance, heroes of spirituality, and heirs to the mission of Prophethood, who convey Divine gifts to the hearts. In regard to some aspects of this mission, a guide is also called a "sitter-on-rug" (*postnishin*), or the "elder one" (*shaykh*). The word *shaykh* is also used in the sense of teacher or professor. A guide favored with special nearness to God and special knowledge from God's Presence, and charged and autho-

---

10 Salim Süleyman Üsküdari (d. 1893) was a Mevlevi (Mawlawi) Sufi poet and writer. He lived in Üsküdar, Istanbul, and was well-versed in both prose and verse. (Tr.)

11 Ruhi of Baghdad (d. 1605) was one of the important figures in Ottoman-Turkish classical literature, who usually wrote about moral issues. (Tr.)

rized with the duty of guidance, is different from an ordinary preacher. Ordinary guides find in themselves the truths to be imparted to others according to their own horizon of perception, and convey them to others in accordance with their capacity. However, perfect guides, like the North Star, direct all to the true way, based on the fundamental sources of the Religion, and present to others whatever should be presented out of the depths of their hearts and spirit. As for those who are both a spiritual Pole (*Qutb*) and a Helper or Means of Divine Help (*Ghawth*), they shape whoever enters their atmosphere in the mold of their own horizon, and rebuild them with the material purely from the Qur'an and the Sunna.

At whatever level it occurs, guidance is the most valued among the duties of servanthood, provided it is done purely for God's sake; and any hero of truth who fulfills such a responsibility is a guide who is an heir to the Prophet, upon him be peace and blessings. However, it should be noted that the companionship of a perfect guide has a particular pleasure of its own and bears signs of a possible "meeting" with God, while it is highly difficult to be able to advance in the company of an imperfect one.

A couplet, whose writer is unknown, reads:

Go to a guide, to a guide, a guide,
A guide has a cure for any suffering, O "father!"

Anwari[12] contributes to this meaning with the following:

The mystery lying in, "You will never be able to see Me!"[13] —
Which signifies the impossibility of seeing God's "Face"—
I was not able to understand it

---

12 Awhadu'-Din 'Ali Anwari is a famous poet who lived in the twelfth century in Iran and Afghanistan. Besides poetry, he was adept in logic, music, theology, mathematics, and astrology. His *Diwan*, a collection of his poems, consists of a series of long poems, and a number of simpler lyrics. (Tr.)

13 It refers to the Prophet Moses' desire to see God on Mount Sinai and God's reply to him, saying: "You will never be able to see Me (while in the world)." See the Qur'an, 7:143. (Tr.)

Before my weeping eyes became the Mount of Sinai
with love for Him.
The mystery of the Cloak in which the People of the Cloak[14]
was covered—
I was not able to understand it before I became happy
in meeting a perfect guide.

Now, without going into the differences that arise from the capacity and amount of knowledge each guide has, or the spiritual gifts that each is favored with, I will try to explain the subject in relation to certain essential elements that are found in every guide.

A guide is one who has sufficient knowledge of the relationship between God, humans, and the universe, and the matters concerning this sphere of the Religion. Anyone who does not recognize God is a denier and an ignorant one; and those who are unable to perceive the relationship between Him and existence are blind and unaware of the real nature of their existence, while one who does not know himself is, in fact, lonely and a stranger amidst existence. All of these types of human beings themselves are in need of guidance.

A guide is a hero of spirituality, one who is a careful student of the Qur'an and the book of the universe, and one who has an inquiring mind which has an acquaintance with existential mysteries. A guide is also a sagacious, insightful one with eyes that are observant of things, a tongue busy with reciting the Qur'an, and ears that listen to it. With sound and accurate sense perceptions, profound and comprehensive observations, and powerful reasoning, a guide is distinguished with the manners that are found in a Prophet at a perfect level. Such a person has a universal viewpoint in dealing with matters, is careful of the intersecting points of the revealed rules and commandments and the Divine laws of creation and life. These indi-

---

14 God's Messenger, upon him be peace and blessings, once gathered together 'Ali, his cousin and son-in-law, Fatima, his beloved daughter, and their sons Hasan and Husayn under his cloak, and said: "O Lord, these are my family." (*Muslim*, "Fadail al-Ashab" 32; *at-Tirmidhi*, "Manaqib," HN: 3726.) After this event, together with the Messenger himself, these people came to be called "the People of the Cloak." (Tr.)

viduals seek only God's good pleasure and approval in conveying to people what God wants them to convey and in communicating whatever is inspired into them to needy souls, thereby considering His nearness in whatever they do and say.

Guides are those individuals who try their utmost to proclaim, on any platform, the cause on which they have set their heart in a mood of dedication, and who mediate between what should be conveyed to others and those to whom it should be conveyed. As they never think of any wage, compensation, or reward, they also attribute any material or spiritual return coming, without expectation, to the sincere efforts of those around them. Without ever appropriating whatever spiritual gifts come to them personally, they regard their followers as a means for the arrival of these gifts. This is, without doubt, self-denial; but in a true guide's sight, it is what an ordinary Muslim should do, not something worthy of acclamation. Such true guides never expect others to appreciate their activities, nor do they aim by them at any worldly or otherworldly outcome, except God's good pleasure and approval. They are always sincere and upright before God, for they are aware that they follow the way of the Prophets and that this way has certain rules to observe, the most important of which is that any guide should pursue only God's pleasure in the act of guiding others.

A guide is also a hero of love and tolerance, one who has full knowledge of his audience or followers with all of their characteristics; a guide keeps them under wings of compassion, shares their joys and grief, congratulates them on their accomplishments, and ignores their faults and deficiencies. Like sources of fragrance, such guides diffuse "incense" to satisfy needy hearts; like candles, they consume themselves to illuminate the dark souls around them, for the well-being of the latter. They find true happiness in the happiness of others and avoid no sacrifice in conveying their ideals. They die in order to revive; weep in order to make others laugh; become tired to enable the rest of others; strive constantly in order to be able to awaken others to eternity—without paying any attention to either sincere or insincere appreciation, or to unfair criticisms. They beg God's forgiveness in the face of compliments, welcome any rightful reactions and criticism, and go on without faltering.

A guide is a wise one equipped with the necessary knowledge of both religious and certain secular sciences to discuss different subjects with an audience and present satisfactory solutions to their problems. In the Naqshbandiya Order, the duty of guidance was not entrusted to those who did not successfully complete all the courses taught in the madrasas or who could not combine spiritual and intellectual enlightenment. Rather, the lodges where the elders or guides of this school taught were each like a fountain of Khadr[15] at which those studying were able to quench their thirst. Any houses of guidance where guides of such caliber did not, or do not, teach are no different from ruins; those who claim guidance in them are deceived and the people who hope for illumination in such centers, which are themselves devoid of light, are indeed unfortunate ones.

Do not offer your hand to whoever claims guidance,
For he may lead you to a slope which is impossible to climb,
Whereas the path of a perfect guide
Is easy enough to follow.

Niyazi Mısri[16]

However transcendent in general knowledge and knowledge of God they may be, in particular, guides are perfect preachers who can combine, in a balanced way, their ascension toward God while still maintaining the level of their audience when conveying to them what they should convey. They always consider the dispositions, feelings, and thoughts of those whose education they have

15 (al-)Khadr is he with whom the Qur'an recounts (18: 60–82) the Prophet Moses made a journey to learn something of the spiritual realm of existence and the true nature of God's acts in the world. It is controversial whether he was a Prophet or a saint with a special mission. It is believed that he enjoys the degree of life where one feels no need for the necessities of normal human life. (Tr.)

16 Mehmed Niyazi Mısri (d. 1694), a Sufi poet who was born in Malatya (Turkey), educated in Egypt, and lived in Istanbul and Edirne. (Tr.)

shouldered, and they avoid causing any misunderstandings or ambiguity in conveying the messages that arise from the particular gifts they have received in the horizon of their relationship with God. A true guide is a strict follower and meticulous student of the Qur'an and is, therefore, obliged to follow the Qur'an in the duty of guidance. Despite being the Word of the All-Great, All-Transcendent One, the Qur'an came to the horizon of the Prophet, upon him be peace and blessings, not in a wholly transcendental manifestation of the Divine Attribute of Speech, but rather, in consideration of the levels of all its audience. Thus, just as the Qur'an addresses humankind according to their many levels of understanding, its first and greatest communicator—and the greatest of all guides—the Prophet Muhammad, upon him be peace and blessings, also considered the different levels of his audience and said: "We, the community of the Prophets, have been ordered to address people according to their capacity of understanding."[17]

Guides speak with the sublimity of their character, the depth of their spirituality, and the language of their actions. They are exceptionally faithful and devoted to God Almighty. It is an undeniable truth that those whose words do not conform to their actions and who are not trustworthy by their own actions cannot have any positive, lasting influence on people; thus, their message cannot be acceptable. The only way for those things that are said to be acceptable to the human conscience is the unshakable conviction of the truth of those things and the practice of them in one's life. It is reported that God Almighty said to the Prophet Jesus, upon him be peace: "O Jesus! First give advice to your own soul, and only after you have accepted and followed it, then give it to others—or else be ashamed of Me."[18] This is in perfect conformity with what the Qur'an quotes from the Prophet Shu'ayb, upon

17 ad-Daylami, *al-Musnad*, 1:398. (Tr.)

18 *Ibid*., 1:144; Abu Nu'aym, *Hilyat al-Awliya*, 2:382.

him be peace: "*I do not want to act in opposition to you (myself doing) what I ask you to avoid.*" (11:88)

> *O God, make us among Your servants who are sincere and who have been endowed with sincerity in faith and in the practice of the Religion, and honor us with following the Lord of those who have been endowed with sincerity, upon him be the greatest of blessings and perfect peace, and on his Household and noble Companions.*

SAFAR (JOURNEYING)

Literally meaning being transported from one place to another, journeying in the language of the Sufis is described as being freed from living a restricted life with carnal or bodily concerns and bounds, and turning to God on the horizon of the heart. It can be viewed and dealt with within the concepts of "journeying toward God," "journeying in God," and "journeying from God."

Turning to God or journeying on His way begins with a person's conscious decision and continues along the bridges of belief, the practice of Islam in daily life, and attaining excellence in one's deeds in awareness that God always sees us and whatever we do. It requires sincerity and purity of intention in faith and the practice of Islam, as well as austerity, asceticism, righteousness, and piety. It continues until the point where the Divine Being, Who introduces Himself to us with the words, *We are nearer to him than his jugular vein* (50:16), favors the wayfarer, who feels invaded by His love and being attracted by Him and experiences an overflowing zeal toward Him, with special nearness to Him. Those who have reached this point and feel this nearness in their spirit cannot help but utter, "There is no longer any space, neither in the heavens nor in the earth!" Without stopping, they continue their journeying, which has now passed beyond time and space.

Journeying occurs at various levels and forms according to how the initiate has been prepared for it, the extent of his own spiritual capacity and, more than anything else, according to the particular gifts with which the One Who is nearer to everything than itself will favor him.

Journeying begins with reflection on the outer world and the human inner world, and by perceiving God's particular manifestation of His mercy and His assistance amidst His overall manifestations of His Names in the light of belief in Divine Unity, and by feeling this particular manifestation in one's inner world with pleasure. This journey, which can be viewed as journeying toward God, continues with the continuous sipping of Divine knowledge by observing His unique stamp on whatever there is in the universe, from the earth to the farthest galaxies. Initiates making this journey never set their hearts on anything other than God, but spend unending efforts to turn to God in their hearts, continuing their relationships with other things and beings only with respect to the fact that they are, in truth, also indicators of God. As long as they feel the breezes that emanate from this proceeding on the way to God in the depths of their hearts or observe their horizon of being favored by God on their peaks, they feel more and more provoked to rise higher and boil from the depths of their hearts in the virtuous circle of observation and pleasure. This state of theirs can be viewed in the light of the verse, *Those who keep from disobedience to God in reverence for Him and piety: when a suggestion from Satan touches them—they are alert and remember God, and then they have clear discernment* (7:201). An initiate who has reached this elevated horizon sees, feels, and evaluates everything differently and displays continuous changes from a lower state to a higher one.

In the second stage of journeying, or in the second journeying, initiates free themselves from different pieces of information that have been collected from different sources and proceed toward unity in thought on the horizon of knowledge of God, exhibiting this unity through all their faculties. This stage can be viewed as "journeying in God," and it consists of an initiate's feeling through the Divine Names the Divine Being Himself called by these Names; and his experiencing the protection and direction of the Divine Attributes; and regarding his innate poverty as a means of pride, continuously progressing toward Him on his particular horizon through the perception of his own innate poverty and helplessness. Initiates in this second stage are always aware of Him, are satisfied with their knowledge of Him, voice Him, and experience themselves in His company at all times. Some call this stage journeying in "the company of the Ultimate Truth." Heroes of spirituality who have reached this peak on the horizon of being aware of the Divine Names watch what is beyond through the prism of the Divine Attributes, and cast their nets of spiritual faculties to catch mysteries. Like sunflowers always turning their faces to the sun, with the eyes of their hearts fixed on a certain point on the horizon, and their consciences conducting business with the Divine Being, they act in great awe of the Divine Presence, shuddering at realizations which they feel according to their level. Every one of their states displays the truth voiced in, *They do whatever they do and give whatever they give in charity and for God's cause, with their hearts trembling at the thought that they are bound to turn to their Lord. It is those (illustrious ones) who hasten to do all kinds of virtuous deeds, and they are in a virtuous competition with one another in doing them* (23:60–61). When they turn their eyes to the sensed existence, they notice the Divine Names; and when they contemplate what exists beyond the sensed existence, they are struck with wonder and amazement.

One drowned in such knowledge of God cannot
distinguish between the Names
and He Who is called by these Names;
The disciples of the guides of the Order of Jilan are
cognizant of such mysteries.

M. Lutfi[19]

The third type of journeying or the third stage of journeying consists of going beyond the difference between the outward and the inward in existence and the Religion, and being favored with the unshakable conviction of and experiencing God's particular

---

19 Muhammed Lutfi Efendi (1868–1956): One of the Sufi masters who lived in Erzurum. He has a *Diwan* containing many beautiful, lyrical poems. (Tr.)

manifestations on oneself and relations with oneself as an individual, as well as the overall manifestations of His Names throughout the universe. This highest point in journeying corresponds to the horizon of feeling absorbed in Divine Existence. This absorption must never be thought of as Incarnation or Union,[20] both of which are false beliefs. Rather, it means going beyond all opposites in the sensed dimension of existence and experiencing the transcendent unity that encompasses and operates in everything. As explained by Jalalu'd-Din ar-Rumi,[21] absorption means that initiates feel annihilated in their horizon of knowledge and love of God. This rank, which is described in the Qur'an (53:9) as nearness to the point where there is *only a distance between the strings of two bows (put adjacent to each other), or even nearer (than that),* essentially belongs to the Prophet Muhammad, upon him be peace and blessings. And those who have reached the final point of nearness to God and sainthood can experience its shadow, each according to their particular capacities, and are freed from all opposites and dichotomies in their hearts.

We can mention another type of journeying. This type of journeying is particular to the heirs of the mission of Prophethood. It consists of turning back among the created after completing ascension to the Creator and feeling absorbed in His Existence. It is such a particular Divine favor that, having set their feet firmly on the Divine Oneness, initiates who are distinguished by it deepen their ascension with "descent," with the zeal of conveying to others all their experiences and the gifts with which they have been, are, and will be, favored. These initiates become the translators of the Creator among the created. This type or stage of jour-

---

20 Incarnation means God's taking the form of a human being and being seen in this form, while Union means a person's joining Divinity or being one with God. (Tr.)

21 Jalalu'd-Din ar-Rumi (1207–1273): One of the Muslim saints and Sufi masters most famous in the West. He is regarded as the founder of the Mevlevi Order of the whirling dervishes, famous for his *Mathnawi*, an epic of the religious life in six volumes. He lived in Konya, Turkey. (Tr.)

neying, which is also called "journeying from God and with God," is the most valuable and meritorious of journeys and is another title to designate the rank of having reached the highest point.

Those who have achieved this last journeying sometimes seem strange and are estranged among people. However, conscious of their being favored with Divine company, they spend lives in an atmosphere where they always feel the breeze of Prophetic congratulations: "How happy are those estranged!"[22] They constantly feel the breezes that flow from the worlds beyond and the next world and they experience both of the worlds together.

Some of the Sufi elders regard the beginning of journeying as "journeying," and its end as "residence." Some others approach both the beginning and end as "residence," while still others see the journey, with all of its stages, to be "journeying."

There are some different considerations concerning journeying that arise from differences of temperaments and schools of Sufism. Believing that they are not directly related with journeying itself in its essential nature, we will be content with briefly mentioning the concept of "journeying in the native land (*safar dar watan*)," which the followers of the Naqshbandiya Order regard as one of the eleven essentials of journeying. We will also give a short definition of the other essentials.

Safar dar watan (journeying in the native land) is used when a traveler toward God is freed from bad morals and the influence of carnal desires, being equipped with angelic attributes. This is in conformity with the saying of the Greatest of Migrants in God's cause, upon him be peace and blessings: "A migrant in God's cause is the one who migrates from what God has forbidden."[23]

The other eleven essentials, each of which is expressed with a particular term, are as follows:

---

22 *Muslim* "Iman" 232; *at-Tirmidhi*, "Iman" 13. (Tr.)

23 *al-Bukhari*, "Iman" 4; *Abu Dawud*, "Jihad" 2. (Tr.)

- *Hush dar dam* (Awareness in every moment): This means that initiates are conscious of what they do and are aware that God sees them at every breath. An initiate who accomplishes this is regarded as one who constantly remembers and mentions God.
- *Nazar bar qadam* (Noticing one's steps): This signifies that travelers toward God are always careful of where they put their feet and how they take each step. It also describes how travelers fix their eyes upon God without ever setting their hearts upon anything or anyone else.
- *Halwat dar anjuman* (Secret meeting amidst crowds): This term, which signifies that an initiate is alone with God while among people, implies the reaction of the Naqshbandiya against seclusion. They maintain that seclusion suggests a secret desire for renown, whereas social life prevents such a desire and is preferable in respect of being beneficial to people.
- *Yad kard* (Remembrance): This term means that travelers toward God should keep their inner world under constant supervision, holding their breath and mentioning God in their hearts. This can also be described as remembrance or mention of God through the heart.
- *Baz kasht* (Distinguishment): This is what is meant in the verse, *When you are free (from one task), resume (another task)* (94:7), and it denotes how initiates resume a new good deed after they finish their invocations. It is the summation of "O my God! You are the One Whom I seek out, and Your good pleasure is what I yearn for."
- *Nigah dasht* (Noticing): This means more than self-supervision and denotes being meticulously careful about one's inner world, trying not to think of, or remember, anything other than God. It varies in degree according to capacities.
- *Yad dasht* (Keeping in mind): This denotes what the Qur'anic term *ihsan* (excellence, perfect goodness) means. It is used to express that initiates should continually act in the awareness that God always sees them and their actions.

- *Wuquf zamani* (Awareness of time): This signifies that initiates who have almost reached the final point in journeying should be awake and employing the utmost care and self-possession, acting with insight at every moment of their lives. It is often regarded as one of the significant spiritual stations toward the final point in journeying.
- *Wuquf adadi* (Awareness of number): This is a term used to describe how initiates should be careful to mention certain words or phrases in the exact number that their guide wants them to.
- *Wuquf kalbi* (Awareness of one's heart): This term signifies that initiates who have reached the final point in journeying should turn to God with all their faculties and concentrate on Him. It is a state belonging to those who have reached the peak.

May God guide us and you to the safe and sound way, and may His blessings be upon our master, Muhammad, full of pity and compassion, and on his Family and Companions, who were noble, godly and virtuous.

WASIL (ONE WHO HAS REACHED)

Wasil denotes a hero of spirituality who has reached the final point in the journey made to attain perfect knowledge of God and is meticulously careful to follow His decrees in parallel with the profundity of that knowledge. A *wasil* has also reached the highest point on the horizon of the heart and spirit, where he or she can observe the Divine manifestations. In Turkish, such an individual is also called an *eren* (one who has attained and been matured, or one with perfect attainment).

With the term *wasil,* we indicate a hero of truth whose particular efforts have been crowned with particular aid, and whose particular instances of turning to God and devotions with particular sainthood, and who has therefore been honored with an indescribable nearness to God. A *wasil* is a sincere one who is continuously drawn toward God in spiritual raptures, and who has programmed his or her will to reach and meet with the Ultimate Truth. Such a one is also a guide who leads others to God without any deviation. Tokadizade Şekip[24] draws attention to this attribute of a *wasil*:

My star was dim and my fortune did not smile on me;
All the days of my life were passing in darkness.
But it was a day when one with perfect attainment came to my aid,
Then I lived glorious days, and I experienced happy ages.

Whether during journeying or upon reaching the horizon of meeting with God, a *wasil* is extraordinarily meticulous in God's

24 Tokadizade Şekip was one of the Turkish poets and writers who lived in Izmir in the first half of the twentieth century. He wrote in favor of freedom during the reign of the Ottoman Sultan Abdulhamid II, and was one of the founders of the Association for Defending the Basic Rights in Izmir. (Tr.)

orders and prohibitions, and tries his utmost to perform the duties of worship fully, constantly considering His inconceivable Grandeur. Even though they are completely sincere and earnest in their devotions, still they tremble with fear that they are unable to observe their duties toward God. With sensitivity proportionate to their efforts, and with a transcending profundity, they do their best to carry out their responsibilities. Such sincere and profound devotions and continuous, earnest efforts receive extra favors from God Almighty. As stated in the Prophetic Tradition, whose meaning is directly from God, *When I love him, I become his power of hearing with which he hears, and his power of sight with which he sees,*[25] the Almighty, with ever-flowing gifts, makes the *wasil* hear what will be heard and see what will be seen, and has such a one travel around the station of being loved by Him to reach horizons where the *wasil* will fully grasp the things which are pleasing to Him.

Though all those who have reached the final point discussed have common perfections, it is a reality that there are some significant differences among them with respect to the specific nature and relative comprehensiveness of their attainments.

Some of them are in unceasing rapture, drowned in the experience of being in the constant company of God, and lead their life fixed on their target with their intellect, logic and reasoning under the direction and protection of Divine manifestations. Any deviation from their target is out of the question, for since their being or self-consciousness has been burned away with the rays of the Divine "Face," they cannot see, hear, or feel anything other than Him and they live in constant spiritual intoxication. Their intoxication is to the extent that they never think of calling at the shores of sobriety or the quays of carnal reason. It can actually be said that even if they want to think of doing so, they are unable to. It is true that some certain temperaments who have reached this rank have suffered some confusion, but

25 *al-Bukhari*, "Riqaq" 38; Ibn Hibban, *Sahih*, 2:58. (Tr.)

this has rarely taken place. Some among this rank may lose their power of reason, which makes humans responsible for their acts, simply because of the intensity of their feelings of attraction toward God; thus, some of their resulting attitudes, words, and acts may be contrary to the rules of Shari'a. The utterances of Jibali Baba,[26] for instance, and words such as, "There is nothing but God in my cloak!", "Glory be to me, how grand I am in respect of my essential qualities!", and "I am the Truth!"—which were uttered by Bayazid al-Bistami,[27] Junayd al-Baghdadi,[28] and Mansur al-Hallaj, respectively, men who were considered to be among the greatest figures of the Sufi way—and other similar statements are effectively attributable to the intensity of the feeling of attraction and to their spiritual intoxication.

Contrary to the exhaustion and calmness caused by unions in physical terms, a *wasil* is always active, as if programmed to act, observe, love, and learn incessantly. This is why there is a continuity in the relationship of the *wasil*'s spiritual life with eternity, while carnal love dies away because of this union. The spiritual union or meeting with God at the end of the spiritual journeying is so different that its pleasure continues to deepen more and more; one who has reached this point experiences ever new instances of union, as if favored with union at every moment. Nasimi[29] voices

---

26 Jibali Baba is one of the saints who lived in Istanbul just before its conquest by the Turks in 1453, and died during the conquest. According to some, he is Jebe Ali Pasha, who was one of the saintly commanders of the Turkish army during the conquest. The district Jibali in Istanbul was named after him. (Tr.)

27 Abu Yazid (Bayazid) al-Bistami (d. 804–874): One of the greatest Sufi masters. He was from Bastam, Iran. Junayd al-Baghdadi said: "Abu Yazid holds the same rank among us as Gabriel among the angels." His life was based on self-annihilation and the practice of devotion. (Tr.)

28 Junayd al-Baghdadi (830–910): One of the most famous early Sufi masters. He lived and died in Baghdad. He enjoyed great respect and was known as "the prince of those having knowledge of God." (Tr.)

29 Imadu'd-Din Nasimi (1369–1417): Azerbaijan's outstanding poet of the fifteenth century, wrote in Azerbaijani Turkish along with Arabic and Persian. He was very accomplished in lyric poems. (Tr.)

this kind of union, which is the highest point to be reached for a traveler toward God, as follows:

The place where I am has developed into no-space;
This body of mine has become a soul completely;
God's Sight has manifested Itself to me;
And I have seen myself intoxicated with His meeting.
A call has come to me from the Truth:
"Come, O lover, you have intimacy with Us!
This is the place of intimacy;
I have seen you as a faithful one!"

In order to be able to reach this point, a very important factor for the traveler, in addition to a particular aspect of human free will, is a feeling of attraction toward God. It is said that a feeling of attraction toward God, the Ultimate Truth, is actually better than the act of worship formally carried out by humanity and the jinn, and this has been circulated among the saints to emphasize that the feeling of attraction toward God is a means of God's nearness, which both humans and jinn can attain through repeated, regular worship.

The feeling of attraction sometimes comes as a Divine favor in return for an initiate's sound intention and steadfastness to reach God, and it serves them for reaching the heaven of perfections in an instant. At other times, it happens in order to save initiates from the troubles of journeying, as God Almighty favors them with the partial or particular manifestation of the truth stated in, *All-Glorified is He Who took His servant for a journey by night* (17:1), carrying them to the point where they can experience God's nearness according to their capacity. In whatever way it occurs, there can be no doubt that this feeling of attraction is a gift from the All-Merciful.

In one of his poems in his *Diwan Kabir*, Jalalu'd-Din ar-Rumi describes an instance of meeting with God, which he attained through such a feeling of attraction, as follows:

The mount of love of meanings has taken away both my reason and heart. Ask me where it has taken them. It has taken them somewhere beyond which you cannot know. I have

> reached under an arch where there is no moon, nor skies. I have arrived in such a world that it is no longer a world. When the All-Beloved Soul appears like the Canopus[30] from the side of the Pillar of the Yemen[31] beyond all terms of quality and quantity, no longer does the moon, nor the sun, nor the pole of the seven heavens remain. The lights of the All-Beloved Soul overwhelm all of them.

The ascension toward God and meeting with Him which was achieved by the great saints, according to the capacity of each, is a manifestation of the Ascension of the Messenger of God and his meeting with God, which is expressed by Süleyman Çelebi[32] as follows:

> At that moment, the Divine Being manifested
> Himself in such overflow that
> There was no longer space or the heavens.

The difference between the ascension and meeting with God that is achieved by great saints who follow in the footsteps of the Messenger, which are a manifestation of his Ascension and meeting with Him, compared to the Messenger's own Ascension and meeting with God, is as great as the difference between a saint and the Messenger.

Among those who have reached the final point of nearness to God are others who, having drowned in the spiritual experience where the existence of all things and beings including themselves is annihilated in the Eternally and Truly Existent One's Own existence, crown self-annihilation in the ocean of annihilation with a return to life in the horizon of sobriety. They do so in order to be able to have

---

30 Canopus is the brightest star in the southern constellation of Carina, and the second brightest star in the night-time sky, after Sirius. (Tr.)

31 The Pillar of the Yemen (*Rukn Yamani*) is the southern corner of the Ka'ba which faces Yemen. (Tr.)

32 Süleyman Çelebi (1351–1422) is the writer of the famous *Mawlid* (whose original name is *Wasilat an-Najat*, meaning "The Means of Salvation"). He lived in Bursa, Turkey. *Mawlid,* which was composed and is widely read in Turkey on certain occasions is a long poetical history of the Prophet Muhammad's life and his matchless virtues and achievements. (Tr.)

others feel the spiritual pleasures they have achieved, through the windows of the states and stations they have attained, and thus they share the favors that have been accorded to them with those souls that are capable of receiving. Thus, as a requirement of being heirs to the mission of Prophethood, they graciously return among us.

These noble servants of the Ultimate Truth are extremely meticulous in observing the Divine orders and prohibitions, both at the beginning and end of their journeying. They never display attitudes or make utterances which do not conform to the rules of the Shari'a, either in their experiences of attraction toward God, or in the peaks of their disclosures and observations of the Divine truths where the lights of the Divine Face burn away everything. Without exhibiting any attitude that is irreconcilable with servanthood to God, they always try their utmost to carry out whatever servanthood to God requires their willpower to do, as decreed in, *And (continue to) worship your Lord until what is certain (death) comes to you* (15:99). They carry out their duties of service according to the depth of their knowledge of God and love of Him, and commensurate with their experiences of attraction. They prefer being servants at the door of the Ultimate Truth to all other achievements and stations, and they always give precedence to servanthood to Him over the rewards that come from Him. Regarding their knowledge of Him as insufficient on any given occasion, they emphasize their inability to give due thanks for God's favors to them. Saying, "We have not been able to worship You as worshipping You requires, O Worshipped One," they confess that they have not been able to do anything worthy of mention in the name of worshipping God. With the words, "We have not been able to know You as knowing You requires, O Known One," they excuse themselves for their lack of sufficient capacity of knowing God. And by uttering, "We have not been able to thank You as thanking You requires, O Thanked One," they sigh with a deep sense of shame as they are unable to give due thanks for the limitless favors of the All-Favoring.

These people of great stature are extraordinarily self-possessed, exceptionally aware, and full of feelings of fear and awe, even when carrying out their duties with the deepest commitment and responsibility. It can be said that their inner worlds are best pictured and manifested by the Divine declaration, *Who do whatever they do and give whatever they give in charity and for God's cause, with their hearts trembling at the thought that they are bound to return to their Lord (remaining anxious, for they are unsure whether God will accept from them and be pleased with them). It is those (illustrious ones) who hasten to do all kinds of virtuous deeds, and they are in a virtuous competition with one another in doing them* (3:114). In any case, God knows the ultimate truth in all matters.

> *O God! Show us the truth as truth and enable us to observe it, and show us falsehood as falsehood and enable us to avoid it. And bestow Your blessings and peace upon our master, Muhammad, whom You have chosen among all creation, made perfectly pure, and favored with Messengership, and on his Family and Companions, whom You have chosen and favored with blessings.*

SAMT (SILENCE)

Literally meaning avoiding speech and keeping silent, *samt* is used by the Sufis to describe keeping silent or preferring silence in self-possession to avoid the useless or harmful utterances that one can make while speaking. Aware of the Divine warning, *Not a word does he utter but there is a watcher by him, ever-present* (50:18), the term *samt* also means that one should speak when necessary and only for the good pleasure of God, uttering words that are pleasing to God. The saying of the glorious nightingale of creation, the Prophet Muhammad, upon him be peace and blessings, "Either speak of good or keep silent,"[33] is a most concise, decisive definition of *samt*, and provides the frame of reference that one should remain within when speaking and keeping silent. We should also remind ourselves of another saying attributed to him: "Let your speech be wisdom, and your silence reflection."[34]

Speaking too much, in particular speaking empty words, is something that has always been condemned and regarded as one of the sinful acts which lead people to perdition. Those who have been initiated into spiritual journeying to God have continuously been warned against speaking too much and against useless words as this is a sinful act of the tongue. It has been emphasized that eating too much, sleeping too much, and speaking too much are each a collar around the necks of the travelers to God, chains on their feet, and handcuffs around their wrists—for they lead one to make frequent mistakes and commit frequent sins. The saying

33 *al-Bukhari*, "Adab" 31; *Muslim*, "Iman" 74. (Tr.)

34 al-Ghazzali, *Ihya' 'Ulum ad-Din*, 1:3; 2:228. (Tr.)

attributed to Caliph 'Umar, may God be pleased with him, "Whoever speaks much errs much,"[35] corroborates this point.

Both the books of good morals and the epistles of Sufism have studied and explained the idea of keeping silent, each from their own perspective, attaching great importance to this virtue by regarding it as important wealth for an initiate, a secret treasure for those who have reached the final point of journeying, and a sign of good manners for every believer.

This does not mean that a believer should keep silent in every case. A believer should speak to advise and promote good or prevent evil, to teach and guide, to remove what is harmful, and to encourage and introduce what is useful. Our religion orders us to utter what should be said to support and establish truth and justice so that everyone can receive their rightful due, and forbids us from keeping silent in such cases. It can be said that however harmful and condemnable it is for one to speak without seeking God's approval or good pleasure and thereby pursuing a lawful purpose, it is equally harmful and condemnable for one to keep silent when and where one should speak. For this reason, although keeping silent is generally approved and advisable, speaking is sometimes more approved than silence. Silence, in other words, while it is not always golden, is sometimes silver. It is of great importance to know where and when one should keep silent, and where and when one should speak. In a Prophetic Tradition, the person who keeps silent where right and justice are violated and truth is desecrated is regarded as a "mute devil"; those who speak false and useless words are considered to be the friends and translators of Satan.

It is both an ethical behavior and indicative of their knowing their place in the "market of thought and speech" that those who should speak are given the opportunity to speak, while others whose speech is not useful should remain silent. In this respect, it has been said:

---

35 at-Tabarani, *al-Mu'jam al-Awsat*, 2:370; al-Bayhaqi, *Shu'ab al-Iman*, 4:257. (Tr.)

If your merchandise is copper, O brother,
Do not offer it for sale in the market.
Leave the market to those who sell jewelry.

Keeping silent in the presence of people with profound spiritual states and wisdom shows that one has good manners and that one respects such profound spiritual states and wisdom. Concerning this, the Shaykhu'l-Islam Yahya Efendi[36] says:

Give ear to the speech of the people of profound spiritual states.
Do not compare their speech to other speeches.
You know, O preacher, that every speech is different from others.

Silence accompanied by self-supervision in the presence of those who have reached the final point of journeying and who have been favored with God's company is also emphasized. This silence of the people of heart, who can recognize people of true merit and worth, means respect for both the hearts where Divine inspirations descend and for the One Who has favored these hearts with satisfaction. They remain silent where they should and prepare the ground for the breezes of inspirations to blow, setting their tables not for the worldly bounties, but for the ever-fresh fruits of Paradise.

It sometimes occurs that the matter to be discussed is so profound that it transcends our horizon of perception to the extent that we should keep silent and invite others around us to silence. Sayings such as, "No need to present our need, for the state we are in is expressive of everything," and the silent prayer, "Consider what a wretched state we are in, and do not leave us alone!" are the voices of such silence. Jalalu'd-Din ar-Rumi makes the following invitation to it:

Look at my pale face, but do not say anything to me!
See my countless pains, but for God's love, do not
say anything to me!

---

36 Shaykhu'l-Islam Yahya Efendi (1553–1644) was one of the most famous Shaykhu'l-Islams of the Ottoman State. The office of Shaykhu'l-Islam was the highest office of religious affairs. Yahya Efendi was also a well-known poet. (Tr.)

Look at my heart in profuse blood, and my tears
flowing like a stream!
But ignore whatever you see, and do not ask how and why!

Common people hold their tongues and only keep silent physically, while those who have certain knowledge of God keep control of both their tongue and heart, and so experience self-supervision in silence. As for the lovers of God, they keep their love and yearning within themselves and so represent the silence of faithfulness. The first of these three groups are saved from blunders of speech and protect themselves from censure and reproach. Those of the second group receive, in addition to what silence itself may bring, the spiritual gifts which come through reflection and self-supervision. As for those of the third group, it is stated in the following couplet:

You say that you are a lover, then do not sigh with the ordeal of love!
Do not make others aware of your ordeal by sighing!

Thus, they are able to keep their secrets in silence and display an example of deep faithfulness.

O God, include us among Your servants, sincere in faith and in the practice of Islam, and those whom You have particularly favored with sincerity; bestow Your blessings and peace upon our master, Muhammad, the leader of those whom You have favored with sincerity, and on his Family and Companions, who both love You and are loved by You.

HALWAT AND *JALWAT* (PRIVACY AND COMPANY)

Literally meaning retreating to a place that is quiet and preferring solitude, *halwat* is used by the Sufis to mean initiates removing themselves from people to dedicate all of their time to worshipping God, and feeling God's constant company in whatever they experience and in whatever state they find themselves in. It also denotes restricting one's powers of sight and hearing to "seeing" and "hearing" only God, confiding in only Him, and devoting oneself exclusively to Him.

What is fundamental for *halwat* (privacy) is that one should purify one's spirit, cleanse one's soul, and turn one's heart and conscience to God exclusively to attain His constant company. As a result of this degree of turning to God and the attainment of His company, a traveler to the Ultimate Truth is supported with certain Divine gifts and favored with breezes of inspiration. It may even occur that they converse with God beyond all terms of quality and quantity—which is called "mutual whispering" by the Sufis. These are all Divine rewards that come in return for one's sincerity and exertion; therefore, expecting and demanding these is a show of bad manners. Thus, worshipping God and exerting oneself on His way in order to be able to receive such rewards represents deviation from the basic aim of servanthood to God and amounts to losing while on the way to winning. The perfected souls feel alarmed even over the coming of such rewards without expectations or demands, trembling with the fear that they have come to lead themselves to perdition, and they themselves are consuming the everlasting fruits of the afterlife in this fleeting world. Therefore, they supplicate to God, saying:

> O God, grant those gifts to those who ask for them;
> Please show me only the way to Your vision (in the Hereafter).

In this way they emphasize their utmost devotion to God without expecting anything in return except for His approval of them as His servants and His good pleasure.

All that we have tried to express so far to describe privacy is what the true travelers on the Sufi way have meant by it. However, some Sufi leaders have narrowed its frame and deal with it as being related to retreating to lodges where initiates undergo willful suffering; during this time, an initiate tries to become accustomed to speaking little, eating little, sleeping little, and remaining alone. This point has already been explained under the headings of *Halwat* and *'Uzlat* (Privacy and Seclusion) and *Chila* (Suffering) in the first and second volumes of this book respectively. The Sufi scholars who approach the matter from this narrow perspective have stressed its universality, mentioning that every religion and every spiritual system gives place to privacy, even if they differ in some secondary matters. They have considered as privacy the Prophet Moses' ten years of residence in Midian and his forty days of stay on Mount Sinai, as well as the Children of Israel's wandering in the Sinai desert for forty years, and the Virgin Mary's retreat which is mentioned in the Qur'anic verse, *We made the Son of Mary and his mother a miraculous sign (of Our Lordship and Power), and We provided for them refuge on a lofty ground of comfort and security with a (water) spring* (23:50), and, finally, God's Messenger's seclusion in the cave of Hira for the purpose of worship. They attach great importance to privacy in the name of spiritual purification. Even if it could be said that all of the events mentioned above do not provide some substantial religious ground for privacy, the importance of privacy serving the heart cannot be denied. The heart is regarded as the "House of God" and in this way can be purified of various attachments to things other than God, being refined and brightened so that it can receive Divine manifestations.

Privacy is important—not in remaining away from people, but as being a means for a "conversation with the All-Beloved" in the house of the heart. From this perspective, we can consider privacy to be a dimension of the spiritual journeying on the way to God and a step toward attaining His company.

Privacy, which initiates try to accomplish through cycles of forty days of suffering, in fact, serves to enable them to achieve refinement toward the purification of the heart, spirit, consciousness, and feelings so that they can turn back among people (*jalwat*) in order to guide them.

Privacy is a way essential to Sufism through which initiates can be refined of the carnal dimension of their nature and discover themselves in the depths of their humanity. Through privacy initiates can also clearly perceive the final purpose of their existence and experience God's particular manifestations of His favors on them through the lens of the helplessness, poverty, and the neediness essential to their very nature. Thus, they turn to God with all of their faculties, in the full conviction of His being the sole source of real power, wealth, knowledge, and all accomplishments.

Privacy does not only consist of constant seclusion from people, as one who went to extremes in solitude said:

> Brothers, my comfort lies in privacy—
> For to whomever I have become a friend,
> They publicized my faults and spread my humiliations around.
> During my entire life, I have not been able to find one—
> One who has been truly faithful.
> For this reason, I have found comfort in privacy.

Although privacy is in appearance a retreat from people, in truth it is a process of being equipped with the necessities of guidance in order to live in people's company.

At the beginning of journeying, those who intend such privacy withdraw to a secluded place, for example, remaining in a mosque for the purpose of worship. They eat little, drink little, sleep little, speak little, and are occupied with the remembrance of God. They never abandon reflection or self-supervision. When they have reached the final point of perfection they return among people and set out to serve them as one from among them. They attain non-existence in regards to their carnal existence and egotism and acquire an ever-active existence through the lights of the Divine existence. In the concepts, thoughts, and speeches of one who has reached this point, the self no longer exists; rather the truth and the Ultimate Truth exist. For this reason, such a person may say, "I no longer exist within me; I am no longer conscious of my existence." In his *Diwan Kabir*, Jalalu'd-Din ar-Rumi describes this feeling of non-existence as follows:

We have been favored with a mystery, a journeying
on the way to the Ultimate Truth.
We rejoice in our non-existence. So, come and
let us remain in our non-existence.
The doors were closed to us before, but when
we were saved from ourselves,
All the doors were opened. Our hearts have been
filled with peace and satisfaction
Because we have remained freed from ourselves on this way.
The All-Beautiful Beloved, Who kept
Himself concealed from us,
Has stroked our face in our non-existence.
We have died for His sake and, in turn, He has
saved us from ourselves.

Jalwat (company) denotes that initiates are freed from self-centeredness or anything that feeds their egos and—having been equipped with God's qualities or way of acting and being polished mirrors to His Names—dedicate themselves to service in God's cause with whatever they have, caring about the eternal happiness of others during their whole life. Another approach to company is that after initiates are freed from relative values that are peculiar to themselves, they then devote their intellect, logic, reasoning, and tongue to the service of humanity in the light of the lamp of Prophethood.

A person who attained company illuminates some of the features of those who have attained it as follows:

> Those who have attained company polish spirits;
> They are those followed by people.
> They have three distinguishing marks:
> Purity of the soul, refinement of the heart, and a polished spirit.
> They are mirrors to the manifestations of the Divine Names.

Whether one prefers privacy or company, the true attainment is servanthood to God, perfectly fulfilling whatever this servanthood requires, and sincere self-exertion to make others know and love Him.

> *O God! Show us the truth as the truth and enable us to observe it, and show us falsehood as falsehood and enable us to avoid it. And bestow Your blessings and peace upon our master, Muhammad, and on his Family and Companions.*

'ILM LADUN (THE SPECIAL KNOWLEDGE FROM GOD'S PRESENCE)

What is meant by *'ilm ladun*, or the special knowledge from God's Presence, is knowledge of the Unseen or knowledge of mysteries, or knowledge which God imparts into one's heart and the truths occurring to it. Primarily included is the knowledge of all the Prophets and Messengers, as well as the knowledge of saints, purified saintly scholars, virtuous and godly ones, and those especially favored with God's nearness. It is the knowledge which God has imparted into their hearts by way of Revelation or inspiration, and therefore it is considered to be some sort of special knowledge from God's Presence. Particularly the knowledge of God's Messenger, the Sultan of *'ilm ladun*, upon him be peace and blessings, whether it relates to the Unseen "absolute" or the Unseen "restricted," is included in this consideration of special knowledge from God's Presence. Süleyman Çelebi expresses this in the following couplet:

> That one who has come is the Sultan of *'ilm ladun*,
> That one who has come is the source of
> the knowledge of Divine Oneness.

That "unique one" of time and space is the perfect treasurer of this knowledge of secrets, and the greatest of those who have drunk out of this pool of special knowledge. Neither the other Prophets, nor the Messengers, nor the saints were favored with special knowledge to the same degree as that of the Prophet Muhammad, upon him be peace and blessings.

The knowledge which a saint claims to have received from God's Presence specially may sometimes be incompatible with the decrees of Shari'a. For this reason, those who do not correct any such knowledge or spiritual discovery according to the basic rules or the fundamentals of the Religion may err and cause their followers to err. However, those others who have established their spiritual discoveries and inspirations on the ground of the basic rules of the Religion always see the physical and metaphysical dimension of existence together at the same time, observe this world and the others like the two faces of a single entity, and offer their students sweet "waters" of Divine gifts from the physical and metaphysical worlds.

In *Surat al-Kahf*, the holy Qur'an mentions a distinguished servant of God favored with special knowledge from God's Presence, one who God's Messenger said was called Khadr.[37] It says: *And they found (there) one of Our servants to whom We had granted a mercy as a grace from Us and taught special knowledge from Our Presence* (18:65). According to the Sufi scholars, the knowledge which God taught Khadr was special knowledge from His Presence. Despite being one of the five greatest Prophets and a perfect guide in Divine truths, the Prophet Moses, upon him be peace, desired to fully comprehend the special knowledge from God's Presence by following Khadr to learn a particular aspect of it. *Sahih al-Bukhari* records a saying of our Prophet, upon him be peace and blessings, which points to the difference between the Prophetic knowledge of Divine truths and some aspects of special knowledge from God's Presence: "Khadr said to Moses: 'O Moses! I have some sort of knowledge from God, which you do not know, and you have some other sort of knowledge which I do not know.'"[38]

The special knowledge discussed is a special favor from God to certain people; others—even though they may be more knowledgeable in different subjects—lag behind these people in respect

---

37 *al-Bukhari*, "'Ilm" 44; *Muslim*, "Fadail" 170. (Tr.)

38 *al-Bukhari*, "'Ilm" 44. (Tr.)

to special knowledge from God's Presence. It is true that in order to be favored with this knowledge, one should have the ability and merit to receive it and enjoy particular nearness to God; but it is primarily a special favor of God to His servants whom He has chosen. For this reason, it cannot be acquired through study, research, or other similar ways. *That is God's grace; He grants it to whom He wills. Surely God is of tremendous grace* (62:4). So, this is a special manifestation of God's grace.

It should be pointed out that although such knowledge is extremely attractive, enchanting, and desirable, and although it is related to certain Divine mysteries, the knowledge of the Religion and Divine truths with which the Prophets were favored is much more elevated than this knowledge; the knowledge of the Prophets is objective, applicable to everybody, and secures the worldly and otherworldly happiness of people. We can explain the difference between these two kinds of knowledge as follows:

Moses's knowledge was the knowledge of the Shari'a, which was absolutely necessary for everybody regarding their happiness in both worlds and was therefore taught to order people's worldly life and secure their happiness in the Hereafter, while Khadr's knowledge was a special favor to know some aspects of the Unseen and certain Divine mysteries. Moses' knowledge related to the rules and judgment by which public order and security could be realized, while Khadr's consisted of some special gifts relating to the metaphysical dimension of life and existence. This second kind of knowledge has also been called "special knowledge that is purely from God's Presence," "the knowledge of truth," and "the knowledge of the inner dimensions of existence." It is a significant source by which one can realize the Divine mysteries. In this respect it is said:

O teacher of religious sciences,
Pay no attention to the knowledge of what people say;
Instead, search for the secrets of the Ultimate Truth
In the special knowledge from His Presence.

Although there is some sort of connection between this knowledge and personal efforts to obtain it, such knowledge cannot be obtained through mere study or efforts, for this knowledge occurs in pure hearts as a Divine gift in the form of a sacred power. It comes directly from God's Presence through the ways of spiritual discovery and inspiration. However, as inspirations coming to the heart manifest themselves in the hearts to varying degrees, so those who cannot continue their spiritual journeying under the guardianship of the Master of creation, upon him be the perfect blessings and peace, may be the target of some suggestions of Satan.

Revelation (*wahy*) came to the Prophets and it is absolutely beyond all doubt. However, inspiration (*ilham*) occurs to saints and it is a broad channel for the manifestations of God's Knowledge. If an inspiration manifests itself in the heart of a human being as a Divine gift beyond his or her willpower, this is called an "occurrence." Satan may mix some things with an occurrence. An occurrence that is certain to have come from God without any interference from Satan can be regarded as special knowledge from God's Presence. The firmest sign of an occurrence having originated in God's Knowledge is its conformity with the Qur'an and the Sunna. It is highly possible that any occurrences which are not in conformity with these two primary foundations or basic sources of the Religion are whisperings or suggestions of Satan or of the human carnal soul. Since occurrences in which Satan and the human carnal soul have interfered bear Satanic and carnal elements, an initiate who has been driven to such an area of deception should immediately turn to God Almighty and regulate his or her state according to the basic rules of Shari'a.

The Sufi leaders call the meanings coming from God's Presence and which echo in the heart "occurrences from the Ultimate Truth," while those known to come from the angels are called "occurrences from the angels," and the "sparks" which come from Satan and the carnal soul and invade the spirit are known as "carnal or Satanic suggestions." To differentiate between these occurrences one must depend on the criteria established by the fundamentals of the Religion and the elevated Sunna of the Prophet, upon him be peace and blessings. We should also point out that although these occurrences can be differentiated through the basic rules of the Shari'a, some others may come as a result of, or lead to, certain secret Satanic goals or ambitions even though they appear to be in conformity with the fundamentals of the Religion. For this reason, only those people who are well-versed in this field can establish the true differentiation.

Since the suggestions of the carnal soul and Satan are outside the sphere of "special knowledge from God's Presence," we will not go into details about them here.

> *O God! Show us the truth as the truth and enable us to observe it; show us falsehood as falsehood and enable us to avoid it. And bestow Your blessings and peace upon our master, Muhammad, and on his Family and Companions.*

WALIYY AND *AWLIYAULLAH* (GOD'S FRIEND [SAINT] AND GOD'S FRIENDS)

Literally meaning a friend, a helper, a loyal one, or a guardian, a *waliyy* is one who is devoted to God with all their emotions and one who is taken by Him as a close friend. Such an attainment is called *wilaya* (God's friendship or sainthood), and the greatest rank in *wilaya* is called *qutbiya* (being a spiritual pole).

Perfect sainthood consists of servants being annihilated with respect to the carnal dimension of their existence and gaining a new, ever-young, and active existence on the horizon of God's nearness through their knowledge of God, love of God, vision of God, and discovery of the Divine mysteries. In the sight of such heroes of spirituality, who have reached the peak where the sun never sets, autumns turn into springs, and annihilation turns into permanent existence, everything is annihilated in God; everything begins and ends with Him, rises and sets with Him, and attains existence through the lights of His Existence. Those favored with such a vision experience existence in a different mood and fashion according to their capacity of perceiving of everything as dependent on Him and observe that every event takes place dependent on the Truth of Truths, Whom they find in their hearts as a "Secret Treasure." Unceasingly thrilling at the lights they observe glittering in the countenances of the mornings and evenings, the depths of the ever-bright heavens, the multi-colored beauties of the seasons that come and go with ever-renewed scenes, the awful appearances of the vast seas and oceans, the flowing of rivers toward the seas with a deep yearning for union, the joyful cries of birds and insects, and the bleating of sheep and lambs, they are overawed by the meanings that pour into their hearts from Him. All the shapes and forms on the horizon of their vision disappear and they find themselves boiling with reflection and pleasure as if they see, feel, and experience Him alone.

Such heroes of spirituality no longer feel zeal, but rather a deep yearning to reach Him, and no longer feel attraction but rather are attracted by Him toward Him. They are completely freed from any kind of heedlessness, with the result that the light of the Ultimate Truth shows itself everywhere. Reason and the spirit are now hand-in-hand and the whole of existence becomes a book to read. All false candles are extinguished, one after another, and it is as if the stars have come down from the heavens to illuminate the entire world. The world with all its worldliness vanishes and is rebuilt with a new design that belongs to the realms beyond. All veils of darkness are rent apart and lights burst forth through the fissures. Everything becomes a friend and a companion to such a hero of spirituality, and the heart finds in everything whatever it looks for, thus being saved from all kinds of loneliness.

God Almighty never abandons initiates who have attained such a degree of God's friendship to their carnal soul, not even for the twinkling of an eye. Since they are always turned to the horizon of obtaining God's approval and good pleasure with all their being, God protects and preserves them with His infinite grace and care. There is no longer any grief or worry; they constantly receive welcome from all corners of existence and they feel spiritual joy in their hearts. As if living in the gardens of Paradise, within the protective walls of, *Know well that the friends (saintly servants) of God – they will have no fear, nor will they grieve* (10:62), far away from the carnal veils of darkness and surrounded by the lights of the All-Merciful—but without ever falling into heedlessness toward the fear and awe of God which they always feel in the depths of their being—they continuously receive promissory messages from the realms beyond and return them with good, righteous deeds.

Although what is primarily meant by *God's friends* is all the believers, as opposed to the enemies of God—for this is what the Qur'an also means by this term—the Sufis give other significant meanings to it. According to them, a friend of God is a person of truth who, through various forms of self-struggle, such as austerity, has transcended the carnal dimension of his or her existence and reached the level of the life of the heart and spirit, thus obtaining God's special nearness. Friends of God have annihilated themselves with respect to their carnal existence, and attained permanence with a new meaning and thus they are favored with God's particular blessings and compliments. They have found whatever they would find and they have been saved from all kinds of pursuits. Without ever aspiring after anything perishable, they say, "Let others have whatever is worldly—God, only, is sufficient for me," and they demand whatever they demand only for God's sake. I think Nabi[39] meant this by the following:

> Do God's friends ever stoop to possessing anything worldly?
> Do they ever endure the burden of people?

Since friends of God always have God as their sole object, and they expect from Him whatever they expect, and thus continuously receive God's favors, it is inconceivable that they should turn to others for their needs or aspirations.

Although all of God's friends are people of deep spirituality, they differ in disposition and temperament, in their relative degree of attainment, and in their duties and missions. This is why they are mentioned with different titles such as the godly, the virtuous ones, those favored with God's special nearness, substitutes, pillars, nobles, custodians, leaders, helpers or means of help, and

39 Yusuf Nabi (1642–1712): One of the most well-known Ottoman poets of the seventeenth century. He was born in Urfa, southeastern Turkey, and emigrated to Istanbul when he was twenty-four. He lived in Istanbul and Aleppo. He usually wrote didactic poems where he criticized certain vices in society and which contained moral lessons. (Tr.)

poles. With whatever title they are called, all of them have—according to the capacity of each—common praiseworthy qualities such as truthfulness, honesty, trustworthiness, sincerity and purity of intention, piety, righteousness, abstinence, asceticism, love, mildness and forbearance, modesty, humility, repentance, penitence, contrition, fear, and reverence. And with the exception of a few extreme "ecstatics" among them, all of them act within the bounds of the principles mentioned.

ABRAR (THE GODLY, VIRTUOUS ONES)

The *Abrar* are the good, virtuous ones who strive to reach God through austerity and moral straightforwardness; they are people of honesty and righteousness, loyal servants of the Ultimate Truth who live a life very carefully in keeping with the ordinances of Shari'a. Some of the godly, virtuous ones who are extremely sincere and faithful in their relationship with the Ultimate Truth are bent on the attainment of personal perfection. Although they pursue God's approval and good pleasure in all of their attempts and actions, they nevertheless aim at their own perfection and seclude themselves from people in pursuit of spiritual gifts and favors to such an extent that they travel from immersion to amazement, and from amazement to utmost astonishment in the waves of the gifts of the "oceans" where they feel that everything has been lost in the Divine Existence. Those who see them think that they are lunatics and mock them. Because of this, and in consideration of how deep they are in their relationship with God, they cannot act as guides for others; the reservations they cause to arise in the minds of others impede this.

There are others among the godly, virtuous ones who always follow the light of the lamp of Prophethood, and therefore act in a balanced way. They plan and put into practice all of their intentions and attempts under the guidance of the Divine Revelation, the heart, and reason. They comprehend and interpret religious matters correctly and without causing any misunderstandings. They always preserve the balance in their observations of the physical and metaphysical realms, or the physical and metaphysical dimensions of things; they correct their intuitions and perceptions in the state of ecstasy and rapture according to the fundamentals of the Religion, and they present their inferences and deductions within this perspective. They see the world from the point of view of Prophethood and, although they always avoid setting their hearts on it, they pay necessary attention to it as it is the place of observation of Divine beauties, the manifestation of the Divine Names, and the arable field of the afterlife. In whatever they do, they aim at God's approval and good pleasure, and eternal happiness, striving in the way of the Prophet to make each second, minute, and hour of their lives into ears of corn that bear seven, seventy, and even seven hundred grains. They actually represent godliness and righteousness and set good examples for people to follow. Wherever they are, they remind people of God, and acting as if an indicator, they cause people to turn to Him in devotion. In short, they are those who are always occupied with good, virtuous deeds; who always dream of godliness and righteousness; who always follow the Creator, the Ultimate Truth, in whatever they do; and who care about the created.

Muqarrabun (Those Favored with God's Special Nearness)

Muqarrabun are higher in rank than the Godly, Virtuous Ones due to their special nearness to God. This exalted title is also used for the most distinguished ones among the Prophets and angels. These blessed ones that are favored with God's special nearness are guides on the way to God, distinguished "lions" in the quarter of the truth, doves who continue their journeying at the peaks, guests who have completed the most important part of the journeying and who have resolved to remain, God's confidants in His "private lodge" who, by virtue of the truths they observe as the gifts of the horizon they have reached, have closed their eyes to fleeting things in respect of their worldly aspects. They are cavalrymen who have defeated the soldiers of carnal desires and caprices with their armies of love and yearning; they are heroes of knowledge of God who have subjected their carnal life to their heart and spirit; they are those who, by having left behind the deserts of mortality to reach the gardens of subsistence by and with God, have found utmost peace and satisfaction; they are heroes of observation and spiritual discovery who have reached the horizon of having a vision of God through God Himself; they are lovers who have appropriated the love of God as the most manifest dimension of their nature; and they are loved ones who are intoxicated with the pleasure of feeling that God loves them. Finally, they are heroes who have been perfectly favored with the compliment that *God loves them and they love Him* (5:54). We see and experience the true color of existence through the lens of their knowledge of God and observe the metaphysical dimension of things with the lights they shed over the face of existence.

Although some reports have been circulated among the saints concerning the number of *Muqarrabun*, it is not possible to say that an exact number has been agreed upon. According to some reports, the *Muqarrabun* consist of three hundred good ones, forty substitutes, four pillars, and two leaders. According to some other reports, they consist of a spiritual pole and four thousand saints. Whatever their number is, all of these heroes of nearness to God are the noblest servants of the Ultimate Truth and they share the same spiritual profundity of the angels.

Accepting that the *Muqarrabun* are composed of four thousand saints, some Sufis classify these distinguished servants of God according to their ranks as follows:

Three hundred of them are *Akhyar* (the good ones who pursue good in whatever they do and say); forty of them are *Abdal* or *Budala* (the substitutes, charged with the administration of spiritual life and acting as veils in the reflection of the Divine

Majesty and Grandeur); seven of them are *Abrar* (godly, virtuous ones who have been able to make righteous deeds and sincerity a deep dimension of their nature); and there are others called by different titles.

Still others make another classification of those favored with special nearness to God, the number of which is unknown. They mention four *Awtad* (Pillars), and *Nujaba* (the Nobles, in the sense of being distinguished in the sight of God), and *Nukaba* (the Custodians, who care for people and the management of their affairs), and, superior to all those mentioned, *Ghawth* (the Helper or the Means of Divine Help), and *Qutb* (the Pole). Some Sufi scholars call all of those *Rijal-i Ghayb* (the Men of the Unseen).

Abdal (The Substitutes)

Substitutes are those pure, honest saints who help people with their affairs without being seen and who function as veils in the reflection of Divine acts. Before the Ottomans, the Iranians called them "the Straightforward," "Easygoing Ones," "People of Light," or "Sufis." Then, this term (*Abdal*) became a name for a spiritual order. Under the Ottomans, some men who were famous for their heroic courage and fearlessness came to be called "Substitutes." In dervish lodges, the term has always been used to describe the "Men of the Unseen."

According to Sufis, Substitutes are saints who avoid fame and who are unknown among people. They always hasten to do good and to help others. They are of two groups. The first group is composed of the saints who have been freed from all evil qualities and equipped with excellence and virtuousness, who resist all kinds of vices and wrongs, and who try to prevent these. The second group consists of those saints who have a particular mission and number three hundred, forty, and seven; they are also referred to by these numbers. Their numbers are not important; what is important is their place and rank in God's sight and the duties they perform.

When one of the Substitutes dies, another one from the subgroup takes his or her place. When one of them leaves his or her place for a duty, either that one sends his double or astral body to perform the duty, or that one departs to perform the duty and leaves his double or astral body behind. (We should remind ourselves here that the idea of a human double or astral body is a matter frequently discussed in parapsychology.)

Some consider the pillars, the two leaders, and the pole as a superior group, separate from the Substitutes: they see the latter as people of a certain spiritual state, while the former are viewed as people of a certain spiritual station. They regard the latter as travelers to God and the former as travelers in and from God.

Those who maintain that there are always seven Substitutes say that they each reside in a different clime or realm, observe and acclaim the Divine acts, and respond to God Almighty with praise and thanks as conscious representatives of the activities of unconscious beings. These seven saints have particular stations, and they are mentioned with the titles they have been given according to their station.

- The first substitute represents the reflection or projection of the Prophet Abraham's heart, and is called by the title, *'Abdulhayy* (the Servant of the All-Living).
- The second has the particular attributes of the Prophet Moses' heart, and is called by the title, *'Abdul'alim* (the Servant of the All-Knowing).
- The third is a mirror of the Prophet Aaron's heart, and the special name of this one is *'Abdulmurid* (the Servant of the All-Willing).
- The fourth reflects the attributes of the Prophet Enoch's heart, and is mentioned with the title *'Abdulqadir* (the Servant of the All-Powerful).
- The fifth has a connection with the heart of the Prophet Joseph, and is known by the title *'Abdulqahir* (the Servant of the All-Overwhelming).

- The sixth is bound to the content of the Prophet Jesus' heart and called by the title *'Abdussami'* (the Servant of the All-Hearing).
- The seventh follows the heart of the Prophet Adam, and is known with the title, *'Abdulbasir* (the Servant of the All-Seeing).

None of these opinions or considerations is based on the Qur'an or the Sunna, but each has its source in the spiritual discoveries of some saints of discovery and is open to interpretation. For this reason, we are not obliged to accept these opinions or considerations as being absolutely true. Nevertheless, whatever their duties, titles, or positions are, and whatever blessings God favors them with, all of the saints are those who have certain degrees of knowledge of God, who are supported by God, and who, with their refined hearts and purified souls, are open to certain Divine mysteries.

Still another consideration concerning the place and duties of the saints known as Substitutes is as follows:

Three hundred of them represent the reflection of Prophet Adam's heart and are mirrors to it, forty of them have a connection with Prophet Moses' heart, seven are affiliated with Prophet Abraham, five with the bosom of Archangel Gabriel, three with Archangel Michael, and one from among them, who is the greatest among them and represents the greatest sainthood, is affiliated with the greatest of all beings, Prophet Muhammad, upon him be perfect blessings and peace. When the last one dies, the one who is superior to all others takes his place, and when somebody from among them dies, that position is filled by another one from another group. Like the number of Substitutes, the opinions about their residences and titles vary considerably.

There are nearly twenty reports from the Prophet concerning the existence of such a group of saints among the Men of the Unseen.[40]

---

40 As for further reference, see Ahmad ibn Hanbal, al-Musnad, 1:112, 5:322; at-Tabarani, *al-Mu'jam al-Kabir*, 10:181, 18:65; al-Munawi, *Fayd al-Kadir*, 3:167–170. (Tr.)

According to these reports, because of their value in His sight, God Almighty sends rain, helps the believers against their enemies, and removes calamities from them. The Substitutes are like a center of gravity for the earth; God employs them as a spiritual means of keeping the earth on its axis and provides for others out of their high place with Him. They forgive the wrong which people do to them; they return evil with good; and they continuously follow the path to Paradise through mildness, forbearance, and generosity. They attach special importance to the soundness and purity of their hearts and they always wish good for Muslims. They have no worldly ambitions, and they avoid quarrelling even with their enemies. They always shun exaggeration in their speech, and they represent the middle way in speech. They avoid religious innovations, and they do not go to extremes in their worship. Of whatever rank they are, they never like or approve of themselves. Resignation to whatever misfortune comes to them from God, utmost care about not committing any action that is religiously forbidden, a deep reverence for and obedience to God Almighty, and never cursing anyone—all these are mentioned among the foremost attributes of the Substitutes.

Some commentators on *Hadith* such as Ibn Taymiyya[41] and Ibn Qayyim al-Jawziyya regard all those reports as fabricated and reject them. Imam Suyuti,[42] another commentator, considers that since the *hadith*s support one another, as a whole, they may be considered as sound as the Prophetic Traditions that have been reported through many reliable chains of transmission. Hafiz Sahawi,[43] following a moderate or middle way, notes that all those reports are

---

41 Taqiyyud-Din Ahmad ibn Taymiyya (1263–1328): A very famous Muslim scholar who was born in Harran in southeastern Turkey near the Syrian border. As a member of the Hanbali School of Law, he defended "return to the Qur'an and the Sunna," being very critical of new developments in thought within Islam over centuries. (Tr.)

42 'Abdur-Rahman ibn Kamal Jalalud-Din as-Suyuti (1445–1505): *The mujtahid* imam, one of the foremost *hadith* masters, jurist, Sufi, philologist, and historian. He authored works in virtually every Islamic science. He lived in Egypt. (Tr.)

43 Hafiz Muhammad Shamsud-Din as-Sahawi (d. 1498): A great *muhaddith*, who lived in Egypt. He was a student of Ibn Hajar al-Asqalani. His famous work is *Maqasid al-Hasana*. (Tr.)

weak in reliability and therefore open to criticism. In view of these different considerations, I leave the truth of the matter to God, saying: "God knows best."

The original Arabic term translated as Substitutes is *abdal*, which is the plural of *badal*. The term *badal* has another plural form: *budala*. This term is used by the Sufis for seven important figures among the "Men of the Unseen." They can change places with unusual speed and can be present in many different places at the same moment. It is not clear whether this occurs by the separation of their double or astral bodies from their original bodies so that they can be manifested in many places at the same time, or by their unusually speedy movement and because they are able to be present in many places, one after the other, within a short time. It sometimes happens that the Substitutes are not aware of this mysterious transportation. The author of *Futuhat al-Makkiyya* ("The Makkan Conquests"), Muhyi'd-Din ibn al-'Arabi, considers that the Substitutes (called *budala*) observe the acts of God Almighty in each of the seven climes. They both observe the acts of the All-Glorified One and appear to be curtains for their reflections, acclaiming them. They receive their spiritual training as Uways al-Qarani[44] did, that is, without being trained by a spiritual master.

Nujaba (The Nobles)

"Nobles" is a title used for the "Fortys," or some among the "Fortys" included in the "Men of the Unseen." According to verifying Sufi scholars, these are the heroes of altruism who have completed their ascension toward God by going down among the people to guide and spiritually educate them. They think of nothing other than guiding people to God; they encourage hearts always to do good, and they erect spiritual barriers before evils. They try to

---

44 Uways ibn Amir al-Qarni or al-Qarani (d. 657): He was born in Yemen. Towards the end of his life, he left for Kufa, in modern-day Iraq. He was one of most outstanding figures of the generation succeeding the Companions. Some regard him as the greatest Muslim saint of the first Islamic century. (Tr.)

confront possible misfortunes through prayers and supplications and they are ready to sacrifice themselves for the good of people or to prevent disasters. Their hearts always beat with feelings of self-sacrifice, compassion, and tender care for others. Since they have dedicated their lives to the happiness of others, they live a life overburdened with the troubles of others and sigh for them. Even if there are times when they feel happy at the news of others' happiness, they are always sorrowful because of what they have witnessed or heard concerning the sufferings of people. In respect of their mission, they are heirs to the Prophets.

Nukaba (The Custodians)

Nukaba are the saints who are always together with people, correcting their faults, and guiding all toward good with mildness and kindness. Although the term is used for those in the Sufi Orders of Rifai[45] and Badawi[46] who have completed their spiritual journeying and have begun the mission of guiding people to God, according to the verifying Sufi scholars they are the purified souls whose spiritual profundity and discovery transcend their scope of learning and sight and who always observe the spiritual domain or realm of existence; by God's leave, they are able to penetrate the hearts of people and what occurs to them. They carry out the duty of some sort of translation between the physical and metaphysical realms, interpreting existence in accordance with their capacity and in consideration of the understanding levels of their audience, and persistently try to find ways to God through everything. In their

45 Sayyid Ahmad ar-Rifai (1119–1183), the founder of the Rifai Order, and one of the greatest Sufi masters in the history of Islam, was born and lived in southern Iraq. He also had profound knowledge of Islamic religious sciences, including especially jurisprudence and *Hadith*. (Tr.)

46 Sayyid Ahmad al-Badawi (1200–1276) was one of the most outstanding Sufi masters, to whom the Badawi Order is attributed. He was born in Morocco. When he was six years old, his family emigrated to Makka. He spent the greatest part of his life in Tanta, Egypt. He was also well-versed in Islamic sciences. (Tr.)

view, the universe is a meaningful book which contains messages within messages, with all its parts making up the words, sentences, and paragraphs. In these ever-wakeful souls and truth-voicing tongues, the truth expressed herein shows itself:

> The universe is a supreme book of God throughout,
> Whichever letter you look at, you read God.

Awtad (The Pillars)

Awtad are the four "Men of God" who are so close to one another that one cannot do without the other. They make their spiritual journeying and carry out their duties under the shadow of the missions of Enoch, Elijah, Jesus, and Khadr, upon them and our Prophet be peace. According to the particular mission of each, they have the titles *'Abdulhayy* (The Servant of the All-Living), *'Abdul'alim* (The Servant of the All-Knowing), *'Abdulmurid* (The Servant of the All-Willing), and *'Abdulqadir* (The Servant of the All-Powerful), and they reflect the spiritual content of Prophets Adam, Abraham, Jesus, and Muhammad, upon them be peace and blessings, or represent the reflections of their truths. Their connection with God is through the lenses of the Archangels Gabriel, Michael,[47] Israfil,[48] and 'Azrail,[49] upon them be peace. They each correspond to a pillar of the Ka'ba, which signifies the door or stairway to that station.

Muhyi'd-Din ibn al-'Arabi is of the opinion that the Pillars are the seven saints who carry out their duties according to a hierarchy that exists among them.

Some call all the saints of God—including the Nobles, Custodians, and Pillars—the "Men of God" in the sense that they

---

47 Michael is the Archangel who supervises the earth with its grass, plants, and animals, and represents or presents to God their glorifications and praises of Him. (Tr.)

48 Israfil is one of the four Archangels. He will blow the Trumpet just before the end of the universe and for the resurrection of the dead. (Tr.)

49 'Azrail is the Archangel charged with taking the souls of human beings. He is the Angel of Death. (Tr.)

are heroes of the truth with certain spiritual power. Their most distinguishing attributes are their deep reverence for God and their feeling of awe before Him; being overwhelmed by the manifestations of the All-Merciful; arousing God's existence and omnipresence in the minds of those who see them; sobriety and dignity coming from the constant awareness of God's company; being deeply ashamed of certain ordinary human acts and states—even though they are lawful; being aware of God in everything in a different wave of sensation; self-forgetfulness when they are aware of God; continuous self-supervision and attributing to Him whatever gifts and blessings they are favored with; and remaining unknown by others. With respect to their being unknown, they are called "the Men of the Unseen" or "the Army of God." In one of his poems, Sultan Mehmed the Conqueror[50] refers to those men who are endowed with a sacred spiritual power and asks for their prayers in carrying out the duty of serving God's Word.

With respect to these men's being able to make the Divine mysteries felt in the hearts of others, they are called "the Men of Conquest"; because of their being unknown or being known only by a few, they are known as "the Men of the Unseen." In regard to their generally living in ecstasy, they are called "the Men of Power," and because they approach everyone with gentleness and tolerance and return evil done to them with good, they are "the Men of Kindness."

Ghawth (The Helper or the Means of Divine Help)

Signifying help, coming to the aid of others, and giving spiritual help, the term *ghawth* is used by the Sufis to denote saints of the highest rank.

A person who has attained this rank has been honored with a particular Divine favor and, by God's leave, hurries to the aid of those in difficulties. Those who do not have this capacity cannot

---

50 Sultan Mehmed the Conqueror (1432–1481) was the seventh Ottoman Sultan, and conquered Istanbul. (Tr.)

be regarded as *Ghawth*; any poles (*Qutb*) who cannot be mirrors for Divine help are not called *ghawth*.

One who combines the spiritual status of being a *Ghawth* with the rank of being a *Qutb* is called *Ghawth-i A'zam* (the Greatest Helper), and if the one who has been favored with the rank of being a *Qutb* is also honored with being a *Ghawth*, he is called *Qutb-i A'zam* (the Greatest Pole). Each of these titles has aspects particular to itself.

Since those honored with these exalted ranks represent the shadow of *Haqiqat Muhammadiya* (the Muhammadi Truth),[51] they are in the company of the Prophet, upon him be peace and blessings, with respect to being mirrors to certain Divine truths. Their part in the universal mission of the Prophet is expressed by Süleyman Çelebi as follows:

I have made your essence a mirror to Me,
And inscribed your name together with Mine.

The status described in, "God has made him a mirror to Him as the Sole Divine Being," primarily and with all its comprehensiveness, belongs to the Master of creation, upon him be peace and blessings, who is the greatest of the Perfect or Universal Men.[52] Each of the other Perfect or Universal Men has a relative, particular part in this great honor.

The Sufis maintain that in every century there is a Helper or Means of Divine Help (*Gwahs*) who is the leader of all the contemporary men of God, the door among people to the attainment of Divine assistance, the moderator of the spiritual realm or domain of existence, and the pivot of Divine gifts and blessings. If

---

51 *Haqiqat Muhammadiya* (Muhammadi Truth): This term is essential to Sufism. It may be translated as the "reality of Muhammad" as God's Messenger, the most beloved of God, the best example for all creation to follow, the embodiment of Divine Mercy, and the living Qur'an or embodiment of the Qur'anic way of life. (Tr.)

52 For a detailed analysis of the Perfect or Universal Man, see M. Fethullah Gülen, *Emerald Hills of the Heart – Key Concepts in the Practice of Sufism,* The Light, NJ, 2004, Vol., 2, pp. 289–302. (Tr.)

a Helper is also a Pole, his title is the Greatest Pole, and his rank is the status of the Greatest Pole.

Such a hero of spirituality who is honored with this rank has such capacities that not only ordinary people like us, but also those who have reached the final point of spiritual journeying are unable to perceive them. This rank is the most comprehensive mirror to the Divine Names, the essence of existence, and the greatest focus of the Muhammadi Truth. By virtue of this distinction, and by God's leave, such a one is an authority entitled to represent the implementation of the Divine decrees under the leadership and protection of *Haqiqat Ahmadiya* (Ahmadi Truth or the Truth of Ahmad)[53] and in the light of the Muhammadi Lamp,[54] upon him be peace and blessings.

The scholarly people of sainthood mention the names of such great saints as 'Abdu'l-Qadir al-Jilani,[55] Abu'l-Hasan al-Harakani,[56] Shaykh al-Harrani,[57] and Imam Rabbani,[58] as those who have attained

53 *Haqiqat Ahmadiya* (Ahmadi Truth or the Truth of Ahmad) is the term used to designate the reality or the essence or the truth represented by the personality of the Prophet Muhammad, upon him be peace and blessings, before his coming to the world and after his departure from the world. In one respect, it signifies the unparalleled sainthood of the Prophet Muhammad. (Tr.)

54 Muhammadi Lamp or the Lamp of Muhammad signifies the light of Muhammad's Messengership or the light of Islam or the way of the Prophet Muhammad, upon him be peace and blessings. (Tr.)

55 'Abdu'l-Qadir al-Jilani (d. 1166): One of the most celebrated Sufi masters. A student of jurisprudence and Hadith, he became known as the "Spiritual Pole" of his age and the "the Greatest Means of Divine Help." Among his well-known books are *Kitab al-Ghunyah*, *Futuh al-Ghayb*, and *Al-Fath al-Rabbani*. (Tr.)

56 'Ali ibn Ahmad Abu'l-Hasan al-Harakani (963–1033) is one of the most celebrated saints. He was born and lived in Harakan near Bistam in Iran. He lived as a poor farmer. He was martyred in fighting in Kars, a city in the farthest northeastern Turkey, and was buried there. (Tr.)

57 Shakyh Hayat ibn Qays al-Harrani (d. 1185), is one of the most outstanding saints in the history of Islam. He was born in Baghdad and lived in Harran near Urfa, in southeastern Turkey. (Tr.)

58 Imam Rabbani, Ahmad Faruq al-Sarhandi (d. 1624): The "reviver of the second millennium." Born in Sarhand (India) and well-versed in Islamic sciences, he removed many corrupt elements from Sufism. He taught Shah Alamgir or Awrangzeb (d. 1707), who had a committee of scholars prepare the most comprehensive compen-

this rank in the history of Islam. These personages, who have combined the rank of being a Pole with that of being a Helper, are mentioned with the titles of "the Greatest Pole," or "the Greatest Helper." As they represent the status of being the Greatest Pole, they are also called "the Pole of the Poles."

With respect to being the representatives of spiritual perfection, they are also regarded as the true heirs to the duties of Prophethood and the special, most distinguished representatives of succession to the Prophet Muhammad, upon him be peace and blessings. It is undeniable that the purification of the carnal soul, refinement of the heart, and spiritual struggle all have an important part in the attainment of this rank. However, it should also be borne in mind that this rank is a special gift of God which He accords to whomever He wills. God Himself declares: *That is God's grace. He grants it to whom He wills. Surely God is of tremendous grace* (62:4).

This elevated rank has sometimes been represented by a single individual, sometimes by a collective personality formed around God's good pleasure through a sincere brother/sisterhood, and selfless unity and solidarity, or, quite possibly, by a community of Muslims which serves the true faith and the Qur'an purely for God's sake.

Qutb (The Pole)

Qutb is the title of one who is the focus of the views of the earth and heaven's inhabitants, the perfect vicegerent of God, the Ultimate Truth, the heir of the Master of creation, upon him be peace and blessings, and the perfect, universal man who always exists among humankind.

After the pride of humanity, the Prophet Muhammad, upon him be peace and blessings, this rank was represented by the first four Rightly-Guided Caliphs in order of succession, who were true successors to the duties of Prophethood. They were followed by

dium of Hanafi Law. His work, *The Letters,* is very famous and widely known throughout the Muslim world. (Tr.)

the greatest scholars or the founders of Islamic Schools of Law, who had the capacity to deduce new laws from the Qur'an and the Sunna, the greatest saints, and the saintly scholars.

Together with the rank of Helper, the rank of Pole is also the greatest of spiritual ranks. While a Helper is primarily distinguished by coming to the aid of others who are immured in difficulties, a Pole may also be favored with the rank of Helper and become a source of spiritual radiance and a reflector of God's gifts. Being heir to the Muhammadi Truth, a Pole represents a reflection of the Master of creation, upon him be peace and blessings, under his guardianship in the age where he lives, and is a successor to him in his duties as a spiritual master.

By virtue of the special gifts with which he is honored, and by virtue of having been equipped with a special capacity in accordance with his duty, a Pole is, like the North Star, a singular, chosen one upon whom the views of all the inhabitants of the earth and heavens are focused. This mysterious power station, which is always open to the metaphysical realms, has effects on the human outer and inner faculties that resemble the spirit's control of the body. This power of penetration comes from this person's knowledge of God; this knowledge of God originates in God's Knowledge, Which in turn has Its source in the Divine Essence. With respect to his own essence, or when left to his own devices, a Pole is like a drop of water—but a drop that contains the entire reflection of the sun by virtue of God's favors upon him. Such a one is nothing but an atom, but that atom reflects all of the heavens. For in their essential nature, Poles are nothing—they are zero—but they are equipped with such essential values and qualities that they reflect eternity.

With one of their eyes always scanning the physical dimension of existence, Poles constantly observe the realms beyond with the other eye, in unceasing pursuit of the radiance of recognition or knowledge of God. They weave the spiritual lacework of existence with the silky threads of wisdom that pour into their hearts and give them to those around them. Like the sun, they always give off light and illuminate all that is around them. And like a surging ocean, they bubble over from within and diffuse life into hearts.

Since Poles have fully developed their innate capacities, they are heroes of extraordinary performance. They are perfect persons whose hearts are mirrors to the Archangel Israfil, and whose power of speech mirrors Gabriel, and whose power of attraction mirrors Michael, and whose power of repelling mirrors ʿAzrail. By virtue of this, they are each, in one respect, a focus of creation as a mirror to all realms, vicegerents of God in their age, special students and representatives of the Muhammadi Truth, rays of the first manifestation of existence beyond time, and luminous, transparent means for the conduction of Divine mysteries to all hearts. Being heirs to the Prophet, they establish new rules to acquire and deepen in knowledge of God and the Religion. The Shiʿa attribute this rank only to ʿAli and the eleven Imams who descended from him through the Prophet's beloved daughter, Fatima, and the last of whom is the Mahdi;[59] this is a restriction. God may accord this honor to whomever He wills among His servants who have been endowed with the necessary capacity and He may make Himself known through them.

The Sufi scholarly saints mention two types of Pole, one being "the Pole of guidance" and the other being "the Pole of existence." The "Pole of guidance" represents the spirit of Prophethood as the owner of the greater rank of Pole, while the "Pole of existence" stands for the inner dimension of the Seal of Prophethood with the title of the Seal of Sainthood. The scholars who have expert knowledge of the matter hold the opinion that although in the same period there may be more than one Pole of guidance, there can only be one Pole of existence. The axis of whichever great angel honored with special nearness to God or illustrated Prophet he journeys around, or the rug-seat of whichever saint he occu-

59 The Mahdi, literally meaning one who guides to truth, is the title of the blessed person whose coming toward the end of time to re-establish the truth of Islam and justice on the earth was promised by God's Messenger, upon him be peace and blessings. (Tr.)

pies, the Pole of existence always turns toward the light of the existence of the Pole of Prophethood, upon him be peace and blessings, and toward his spiritual assistance.

Although there are Sufi scholars who mention some people as the Poles of existence who have existed since the Prophet Adam, upon him be peace, this view has not received much acceptance. The majority of the experts in this matter agree that in every age the Pole of existence is mentioned with the title of *'Abdullah* (the Servant of God) and *'Abduljami* (the Servant of the One Who Has All Excellences in the Infinite Degree).

All the information given so far is based on the spiritual discovery and observation of some talented saints. For this reason, more or less space can always be assigned to the subject. There may even be those who say different things on this matter. God knows best. Therefore, what I should finally do is to entreat God Almighty, saying:

Our Lord, take us not to task if we forget or make mistakes! Our Lord, forgive us, then, our sins, and blot out from us our evil deeds, and take us to You in death, in the company of the truly godly and virtuous.

> *O God! Show us truth as truth and enable us to observe it, and show us falsehood as falsehood and enable us to avoid it. And bestow Your blessings and peace on the Sole Owner of the subtle essence and meaning of being, Muhammad, the sun of the heavens of mysteries, the object of all lights, the pivot of the Divine Majesty, and the axis of the sphere of the Divine Grace and Beauty, and on His Family and Companions, who are the stars of guidance and the springs of assistance.*

FAYD AND *TAJALLI* (EFFUSION AND MANIFESTATION)

Fayd literally means the effusion of blessings, profusion, abundance, and increase. Giving existence to something and equipping it with all the particularities and necessities of being existent, and favoring a person with inspirations and spiritual gifts to deepen him or her spiritually are also included in the meaning of *fayd*, but these aspects belong only to God as the Lord of all creation.

The term *fayd* is also used in some noun phrases with a wide range of meanings as a modified noun. For example, God's all-holy manifestations of origination without anything preceding them to be imitated, His creation, generation and causing things to grow, the granting of life and death, and providing, are all called "effusions of creation"; the inspirations coming from God, the Ultimate Truth are known as "Divine effusions" or "spiritual effusions of the Lord"; a person's being favored with Divine gifts according to his capacity is termed "effusions of capacity"; the spiritual pleasures coming from knowledge and love of God are "effusions of worship"; heart-felt care and concern in the degree of love and yearning are "effusions of love." Everything with which all existence is favored—from the blessings in the initial determination of natures and forms during the phases of creation to the blessings manifested as the laws of the operation of the universe and the lives of beings, and thereafter to the Revelations, inspirations, and sensations that have been sent to human beings—all are effusions of different wavelengths.

Every existent thing or being is created through the profuse manifestations of His Light as a pure blessing, as based on His eternal Will and in accordance with the determinations of His Knowledge. Every existent thing or being is given a particular, perfect form, a particular nature, a particular capacity, and the necessary equipment. During the existential course, existence is endowed with the miracle of life and with a tendency to journey toward metaphysical dimensions that will secure it new gifts. Those endowed with consciousness and free will have been shown the beginning, the end, and the goal of existence through death and the life to follow it, and reminded of what they need the most by being provided materially and spiritually. Through all these vital gifts that have been accorded to existent things and beings and which come in different wavelengths of Divine manifestation, a new door has been left ajar toward the Hidden Treasure.[60]

The first signal of the existence of things and events came from the Most Sacred Effusion, or the most sacred initial manifestation of the Divine Being. Through the Sacred Effusion, or God's sacred manifestation of His Attributes, the archetypes of existence, whose coming into existence was willed, were given the signal of being clothed in external existence, and the course of coming into external existence began for the archetypes that were endowed with the possibility of existence. Then, every would-be-existent thing and being started the journeying of existence with the potential with which it had been endowed, in the expectation of new effusions to develop.

The Most Sacred Effusion, which serves as a veil before the Honor and Grandeur of the Real Agent or Originator of existence, is the manifestation of the essences of all the creatures in Divine Knowledge as archetypes or that these essences are given each a particular nature and/or identity. This appearance of these realities in Divine Knowledge, or the initial growth of existential essences, occurred in accordance with the potential appointed for each being in eternity. Thus, with the exception of the unusual, miraculous

60 The term "the Hidden Treasure" is used for God as based on a *hadith qudsi*, the Prophetic saying inspired in him directly from God Himself: "I was a Hidden Treasure; I willed to be known and created the universe." (Tr.)

disposals of Divine Power, each being is restricted in the potential that has been accorded on it. The poet, Beligh,[61] says:

> The effects of Divine effusions differ according to the
> capacities of every being;
> A pearl-oyster receives pearls from the rain of April,
> but a snake, poison.

The Sacred Effusion has been considered to be the manifestation of the Divine Will and Power that appoints every thing and being of archetypal existence as a particular form and external existence. We can explain the matter more clearly as follows:

The contingent essences, or the essences of contingencies, are reflected upon the "ideal" lines, pages, and booklets of existence through the Most Sacred Effusion. They are clothed in external existence through the Sacred Effusion and take on the forms of the letters, words, sentences, and books of the Tablet of Confirmation and Effacement,[62] being elevated to the rank of serving as mirrors to the Eternal All-Observer.

---

61 Muhammed Emin Beligh (d. 1760) was an Ottoman poet who was born in Greece and lived in Istanbul and Greece. He lived a poor life and wrote a *Diwan*, collection of poems. (Tr.)

62 The origins, sources, and seeds from which God Almighty shapes things and/or beings with perfect order and art show that they are arranged according to a "book of principles" contained in Divine Knowledge. The seeds contain the plans and programs of beings or things that will come into existence. To give a more concrete example, a seed contains or even constitutes the plan and program according to which a tree may be formed and, furthermore, is a miniature embodiment of the Divine principles that cause the tree to come into existence and determine this plan and program. The archetypal plan and program of the Tree of Creation as a whole, which spreads its branches through the past and future and into the World of the Unseen, is called the "Manifest Record," and the Divine principles that determine this plan and program constitute what the Qur'an calls the "Supreme Preserved Tablet" that is contained in Divine Knowledge.

The life history of, for example, a plant or tree from its germination under soil until it yields fruit is the developed form of its seed, and this complete life history with all its cycles is summed up in its fruit, rather in each seed in its fruits. We call this active life history of a living thing or being its "Destiny Practical" or "Manifest Book." With every thing and event in it, the universe has its own "universal" Des-

The difference between these two effusions can also be clarified as follows: The initial manifestation, which causes the realities in the Divine Knowledge to be determined or appointed as archetypes with the potentials particular to each, is the Most Sacred Effusion; the second manifestation, which serves as a veil before the acts of the All-Originator in giving external existence to each archetypal essence according to its original potentials or capacities, is called the Sacred Effusion. According to the Sufis, just as the essential realities or the essential existence of future things and beings in Divine Knowledge is different from their external existences, so also do the sources of these two sorts of existence and the realms of the manifestations responsible for each differ from each other. Thus, while the Most Sacred Effusion manifests itself in the essential realities or pure essences in the Divine Knowledge, the Sacred Effusion acts on the archetypes, with their natures and forms to come forth into external existence.

---

tiny Practical, which is the "universal" Manifest Book. The "Manifest Record," which is written by Divine Knowledge, relates to the origins of things or beings, while the "Manifest Book" relates to their entire life histories and is a notebook written by the Divine Power.

Through the dictates of the Manifest Record, that is, through the decree and instruction of the Divine Knowledge and Destiny, the Divine Power uses atoms to create or manifest the chain of beings, each link of which is His sign, on the metaphorical page of time, which is called the "Tablet of Effacement and Confirmation." Thus, atoms are set to move so that beings may be transferred from the World of the Unseen to the material, visible world, from (the Realm of) Knowledge to the (Realm of) Power.

The "Tablet of Effacement and Confirmation" is the tablet on which events and things or/and beings are inscribed and then removed or effaced according to the dictates of the Supreme Preserved Tablet contained in Divine Eternal Knowledge. Therefore, it displays continuous change. The Tablet of Effacement and Confirmation constitutes the essence of time. Time, a mighty river which flows through existence, has its essence in the Divine Power's inscription of beings and in the "ink" It uses.

Similarly, God also has archetypal principles for human earthly life, all of which are called the "Mother of the Book." He lays down these principles as commandments or laws during human history as suited to the particular needs of the time and the people concerned. For this reason, every age or appointed term has its own Revelation and laws. God sent them down with succeeding Messengers in a way that culminated in the Qur'an as the final form of the Divine Message. (Tr.)

Philosophers think differently from the Sufis about effusion. Although this is not something that is being discussed in this book, I will briefly mention their approaches, starting from the earliest times.

Some of the philosophers use the terms "effusion" and "manifestation" identically and mean "emanation" by both. That is, according to them—God forbid such an assertion!—existence has emanated from God, and what is meant by "effusion" or "manifestation" is that emanation.

Others among them rightly attribute effusion to the Divine Will and Decree, but place several intermediaries of creative effect between God's initial origination of things and events and their coming into existence.

Still others restrict themselves to the external existence of things and events, and conclude that—God forbid such a conclusion!—the aforementioned Divine effusions occur naturally and necessarily. That is, according to them, God naturally and indispensably originates things and events. Thus, they ignore the absolute freedom of the Divine Will in doing or not doing something.

Others conceive of the Divine Being only as the First Cause, without personal existence, and claim that every thing and event emanates from this Being in a certain order.

Still others attribute the initial effusion or, in their terminology, emanation, to an Intellect, which they call the First Intellect, and they talk about a trinity: (1) the Intellect itself, (2) the Intellect's thought of an initial cause, (3) a second Intellect's emanation from this thought.

Yet others think of many Intellects (the Ten Intellects), from the first one to the supposed spirits of realms or spheres of existence, and thereafter to the Active Intellect. They also insert a Soul among those Intellects.

All such assertions by philosophers imply a random guessing at the Unseen, and they are impossible to reconcile with the essence of the Religion. Furthermore, they are of no practical use for true or sound knowledge and faith, knowledge of God, or spiritual pleasures.

Even though some Muslim thinkers have, now and then, busied themselves with such matters, neither these philosophies nor similar trends of thought have made any contribution to Sufi life or experience, which is another way of expressing the Islamic life of the heart and spirit. More than that, they have muddied some simple minds, damaged the spirit of some principles of faith, and caused several trends of falsehood to emerge.

We also come across some Sufi guides who are reported to have written or talked about emanations from God and His self-manifestation as a visible Being. I think that either such contorted ideas have been inserted into their works by others, or they themselves have approached the matter from a different viewpoint in relation to the Divine Oneness and Will and have lapsed into seeing such approaches as harmless. For neither the Qur'an nor the Sunna contain such considerations, nor did the scholars of the earliest times make any mention of them. For this reason, such philosophical approaches to creation can only represent some contaminated information that has found its way into our religious heritage from the legacies of earlier traditions.

As Bediüzzaman Said Nursi points out, the false doctrine of "only one entity emanates from one entity" lies in the essence of such trends of thought. They regard the All-Independent, absolutely Powerful Lord of the worlds to be in need of some powerless means or intermediaries, and present material or immaterial causes, which are in fact veils before the acts of His Lordship, as if His partners. To explain further, these approaches accept the existence of an Intellect besides God, an Intellect which emanated from Him, and they consider God to be inactive—God forbid such conceptions!—ascribing His dominion over all parts and dimensions of existence and all His acts to different means and causes. This is impossible for any believer in God to accept.

As the explanations of the Qur'an and the Sunna concerning creation are so clear as to cause no misunderstandings, so too are the views and conclusions of true Muslim thinkers and scholars regarding this matter so obvious that they make no way for such misconceptions. According to the Qur'anic way of thinking, or the Islamic viewpoint, whatever exists—with all its punctuation, letters, words, sentences, paragraphs, and parts—has been created by the All-Sublime Creator, and receives from Him whatever it needs to subsist; and all that exists is under the control, direction and disposal of His Will and Power at every second of its life, without excluding the partial, free will of conscious, responsible beings. The creation and direction of all the visible and invisible realms of existence belong to God, Who is the sole Source of all gifts and blessings that reach every existent thing and being. With the exception of some misunderstandings that arise from certain ambiguous expressions, all the explanations concerning this matter agree upon this cardinal truth. Sound minds have thought so, sound senses have received the same sensations, and the order, harmony, and instances of wisdom in existence have always expressed it.

Everyone who is able to observe carefully will feel and see that everything—from the multicolored faces of flowers, which send smiles to passers-by, to the swaying of trees in the manner of brides, from the frightening roars of thunderbolts to the delicate, penetrating songs of birds and insects echoing in our souls, from light, heat, gravity, electricity, and chemical processes to biological activities, from humans' observable potential and abilities to their feelings and conscious, spiritual activities—all indicate and bear witness to the Existence of God and His absolute dominion over all things and events. Everyone will feel and see this truth and quiver in awe.

If humans can evaluate the sounds and scenes which come to their ears and touch their eyes by passing through the sensitive filters of the conscience—the sounds and scenes from the terrifying roars of the seas to the enchanting howls of the forests, from the contemplative silence of bays and coves to the awe-inspiring stature of mountains, from the flirtatious gestures of multicolored flowers to the loving kindness of birds and insects, from the world that is a book to study, an exhibition to watch, a palace to visit, and a field to sow and harvest, to humans, who are honored with abilities, to numerous subtle purposes for and instances of wisdom in the existence of all these things—then they will be able to feel and understand that all these have originated from the Sacred and Most Sacred Source of effusion through the Knowledge and Will of God, and go into raptures at the knowledge of the love of God and yearn for Him and for the spiritual pleasures that invade their spirits.

In short, whether spiritual or material, animate or inanimate, large or small, every existent thing or being has come into existence through an effusion from God and continues to exist through constant manifestations that originate in Him, thus pursuing a fixed goal. Coming into existence from non-existence depends on a certain effusion and manifestation, and taking care of every thing or being that has been sent into existence is dependent upon another, different effusion and manifestation. Furthermore, the opening of ways to belief, knowledge of God, and love by means of the Prophets is the result of another gift of effusion—while it is yet another gift of effusion that the same truths brought by the Prophets are presented by saints, verifying, saintly scholars, and true guides to the level of comprehension of every age according to changing time and conditions. It is also another, particular effusive gift that all the means and possibilities down to the slightest ones are used to form a pool of mysteries and enable everyone to benefit from them.

The Creator has boundless gifts that come in effusion,
And in every effusion is a different manifestation.
Whatever we see is a mystery throughout,
Every mystery is clearer than the other for those who are aware of it.

Our Lord! Grant us mercy from Your Presence and arrange for us in our affairs what is right and good!

Our Lord! Grant us a way out and salvation in our affairs!

Bestow your blessings and peace on our master, Muhammad, and on his Family, and Companions, all of them!

TAJALLI (MANIFESTATION)

Tajalli has several meanings such as being uncovered, coming forth, appearance and development within a certain framework and, to a certain extent, Divine Attributes and Names revealing themselves through their works individually or collectively, Divine mysteries and lights making themselves felt in hearts with certain signs, numerous unknown states and particularities that pertain to the Unseen coming to be known through the conscience and seen with the eye of the heart, and spiritual enlightenment through a continuous, sound relationship of servanthood with God Almighty. This term, which has the same meaning as the terms "dawning," "enlightening," and "illuminating" when used for people as objects, is also used for God with some modifiers, such as "the manifestation of the Divine Being or the Divine Essence," "the manifestation of Divine Essential Qualities," "the manifestation of Divine Attributes," "the manifestation of Divine Names," "the manifestation of Divine works," and "the manifestation of Divine acts." There are a few who mention the manifestation of Divine Essential Qualities, and some include the manifestation of Divine works in the manifestation of Divine acts.

The Manifestation of the Divine Being or The Divine Essence

This is a direct manifestation of the Divine Essence beyond all terms of quality and quantity. It is thought about without considering any of His Essential Qualities and Attributes. This manifestation occurs in the realm of acts through the mediation of Divine Attributes and Names. Not only can we not know what this mediation really is like or how it occurs, neither has anyone ever been honored with the perception of the manifestation of the Divine Essence. Those who follow the way of the Master of creation, the Prophet Muhammad, upon him be the most perfect blessings and peace, and make their spiritual journeying under the light of the Religion he brought, always behave like our master Abu Bakr, who said: "Perception of the Divine Essence is admission of our incapacity to perceive Him." They have tried to extinguish the fire of their wonder in the face of such subtle and transcendent matters by thinking as follows:

Perception of transcendent matters
Is not a matter for our incapable reason,
For these scales cannot weigh up such great load.
Ziya Pasha[63]

Like other subtle matters that concern the Divine Being, the manifestation of the Divine Essence is so incomprehensible that the words uttered and articles written about it only add to its imperceptibility. What follows is one of them, which was written by Yazıcızade, the author of *Muhammadiya*:[64]

Since His Image was engraved in my heart,
It has obliterated whatever there was of His Names and Attributes.
I am completely drowned in the ocean of His Oneness,
If only I could take some pearls from this ocean of union.

Muhyi'd-Din ibn al-'Arabi spoke more astonishing words to be able to clarify what is impossible to clarify:

When the all-embracing Light (His universal
manifestations of Oneness) entirely revealed Itself to me,

---

63 Ziya Pasha (1825–1880) was one of the influential political and literary figures of nineteenth-century Ottoman Turkey. He published *Hurriya* (Freedom) newspaper (Tr.)

64 Yazıcızade Muhammed Efendi (d. 1451). One of the important Sufi and literary figures in the fifteenth-century Ottoman Turkey. He lived in Gallipoli. Muhammediye, which is about the life and excellencies of the Prophet Muhammad, is his most famous work. (Tr.)

I began to observe Him in every face. (He reflects his own impression.)
Whoever goes and enters that glorious Ka'ba,
Can turn in all directions to face Him.

Every observation outside the framework of the perception of our incapacity adds greater astonishment to our wonder and increases our feelings of being awestruck.

The Manifestation of Divine Essential Qualities

This is the manifestation that is beyond all veils; it is considered to be the origin of the Divine Attributes that are derived from the Essence of the Divine Being. This manifestation—God knows best—is the origin or source of the capacities and potential of creatures. As declared in, *Every (moment of every) day, He is in a new manifestation* (55:29), the Almighty Divine Being has limitless manifestations, observable or unobservable, universal or particular, which pertain to His Majesty or Grace. Only a few among the profound scholars of truth can perceive these manifestations to some extent. If we do not strictly follow the all-illuminating way of the most perfect Guide, upon him be the greatest of blessings and the most comprehensive peace, concerning the manifestation of both the Divine Essence and Divine Essential Qualities, it is inevitable that we will fall into confusion, even into deviation or misguidance. It is in such confusion and deviation, caused by the lack of guide, that lie the delirious utterances and statements we encounter in the history of thought. A leading figure in the school of Sufism severely warns those who cannot perceive that they are only mirrors reflecting Divine gifts and blessings and therefore they display affectation. He says:

He supposes the spirit to be the Divine Being Himself;
"I am the Truth," echoes in his utterances.
Whoever utters, "I am the Truth," without being a Mansur,
Becomes an unbeliever in God in spirit and body.

The Manifestation of Divine Attributes

This means that any of God Almighty's Attributes manifests Itself in the heart of an initiate. Such an illumination in a heart that is capable of receiving or reflecting it—whether we regard that heart to be a mirror or receptacle—is a great favor. One who has almost reached the final point of spiritual journeying and has been honored with this favor rises to the point of being a polished mirror for the Divine lights, mysteries, and blessings that transcend the limits of his or her own nature, and becomes a receiver and transmitter of the lights belonging to Divine Attributes. Such a one begins feeling, seeing, and hearing differently, and displays many other differences. If, for example, the Attribute of Hearing manifests Itself in a human being to the fullness of their capacity, like the Prophet Solomon, upon him be peace, he or she can hear the voices or sounds of many things and beings, decipher many secrets, and build relationships with them within the bounds of their world. Actually, an initiate whose horizon has been illuminated through the manifestations of the Ultimate Truth begins to see what is unseen, to hear what is unheard, and—provided this favor continues—lives beyond the limits of his nature, achieving transcendent accomplishments. Yazıcızade Muhammed Efendi portrays such a hero of manifestation as follows:

Your Graceful Face has appeared again from
the Castle of Majesty;
Being a lover, I again find myself sighing because
of the eternal Wine;
The veil from my eyes has been lifted again,
And from my heart the veil of ignorance —
The All-Beloved has once more called me with
a transcendental call.

The Manifestation of Divine Names

This manifestation, which denotes that initiates discover the meanings and works of some of God's Names in their hearts, is an intermediate post where talented initiates who have gone beyond the manifestation of Divine acts without encountering any problems in the journeying temporarily halt toward the horizon of the manifestation of Divine Attributes. Initiates stop by this post temporarily, perfect their equipment through Divine gifts, and go on toward another horizon where they will be honored with new favors. If such talented ones, whose hearts have flourished through the manifestation of some of the Divine Names, ask God for something by the grace of the Name on Which the procurement of that thing depends, just at the moment they feel the effusions of these Names in their spirit, certainly God answers their appeal purely out of His Grace. Asking is from us, while answering and giving are from Him:

When God manifests Himself with His favor,
He makes everything easy;
He creates the means for attainment, and grants it instantly.

Whatever we are trying to present concerning all the types of manifestation is pure grace beyond all human means; it can be assessed at its true worth through the criteria of an appreciative heart and comprehended by those who have sufficient knowledge of the heart and its states. Only those with an aware heart can understand whatever is asked about this matter and know the answer to be given. A man of deep spirituality, whose identity is unknown, says:

My tongue is silent about it;
It is something beyond expression.
O saintly one, this is a spiritual state, so
Only those aware of the states of a heart can understand it.

The Manifestation of Divine Works

This expression denotes that whatever is and takes place in the corporeal realm is a work of Divine Power. In its most complete and perfect fashion, this manifestation shows itself on the human face. Humans are the most comprehensive mirrors that reflect the All-Merciful, All-Compassionate One.

The Manifestation of Divine Acts

This expression is used to mean that initiates are aware of some of the Divine acts in their hearts. This is a significant Divine favor. However, it is a reality that those who cannot strictly follow the rules of the Shari'a and the Sunna of the Master of creation, upon him be peace and blessings, in their spiritual journeying may deviate at this point. Those who act as mirrors for Divine acts can fall into the error of falsely attributing to themselves some Divine acts or disposals that they feel are taking place dependent upon their own will and choice. This is nothing less than loss in the place of gain, and this may cause eternal ruin if such people do not immediately turn to follow the Prophetic way in all of their acts and feelings.

Initiates must attribute to God whatever attainment they are favored with and whatever gift comes as a reward for that attainment. Without ever abandoning self-supervision or self-criticism, they must ascribe to themselves nothing more than being a mirror which God uses to reflect some of His acts, works, Names or Attributes. They must not attempt to lay claim to anything with which God has favored them, and they must know that when they see themselves as real agents of such extraordinary blessings, one of the following two results will occur:

1. All the gifts or blessings will cease to come.
2. The gifts or blessings will cause a gradual slide to perdition.

Either of these two results means falling far from the source of the effusions. For this reason, initiates must choose modesty and nothingness in the face of the Eternal One and attribute to Him all their attainments. In this respect, the words of Gawsi are very beautiful:

> You do not manifest Yourself while I am appearing on the screen;
> My non-existence is the condition for Your manifestation of existence.

In addition to the Divine manifestations of Essence, the Essential Qualities, Attributes, Names, works, and acts, Sufis speak of the manifestation of Divine Grace and the manifestation of Divine Majesty.

The Manifestation of Divine Grace

This denotes God's particular manifestations of grace, favoring, care, compassion, and so forth, on an individual thing, being, group or community.

The Manifestation of Divine Majesty

This is regarded as the most comprehensive and greatest manifestation of the Divine Proper Name—Allah (God)—and it is used to express the Necessarily-Existent Being's all-inclusive manifestations of grandeur, glory, and being the All-Overwhelming and All-Compelling.

The first of these two types of manifestations is connected with the Divine Name the All-Compassionate (*ar-Rahim*), and the other is connected with the Name the All-Merciful (*ar-Rahman*).

Some Sufis consider "manifestation" only as Divine effusions that appear in the hearts of believers and focus on such lights of the Unseen in the name of "manifestation." The manifestation which they regard as being the emergence of the lights of the Unseen develops according to the capacity of each person; and in the most talented ones, it shows itself perfectly in a way that indicates the essence and source of everything. All of the human beings' inner senses are fed with these lights and *al-latifa ar-Rabbaniya* (the spiritual intellect) is transformed into a "house of God" with them; *sir* (the faculty of the secret—the spiritual faculty that is more subtle than the heart) becomes a point of observation of some transcendental truths, while *khafiy* (the faculty that is more subtle than the "secret") becomes a bay of private meeting, and *akhfa* (the most subtle faculty) becomes a place of union. We could give more information about these faculties, but it is better to stop here.

> *O God! Make us of those of Your servants who pursue sincerity, and whom You have favored with sincerity and purity of intention, and who have achieved piety and righteousness, and abstinence from all forbidden things, great or small, and whom You have made near to You. And may God's peace and blessings be upon our master, Muhammad and his Family, and Companions, all of them.*

WAHY AND *ILHAM* (REVELATION AND INSPIRATION)

Revelation and inspiration are two subjects that have been much discussed in Islamic religious sciences, as well as by Sufis, as they are each an important dimension of effusion and manifestation. The Sufis have mostly recollected Revelation and inspiration when manifestation is discussed, and since the former ceased after the migration of the Last of the Prophets, upon him be peace and blessings, to the eternal world, the latter has been the focus of discussions concerning the subject.

Telling someone about something, suggestion or gesture, sending a messenger, speaking to someone so privately that no one else can hear, conveying knowledge and information into someone's heart that one would otherwise be required to study, directing some being to act in a certain way without the will of that being, and enabling that being to succeed in some tasks or activities—all these are some of the meanings of Revelation and inspiration.

According to the methodologists in Islamic religious sciences, Revelation means that God conveys or imparts some knowledge from His Presence to His Prophets with or without a means. It is also used for the spiritual words that He puts into the hearts of the Prophets in ways unknown to us. The one who is nearest of all to God, upon him be peace and blessings, who was honored with all types of Revelation, said: "The Spirit of Holiness has been breathed into my spirit." Thus, he stated that Revelation is a spiritual communication between God and His Prophets; however, he made no further explanation as to how it occurs.

Revelation, which can be described as breathing into hearts, occurs within a wide area, ranging from various manifestations to the Master of creation, upon him be peace and blessings, to the inspiration in the heart of the mother of the Prophet Moses, as stated in the verse, *We inspired into Moses' mother* (28:7), and thereafter to what we can define as God's direction or guiding, which is mentioned in the verse, *Your Lord has inspired the honeybee* (16:68). Revelation sometimes occurs as a suggestion through a single sound, gesture or hint, without speech. So, when we mention Revelation, we may sometimes mean this, without meaning Revelation in the religious sense. The revelation mentioned in the verse, *So he (Zachariah) came out to his people from the sanctuary, and revealed (signified) to them: "Glorify your Lord at daybreak and in the afternoon"* (19:11), and that in the verse, *The satans reveal (do whisper and make suggestions) to their confidants to contend with you....* (6:121), are of the kind that mean suggestion, signifying, and whispering.

Revelation, in the sense that God Almighty speaks to His Prophets, occurred in any one of the three ways below (42:51):

- *It is not for any mortal that God should speak to him unless it be by Revelation*: That is, God Almighty directly puts His message in the Prophet's heart and the Prophet knows that this message is from God.
- *Or from behind a veil*: That is, the Almighty conveys His decrees to His chosen servants through their internal and external receptors such as their ears and inner senses.
- *Or by sending a messenger (angel) to reveal, by His leave, whatever He wills (to reveal)*: That is, the Almighty charges one obeyed and trustworthy (angel) who is embodied in a certain form.

God Almighty conveyed His messages to the Prophets, His noble servants, in one of these three ways. In most cases, He employed an angel. According to the Qur'an and the Prophet's authentic Sunna, this angel is Gabriel, whom God describes in the Qur'an as one that is obeyed and trustworthy (81:21). This is the soundest and most elevated way of Revelation. In addition, such a being, mediating between God and His Prophets, is a witness on behalf of the Revealer for those who received the Revelation. So, revealing through an angel is regarded as the main means of Revelation.

Although Revelation came to the great ones among the Prophets mostly by means of an angel, Revelation is also an interactive phenomenon between God and the hearts of His chosen servants. This point is worth deep consideration. Such a transcendent interaction is a special, most elevated favor of God to those who are qualified for it; there is no other rank in the world comparable to it. This interaction occurs in the form of Revelation with the Prophets and of inspiration with the saints. Although Prophets and saints appear to share the same heavenly table in being favored with this metaphysical interaction, Revelation is an objective address which is clear in meaning and binding as a Divine message, one that is witnessed and confirmed by the One Who sends it, as well as the one who conveys it. As for inspiration, it is of a particular nature, open to interpretation, and since it is not conveyed by an angel, it is neither witnessed nor confirmed. Therefore, it is not a binding Divine message.

Both Revelation and inspiration indicate the metaphysical, angelic aspect of humanity. As stated in, *I have breathed into him out of My Spirit* (38:72), it was by virtue of this breathing as a spiritual means or reason that the Prophet Adam, upon him be peace, was favored with vicegerency or regency on the earth. This breathing, which was the origin of the human spirit and therefore human life, is comparable to Revelation. Just as the spirit is the source and mechanism of human life, so too is the Revelation a source and mechanism of the spiritual life of humanity, as it can be seen that God sometimes uses spirit in the same meaning as Revelation: *He conveys the spirit (the life-giving Revelation, from the immaterial realm) of His command to whom He wills of His servants* (40:15).

In the person of the Prophet Adam, upon him be peace and blessings, humankind has been honored with both of these favors. That is, Adam and his descendants were equipped with potential vicegerency through God's initial breathing into them out of His "Spirit," and then some among them were qualified to be honored with Prophethood, or sainthood, by God's sending them Revelation or inspiration. This can also be viewed as a three-step development.

First, God Almighty honored matter with the human spirit through His initial breathing of spirit into it. In the second step, human nature was purified of bad morals or vices and directed toward virtues and therefore toward true humanity by God's breathing something of Revelation or inspiration into it. In the third step, those whose nature was perfectly purified were made, through special favors, the doves in the realms where spirits fly.

Based on this reality, we can say that generations that are not trained and fed by Revelation cannot attain true or perfect human life, nor can those whose breasts do not effervesce with inspiration be honored with vicegerency in the sense of improving the earth with truly useful and necessary operations. In fact, Revelation is an absolutely necessary foundation for the intellectual and spiritual life of humanity, and inspiration is the means by which Revelation develops and flourishes over time to meet the necessities and intellectual levels of every age.

Inspiration, this extremely important source which is based on the Qur'an and the Sunna and which finds its true worth in conformability with them, keeps silent where it must do so out of respect for the Qur'an and the Sunna, speaking only based upon them, and never attempts to transgress them or use them to confirm any possible errors. Although it is not a source of objective knowledge, it has always served as a source of recourse, like a spring of sweet, fresh water. Some distinguished scholars have regarded inspiration to be among the stipulations that are necessary to do *ijtihad*, that is, to deduce new laws based on the Qur'an and Sunna to meet the emerging requirements in every age, and have thus evaluated it as the deciding factor when there are conflicting views.

Saints pay greater attention and value to inspiration and assign an even broader area for it. The breadth of the area where inspiration is applicable depends on our scope of knowledge and ability to use it. We can consider this as transforming knowledge into actions and deepening in inspiration through knowledge of God so that we are able to be open to Divine favors. We can liken this process to winds that move clouds of rain. As long as these winds blow or are blown, inspiration pours like heavy rain. When it does not come like heavy rain, it comes in drizzles. The Master of creation, upon him be perfect blessings and peace, proclaims: "God inspires what they do not know in the ones who practice what they know." This can be viewed as a wonder of knowledge. Those who have expert knowledge of the matter call the acquired knowledge that causes inspiration to come "the knowledge of what is outward and explicit" or "the knowledge acquired," while the knowledge that arises through inspiration is considered to be "the knowledge of what is inward and implicit" or "the knowledge bestowed as a pure favor."

Inspiration is acceptable and regarded as sound so long as it is in conformity with the indisputable principles and foundations established by the Qur'an and the Sunna, and as long as it can be viewed as an origin of rules of a secondary degree. However, it is of a subjective character, and therefore it is not binding on others. But the Revelation which comes to the Prophets, is an objective, binding phenomenon. Revelation takes place beyond the spheres of the human soul and sensations, and its certainty transcends the conviction which comes from mere knowledge. As mentioned above, it usually occurs by means of an angelic envoy. As for what is stated in the verse, *And He revealed to His servant what He revealed* (53:10), it is one of the ways in which Revelation comes. This verse, as particularly related to the Prophet Muhammad, upon him be peace and blessings, expresses a direct, heavenly, unique favor—an extra reward—in accordance with the spirit of the Ascension, for the hero of nearness to God. The angel who brought the Revelation of the Qur'an taught the Prophet how to recite it. This was guidance in a particular field of one who was superior in general terms by one who was inferior.

Muhyi'd-Din ibn al-'Arabi regards Revelation as a development from the rank of absorption,[65] or concentration on the

---

65 For the rank of absorption *(Maqam Jam')*, see M. Fethullah Gülen, *Emerald Hills of the Heart – Key Concepts in the Practice of Sufism,* The Light, NJ, 2004, vol. 2, pp. 199–205. (Tr.)

Divine Being, toward the rank of elaboration, where the Divine Being manifests Himself with His Speech. According to him, whatever there is in the name of existence consists of a development from a concentrated or compacted form toward elaboration or expansion. Another important one who was aware of the Divine mysteries interprets the phenomenon of Revelation as transition from existence as knowledge to existence perceived. This second interpretation can be viewed as the willful, direct, or indirect effusion of Divine Knowledge in the form of Speech to one endowed with the required intellectual and spiritual equipment.

Another phenomenon discussed in connection with inspiration is that of imparting information. Inspiration is knowledge or perception that radiates in the heart as a Divine grace. It cannot be the source of any objective, binding religious rule, although it can be seen and accepted as a means of illumination and clarification in some respects by those who receive it and those who follow them as guides. Imparting information occurs in parallel with, or is proportionate to, human effort. Without any efforts on the part of a human being, imparting information cannot occur. However, inspiration is a Divine gift in which human effort has little part. Unlike Revelation, inspiration comes without any intermediary and is a special, direct way of communication. According to the majority of scholars, the angels of Revelation do not come and bring messages to people other than the Prophets.

Both Revelation and inspiration are special favors of God to those endowed with the special intellectual and spiritual equipment for receiving them. The purpose for these favors is to convey God's decrees to His servants. Both Prophets and saints approach Revelation and inspiration in terms of their responsibility to personally practice and represent God's decrees in their lives and convey them to others, without ever thinking of boasting about them, or seeing them as a means of special rank.

As 'Abdu'l-Wahhab ash-Sharani[66] points out, both feeling and receiving the Divine effusions of Revelation and inspiration require a special disposition, as well as intellectual and spiritual endowments. It is by developing such intellectual and spiritual endowments that Prophets or saints train some of their emotions and faculties which are regarded as the origin of certain vices in human nature, and restrict them in such a way that they are able to use them as required by the Divine purpose for their creation. This is also the way in which they develop or deepen in spirituality. Human beings rise to the point where they can perceive the metaphysical breezes that blow in different wavelengths in proportion to their struggling against or training the faculties that are the origins of vices in their nature; these breezes stimulate the spirit toward moral and spiritual perfection. Such people can even rise to the horizon unrestricted by the measures of our time and space, where they can acquire knowledge of many things pertaining to the Unseen.

The Prophets are incomparable heroes of this attainment. After these most illustrious servants of God come the saints and the purified, exacting scholars, who are regarded as His other noble servants in the heavens and on the earth. Divided into such classes of the godly, virtuous ones and those favored with God's special nearness, these noble servants of God receive and convey God's decrees like a central system, and give guidance to those traveling on the way to God.

> *O God! Show us the truth as truth and enable us to observe it, and show us falsehood as falsehood and enable us to avoid it. And bestow Your blessings and peace upon our master, Muhammad, and on His Family and Companions, altogether.*

---

66 Imam 'Abdu'l-Wahhab ash-Sharani (897/1492–973/1566): A great scholar of the sixteenth century. He lived in Egypt, and wrote books on jurisprudence, theology, Sufism, medicine, and grammar. *Kitab al-Mizan* ("The Book on Balance") is his most famous book. (Tr.)

A'YAN ATH-THABITA AND *'ÂLAM AL-MITHAL* (ARCHETYPES AND THE WORLD OF REPRESENTATIONS OR IDEAL FORMS)

In Sufi terminology, archetypes are the established, existential origins of things in the realm of Divine Knowledge. They consist of the manifestations of the Divine Names in the realm of Knowledge, and they denote the existential essences that pertain to the origins of contingencies. Although the relationships of these spiritual forms or existential essences in the realm of Knowledge with the Divine Being seem to be within the frame of time, they are beyond time. The limitless content of Divine Knowledge is different from the existential essences that are individually or collectively identified within the frame of time. Even though whatever exists in Divine Knowledge has some sort of individually or collectively identified existence, it is equally possible whether it will be brought into external existence or not within the dimensions of time and space.

It is a fact that whether they are Sufi leaders or theologians, those who have expert knowledge of this subject have lacked the words with which to express the issues that pertain to the transcendental dimensions of existence; indeed, they take great care in order to avoid any confusion. As mentioned before under the title of Effusion, they call the Divine manifestation on the archetypes, which is a Divine mystery whose essential nature we cannot know, the Most Sacred Effusion, while the manifestation considered to be the origin of the archetypes emerging as existent beings and things within the dimensions of time and space is termed the Sacred Effusion. By such designations, scholars not only remind us that the archetypes and the contingencies that have been brought into the time and space-bound realm of existence are different from one another, they also focus our attention on the difference between manifestation (*tajalli*) and emergence (*zuhur*), thus stressing the Qur'anic truth concerning the beginning and process of the creation of the universe. This truth can never be reconciled with the philosophical approaches of monism and pantheism.

I think that since some cannot avoid going into extremes, they cannot preserve balance in approaching the most sublime Divine truths and thus fall into many grievous faults. Those who concentrate on the all-encompassing Divine Will and the all-overwhelming Power ignore the universe and view all things as if they were God's incarnates, while others who focus on things and beings themselves, together with the apparent causes for their existence, take on views of naturalism or materialism. However, the unity or uniformity of or the interconnectedness in existence comes from the unity of the Origin of manifestation, while the almost limitless variation among and multiplicity in things and beings issue from the different dispositions or operations of the archetypes in the Divine Knowledge by the Divine Will and Power.

Self-existence with all its parts is one thing; things and beings appearing in different mirrors of existence in all their varieties through the manifestations of the Divine Knowledge and Existence is another. If we can perceive this difference, we will be able to notice the aspects of existence which lead some to the doctrine of the transcendent Unity of Being, and some others to the Unity of the Witnessed, and understand the difference between the essence and the form, and between the One Who gives existence and makes subsist and those who are brought into existence and made to subsist. We can explain the differences in question in plainer terms as follows:

Things and beings are not existent by or on account of themselves, but they exist by God's bringing them into existence or by being the shadows of the light of God's Existence from behind numerous veils. Apparent or superficial existence is one thing, and real, substantial existence is another. Forms and appearances are reflections as gifts from Him; they are neither identical with Him nor independent of Him. He said to them, "Be!" and they were. When He cuts off His effusion, they will disappear. Assertions such as Divine incarnation, existential union with Him, being an embodiment of Him, and His being a pervasive Soul—these and other similar assertions are all false. What gives external existence to all things and beings are the manifestations of His Attributes and Names:

> If you focus on the forms, you will see that both you and I exist—
> But in absolute, transcendent reality, neither you nor I exist.

Now, as it is the All-Living, All-Subsisting One Who gives existence and subsists, who can have the right to claim self-existence? Everything's existence depends on His Existence and Knowledge; whatever exists is a mirror in which His Names manifest themselves as being ultimately responsible for anything that occurs in it. Humanity is the most comprehensive and polished of these mirrors, and the Master of creation, upon him be perfect blessings, is the most perfect and complete of these. What follows is an anonymous couplet expressing this:

> Whatever exists in the universe is a mirror and subsists by Him;
> It is God Who is constantly reflected in the mirror of Muhammad.

Without considering the First Identification, the archetypes are contingencies which are regarded as non-existent in one respect. When they first emerge, they are hidden and not known; and when they are sent into existence, they continue their non-existence on account of themselves. They serve as veils for the manifestations of Divine Knowledge and Existence. As this service of veiling is, in the words of Bediüzzaman, required by the Divine Dignity and Grandeur so that those who reason superficially should not see the Hand of Power as directly related to certain seemingly insignificant or vile things and affairs, it must also be in order to guide humanity, which has been honored with vicegerency—the administration of the earth according to God's law—to be careful about their considerations of the Divine Being and His manifestations.

As in the world, which is the realm of existence and decline, the manifestations of the Divine Majesty and Grace also follow one another in the realm of the archetypes. While the Divine Majesty manifests Itself to destroy, the Divine Grace invents. These manifestations continue after those of archetypes which have been decreed to be sent into the realm of perceptible existence have been clothed in existence. It can be said that every existent thing bursts forth out of the spring of archetypes and becomes an "ideal reflection or representation," or "form." Then, these forms are clothed in perceptible existence.

All of the attributes to be manifested by beings in the corporeal world, including conflicting ones such as light and darkness, good and evil, bliss and wretchedness, have already been determined while they are in the World of Representations or "Ideal Forms." However, a conscious, responsible being's nature as good and blissful or evil and wretched is determined according to his or her future choice in this corporeal world. No one other than the All-Knowing of the Unseen can judge them until their state becomes apparent in the corporeal world. However, God may inform some of His "purified, chosen servants" about their "future" states and natures while they are in the World or Realm of Representations or "Ideal Forms." This is an exception and therefore beyond the sphere of our duties or responsibilities. The statements or declarations of the All-Knowing of the Unseen in the Qur'an in reference to these are sometimes about their states in the Realm of Representations, and sometimes about those in the corporeal world. So, those unaware of this fact may confuse one with the other. For example, the Qur'an's declaration regarding Satan to mean, *He was from among the unbelievers,* without considering his rebellion, is concerned with the archetype of Satan, while its description, *He grew arrogant and became one from among the unbelievers* (2:34; 38:74), is about his state after he rejected God's order when, therefore, the signs of his rebellion appeared.

Some saints can at times observe the states of the archetypes plainly or in the form of symbols as in dreams. This is a special, extraordinary favor from God to them. God sometimes informs them about certain future events and so reminds them of some points peculiar to them. It sometimes occurs that the Almighty sends these heroes of self-possession some signals regarding impending dangers, directing their hearts to prayer and supplication. At other times, they are reminded of the necessity of preserving the balance between the means and material causes and the Causer of causes, being called to focus on the Divine absolute Unity.

The information and observations mentioned concerning the archetypes are usually presented to God's specially chosen, purified servants in the forms of "ideal" tablets. These tablets are manifested either identically with their future, corporeal existential forms, or in symbols according to their meaning and contents. Symbolic representations require interpretation, like unclear dreams. Their interpretation is possible through knowing or discovering the key words or terms in the Qur'an and the authentic Prophetic Traditions. Any interpretation made without this knowledge means "throwing random stones at the Unseen" and therefore amounts to disrespect for the All-Knowing of the Unseen.

The realm or the world where the immaterial forms or models belonging to the archetypes are reflected and represented is called "the World or the Realm of Representations or Ideal Forms," and the forms or reflections in this World are termed "the ideal or reflected forms." The perceptible, corporeal forms are the shadows of these ideal or reflected forms. Some of the ideal forms are purely spiritual, while others have some perceptible figures. The realm where the former reside is called "the World of Absolutely Ideal Forms," while the realm where the latter reside is known as "the World of Specified Forms."

Some see the World of Representations or Ideal Forms as the representations or reflections of corporeal forms and events in our world of sensations in their particular energetic covers. This can be exemplified by the appearances of spirits and angels in certain forms in our world. There are so many simple (not composite) natures which belong to the Realm of the Spirit and the Divine Commands or the pure, primordial natures as the first results of the Divine commands that they can appear in the corporeal world in certain forms by God's will; they appear in the corporeal world to the extent allowed by the Divine Names primarily manifested on each. They can appear and exert some influence on the physical world as mere causes. There are many reliable Prophetic reports that knowledge appears in the form of or is represented by milk, and that Islam is symbolized by a splendid container; the Qur'an, as honey or an orange; and the feeling of enmity, as snakes or vermin.

Some Sufis see the Realm of Representations or Ideal Forms as broader and maintain that this realm is the intermediate between this world and the Hereafter, and between matter and spirit, and the realm of immaterial sacred spirits. According to these considerations, the World of Representations or Ideal Forms is an intermediate bridge over which meanings or purely spiritual identities pass in order to attain a new identity and nature; it is a mysterious corridor between the physical and metaphysical worlds, a veil between two different dimensions, a point of meeting for abstract truths and concrete realities, and the horizon that separates the perceptible and imperceptible from each other. There are some who see this world as a realm where meanings or abstract truths begin to be clothed in worldly existence. Abstract or immaterial identities become familiar with the silky robe of external or perceptible existence in this intermediate realm, and they set off toward further realms from this dock with the equipment that they have been given.

Dictionaries of religious terminology define the intermediate realm also as the special corridor that connects this world and the Hereafter, or the process that begins with death, continues with the life of the grave, and ends in the Resurrection; or as the point where the world of spirits and abstract meanings meets with the corporeal realm, or as the passage between the horizon of the heart and spirit and the carnal life.

Not only is every ramp or platform from which things and beings jump to another stage—where they will be given a different nature and identity during their journeying of existence from the "initial or first identification or determination" to corporeal life—called the Intermediate Realm, but the realm of life beginning with death is also known as the intermediate life. According to the first meaning, the intermediate life is a bridge between the spirit and the body or between the abstract and the concrete. According to the second meaning, it is like a waiting lodge that resembles both the Unseen and the corporeal realms at the point where the world and the Hereafter meet. Everyone will pass across that bridge and those whom God wills will call at that waiting lodge and afterwards go on toward the other world in different ways, according to their equipment or acquisitions.

Some Sufis mention another intermediate realm which they call *Barzakh Jami'* (the Encompassing Intermediate Realm). This is a term used to denote the original or essence of all the intermediate realms, which is another name for *tajalli wahidiya* (God's manifestation of all His Names throughout the universe or on an entity), or *ta'ayyun awwal* (the initial or first identification). The Encompassing Intermediate Realm is also called "the First Intermediate Realm," "the Grandest Intermediate Realm," or "the Greatest Intermediate Realm." The essence of this Realm is the meaning or spirit of humanity and its seed and fruit is *haqiqat Ahmadiya* (the Ahmadi Truth or the Truth of Ahmad).[67] In the words of Bediüzzaman Said Nursi, the Prophet Muhammad's light is the ink of the Pen of the Author of the universe. It is also the seed of the fruit of the tree of creation, the key to all the Gardens of Paradise, the insurmountable wall before Hell, the alchemy of the happiness of hearts, and the genuine, sole guide to human excellencies and perfections.

May perfect blessings and peace and the most honorable of benedictions be upon him and his Family and Companions.

---

67 For *haqiqat Ahmadiya* or Ahmadi Truth or the Truth of Ahmad, see note 53. (Tr.)

HEAVENLY OR ELEVATED REALMS

Just as the Creator has limitless Names, so too do these Names and the Attributes in which the Names originate possess the realms of manifestation in the greatest degree, the secondary degree, the third degree, and so on. The realms that are heavenly transcend our horizon of perception and they are of transcendent meaning and content. Although we can have some degree of exact knowledge about the Corporeal or Visible Realm (*'Âlam Mulk* or *Shahada*), it is extremely difficult to be able to have or give definite knowledge about the nature or number of the heavenly realms, such as the Realm of the Transcendental Manifestation of Divinity (*'Âlam Lahut*), the Realm of the Transcendental Manifestation of the Divine Mercy and Compassion (*'Âlam Rahamut*), the Realm of the Transcendental Manifestation of Divine Attributes and Names (*'Âlam Jabarut*), and the Realm of the Transcendental Manifestation of Divine Commands (*'Âlam Malakut*). All the considerations concerning these are based on spiritual discovery and observation in conformity with the essential principles of Islam that have been established by the Qur'an and the Sunna.

From the perspective of Islamic epistemology, whether visible or invisible, transparent or opaque, observable or unobservable, animated or unanimated, from this world or other world, everything is an *'âlam* (realm or world). Derived from the same root word as *'alam*, meaning a sign or mark, everything and what lies beyond it is a sign for the existence of the Divine Being, a document of His acts, a mirror to His Perfection, a register of Destiny, a site where the relevant Divine determination is manifested, and a location for the manifestation of Divine Attributes and Names. For this reason, whether visible or invisible, everything bears traces belonging to or is a sign for the Divine Being; therefore, it is regarded as an *'âlam* (realm, world). Its plural is *'awalim* or *'âlamin*. While the incorporeal entities, such as intellect or reason, spirit, soul, consciousness, feeling, and perception—which come into existence by His mere command "Be!"—are considered to belong to the Realm of the (Initial Manifestation of) Divine Commands (*'Âlam Amr*), all corporeal, compound, or composed and decomposable entities contained in time and space are regarded as constituting the Realm of Physical Creation (*'Âlam Khalq*). These two realms—the Realm of the (Initial Manifestation of) Divine Commands and the Realm of Physical Creation—are also dealt with under the titles of the Unseen Realm or World (*'Âlam Ghayb*) and the Visible or Corporeal World (*'Âlam Shahada*), respectively. All other realms are included in these two main realms.

The Unseen World is the realm which we cannot perceive with our five external senses. Including in particular the realms that are mentioned above as heavenly realms, many other inner and transcendent realms—such as the Spiritual Realm, the Realm of the Spirit, the Realm of Representations or Ideal Forms, and the Intermediate Realm—are considered to be realms that belong to the Unseen World.

As for the Visible or Corporeal World and the question of how many corporeal worlds there are, such as those called the Realm of Physical Creation, the Realm of the Divine Property and Dominion, the Realm of Matter, the Realm of Physical Bodies, the Realm of Physical Forms, and the Realm of Density, these are all titles given to that World from different viewpoints. And even though they are mentioned with different titles, the Unseen World and the Visible or Corporeal World—or the World of (the Initial Manifestation of) Divine Commands and the World of Physical Creation—are concentric realms, the former being the inner dimension of the latter, and the latter being the outer dimension of the former. However, all the realms, both those mentioned and not mentioned, have characteristics particular to each and are different from others, as they are the domains where Divine Attributes and Names are manifested and God acts as the Lord of all the worlds in different degrees and ways.

According to verifying scholars, existence, including in particular humankind, has different degrees or stages of birth. They are as follows: The first of these degrees or stages is the stage of the initial, transcendental manifestation of the Divine Attributes and Names, the second is the emergence of Divine Commands in the rank of the transcendental manifestation of Divine Attributes and Names, and the third is the appearance of physical substances and bodies in the horizon of the manifestation of Divine Commands. And even though this development or expansion may seem to have the same meanings as the ideas of "descent" and "ascent" in some Sufi and philosophical schools, they are actually different.

The degrees or stages mentioned are titles in the determination and identification of different ranks in the process of creation. They also point to the stations which initiates are bound to reach and pass during their journeying to the station of subsistence by and with God. An initiate ascends toward the imperceptible, indescribable, and transcendental manifestation of the Divine Being through the realms of Divine works, acts, Names, and Attributes successively. We can also view this as journeying in the attainment of knowledge of God and spiritual pleasure through the realms of Corporeal Existence, the Initial Manifestation of Divine Commands, the Transcendental Manifestation of Divine Attributes and Names, and the Transcendental Manifestation of the Divine Mercy and Compassion—as high as the Realm of the Transcendental Manifestation of Divinity, which is considered to be the horizon of "annihilation in God" and "subsistence by and with God." Subsistence by and with God begins by having glimpses of the Realm of the Transcendental Manifestation of Divine Commands, and goes on rising higher and higher, reaching the rank of living at the level of the heart and spirit. When initiates reach the point where they can perceive that their existence is a shadow of the light of His Existence, this journeying then, in one respect, ends.

Now, from the horizon of our perception, let us try to see into the stations or stages of this journeying, from the highest down to the lowest, with the distinguishing features of each.

'Âlam Lahut (The Realm of the Transcendental Manifestation of Divinity)

This is the highest, all-encompassing realm where the Attributes and Names of the Divine Being, Who is beyond all perception and conception and therefore is known or recognized through His Names and Attributes, and Whose existence is proven by His works, are manifested beyond all terms of modality or quantity and quality. This manifestation is also known by other titles, such as the Unseen of the Whole Unseen, the Absolutely Hidden Treasure, the Realm of Absolute Existence, the Unseen Absolute, and the Truth of Truths.

Another approach to the Realm of the Transcendental Manifestation of Divinity is that it is an absolutely transcendental realm that is related to Allah (God)—the Proper Name of the Divine Being that contains all other Names—on Which the existence and subsistence of all other realms—with all their distinguishing features, as well as the things and beings they contain—depend. It is also the first-rank source of radiance for our thoughts, feelings, and sensations, and for all the actions we perform with our inner and outer faculties. All of the Divine Essential Qualities, Attributes, and Names are concentrated and intersect in this realm. Being the infinite realm for the Divine Being's initial manifestation beyond all modality or all terms of quantity and quality, this realm also encompasses all of the other realms. Since it is the realm for this manifestation, it reminds us of our servanthood and duty of worship. That is, as Divinity connotes being the Worshipped, Sought, and Loved One, this realm implies the duty of worship to God the Ultimate Truth, according to the relevant commands of the Qur'an. Purely being the Divine Being, God is also the All-Worshipped, Eternally-Sought, and All-Loved One.

The Initial, Transcendental Manifestation of Divinity is an all-encompassing mirror to the Divine Being and therefore it is eternally unchangeable. As this manifestation is a mirror eternal in the past, It denotes a manifestation that is also eternal in the future. In the course of history, different ways of worship and servanthood have been born from human thought and they have led to the fabrication of many objects of worship. However, all these human-generated ways of worship and human-fabricated objects of worship have been forgotten, and only the Unique, All-Majestic One of absolute Transcendence, Who has All-Lofty Attributes and All-Beautiful Names, has remained. He has no beginning at all; since He is thus, He is eternal, with no end at all. He exists eternally, and both His non-existence and impermanence are absolutely inconceivable. And the Realm of the Transcendental Manifestation of Divinity is the most polished mirror of His manifestation as the Divine Being, Who has all the Attributes mentioned.

'Âlam Rahamut (The Realm of the Transcendental Manifestation of Divine Mercy and Compassion)

All animals and vegetables on the earth are honored with life as pure favor of the Creator; their survival and multiplication in a determined, harmonious system are also pure favor, and they receive numerous other favors during their lives; humans are equipped with many special faculties and attributes, in addition to those they share with animals, and they receive special mercy, tenderness, assistance, and care—all such and other favors unmentioned which are accorded to living creatures overflow from *'Âlam Rahamut*, where the first, transcendental manifestation of Divine Mercy and Compassion occurs. This can also be explained as follows.

God Almighty's concentrated manifestation of all of His Attributes and Names and, particularly, His being the Eternally Besought-of-All on the whole of the universe is a manifestation of His Divinity or *'Âlam Lahut*; while the fact that every entity benefits from His Mercy, Compassion, Preservation, Help, Care, and Protection according to its capacity, is a manifestation that issues from the horizon of *'Âlam Rahamut*. This realm is absolutely connected with the Divine Attributes and Names. In relation to God's being the All-Merciful, it is the most unique sphere of the Essential Attributes of the Divine Essence, while in relation to His being the All-Compassionate, it is the realm where the Attributes derived from God's acts (they are almost infinite, such as Providing, Creating, Sustaining, Forgiving, etc.) manifest themselves.

This realm can also be viewed as the initial manifestation of the limitless Divine Mercy, Which surpasses His sacred "Wrath," in a way that identifies or determines every formation. As God's being the All-Merciful (*ar-Rahman*) expresses His all-encompassing, limitless Mercy, the realm where this Mercy manifests Itself is certainly an all-embracing realm of Mercy. Since God's being the All-Compassionate (*ar-Rahim*) denotes those acts of His that issue from His Mercy, the Realm of the Transcendental Manifestation of His being the All-Merciful can be viewed as the source from which God's particular mercy (compassion) reaches all things and beings individually according to the capacity and merit of each individual from the stage of existence in God's Knowledge to their corporeal existence. This Realm relates to eternity in the past from the perspective of God's being the All-Merciful (*ar-Rahman*), while from the perspective of His being the All-Compassionate (*ar-Rahim*), It relates to eternity in the future.

The favors that come to every creature at the beginning of its existence, in return for having done nothing, issue from God's All-Mercifulness; no creature is deprived of these. The existence of every creature, the life span, and particular physical form accorded to it, along with all the faculties, urges, and desires with which it is endowed to survive and multiply—all its vital necessities and the possibilities created to meet them—these are all favors that issue from the Realm of God's All-Mercifulness. As for the favors that come in return for every creature's labor, strife, and efforts, including eternal happiness in the other world for conscious, responsible beings and their being honored with the vision of God, they have their source in God's All-Compassionateness.

Both the Realm of the Transcendental Manifestation of God's Divinity and the Realm of the Transcendental Manifestation of Divine Mercy and Compassion, or God's being the All-Merciful and the All-Compassionate, are realms that are related to God's knowledge of everything and to His making Himself known through His manifestations of Mercy, Care, and Helping; He thus prepares hearts for perfect servantood to Him through worship and obedience.

'Âlam Jabarut (The Realm of the Transcendental Manifestation of Divine Attributes and Names)

This realm is the realm where Divine Attributes and Names manifest themselves transcendentally. It also known by other titles, such as the Realm of Unity, the Grand Intermediate Realm, the Truth of Ahmad, the Grandest Spirit, the Universal Spirit, and the First Shadow. Some Sufi scholars view this Realm as the Realm of Divine Grandeur and Power, which is situated between the Realms of the Manifestation of Divinity and the Manifestation of Divine Mercy and Compassion, or between the Realms of the Manifestation of Divinity and the Manifestation of Divine Commands. It is certain that this Realm, like the others described above, is a heavenly and spiritual one. It is also certain that it has nothing to do with Egypt's Hermes Trismegistus'[68] considerations of realms, or Plato's Realm of Ideas. According to Ibrahim Haqqi of Erzurum, this Realm is above the Divine Supreme Seat and below the Divine Supreme Throne—I do not know what he means by "above" and "below"—and views all other Realms from "above."

---

68 Hermes-Thot was an Egyptian sage who lived in pre-historic times. In order to separate him from the Greek Hermes, he is also called Hermes Trismegistus. According to certain historians, he was a monist. (Tr.)

From the perspective of all the considerations mentioned, the Realm of the Transcendental Manifestation of Divine Commands (*'Âlam Malakut*) is a realm "below" the Divine Supreme Seat and beyond all conceptions, while the Realm of the Transcendental Manifestation of Divinity (*'Âlam Lahut*) is above all other realms—beyond any consideration of "over" or "above" and "below"—and relates to "God's seating Himself on the Supreme Throne." As for the other two Realms of the Transcendental Manifestation of Divine Mercy and Compassion and the Transcendental Manifestation of Divine Attributes and Names, the former is the realm of growth and development on the part of the manifestation of Mercy and Compassion, while the latter is the realm of Divine Grandeur and Dominion before, or next to, the former.

Divine Destiny and Decree have a particular relation with the Realm of the Transcendental Manifestation of Divine Attributes and Names. This relation also encompasses events associated with persons. When all things and events are considered, the Realm of the Transcendental Manifestation of Divine Attributes and Names is a pure, spiritual realm. Therefore, it is higher than the Realm of the Transcendental Manifestation of Divine Commands and the Corporeal Realm. All things and events are identified in this realm in the entirety of each, while they are individualized and particularized in the others.

'Âlam Malakut (The Realm of the Transcendental Manifestation of Divine Commands)

Also called by other titles such as the Realm of the Initial Manifestation of Divine Commands, the Realm of Spirits, the Intermediate Realm, the Horizon of the Final Identification, and the Relative Spirit, the Realm of the Transcendental Manifestation of Divine Commands is the final and lowest order or level of immaterial entities, and it can be considered as the roof of the Corporeal Realm. This classification is according to the order or ranks of the manifestations of the Divine Essence, Attributes, and Names. It is not based on a decisive statement of the Qur'an and the Prophet, upon him be peace and blessings, but on spiritual discovery and observation and on interpretation and inference founded upon the fundamental, unchanging principles of the Religion.

The Realm of the Transcendental Manifestation of Divine Attributes and Names, the Realm of Divine Commands, and the Realm of Corporeality exist as the inner or outer dimension of one another, or as one within or above the other. That is, if the Realm of the Transcendental Manifestation of Divine Attributes and Names is a separate realm, then each of the other two realms are dimensions of it. The first of these three realms is a realm of natures, and thus does not have an external existence. Everything exists in it as a determined nature, while it is clothed in a form—or in corporeal existence—in the other two, respectively.

All four realms being discussed are transcendental realms in which the exact divisions of place and time—such as top and bottom, above and below, front and back, in front or behind, day and night, and yesterday and today—are beyond consideration. Therefore, a heart that has developed or advanced far enough on the way of spirituality can experience yesterday together with today, and today together with tomorrow, transcending the boundaries of time.

The human rank or mission of vicegerency on the earth relates to the heart and its relationship with the Realm of the Transcendental Manifestation of God's Commands. Although humans belong to the corporeal realm with respect to their bodily existence, as far as the inner dimension of their existence is concerned, they belong to the Realm of the Transcendental Manifestation of Divine Commands. We can even say that human bodily existence corresponds to the Corporeal Realm, while the inner dimension of human existence corresponds to the Realm of the Transcendental Manifestation of Divine Commands. This same relationship also exists between the universe and the Divine Supreme Throne, and between the earth and the Ka'ba. A heart that is open to the Realm of the Transcendental

Manifestation of Divine Commands is more spacious than the earth—while even a large body is more cramped than a cup. Human corporeal existence is the place where sensations are imprisoned and concentrated, but the spiritual dimension of existence is where human spiritual and intellectual faculties develop and expand. The gifts and radiance coming from the Realm of the Transcendental Manifestation of Divine Commands are the source of wealth and power for a spirit, and no one is thought to be able to remain indifferent to it. Anyone completely cut off from this realm has entered a way that will lead to complete loss and ruin.

Both the corporeal and incorporeal dimensions of existence have fully and most perfectly been manifested on the Master of creation, upon him be perfect blessings. With respect to his bodily existence, he is the most perfect; also, he is the incomparable representative of the spirit of Islam regarding the spiritual dimension of his existence, which is reflected in his conduct. His Ascension beyond the realms—as high as the insurmountable boundary between Divinity and servanthood—is the wonder or miracle and expansion of his spiritual existence. Truly, through the Ascension, he was favored with the full, unparalleled attainment of spiritual visions and observations, and he rose to the rank of being the pride of the inhabitants of both the heavens and the earth.

Vision of God, the Ultimate Truth, Who is beyond any concept of modality, has different ranks or degrees. The vision of Him from the horizon of belief in Him as the sole, ultimate Agent of all actions in the universe is of the first or lowest degree; the vision of Him from the summit of belief in Him as the sole, ultimate Owner and Giver of all the attributes that are shared by all existence is of the second degree. Experiencing the pleasure of the vision of Him from the peak of belief in Him as the sole, truly Existent Being is of the highest degree. However, there are veils in human nature that prevent these visions, from those which arise from the veils formed of feelings, imagination, fancy, and whims, to those which are produced by failing to observe the criteria of the Shari'a and the balances established by the Sunna and by making some utterances or assuming some attitudes incompatible with essential Islamic principles.

When the hearts that are not prevented by such veils from being elevated rise and are purified of the dirt of attachment to all things other than God, they become bright, polished mirrors to the various truths including even the Ultimate Truth of Truths. They reflect the lights of the Divine Essence and Attributes; they get in contact with the Realm of the Transcendental Manifestation of Divine Commands; they speak with the voice of the Realm of the Transcendental Manifestation of Divine Attributes and Names; they build relations or transact "business" with the Realm of the Transcendental Manifestation of the Divine Mercy and Compassion; and they reach a point where they are favored with reflections from the Realm of the Transcendental Manifestation of Divinity. As a consequence, the heart begins to beat with the messages of the Realm of the Transcendental Manifestation of Divine Commands, and the spirit starts inhaling the breezes of the Realm of the Transcendental Manifestation of Divine Attributes and Names, while the secret—the inner faculty that is more refined than the heart—commences experiencing feelings related to the Realm of the Transcendental Manifestation of Divinity. The first of these attainments is described as "the victory near," the second, as "the victory manifest," and the third, as "the victory absolute."

O God, O Opener of doors! Open our hearts and other outer and inner faculties and senses to belief, the practice of Islam, and excellence in servanthood to You, and enable us always to do what You love and are pleased with! And bestows blessings and peace on our master, Muhammad, who is honored with all virtues and faithfulness, and on His Family, and Companions.

AHADIYA AND *WAHIDIYA* (UNIQUENESS OR ABSOLUTE ONENESS AND UNITY)

Ahadiya literally means oneness, or singleness, without having a second or like. It denotes oneness in order to emphasize uniqueness, or that God is One Who has no like. Because of this, when we say that God is *Ahad* (Unique, Absolutely One), we mean God's Uniqueness, or that there is none comparable to or like Him. And we use the term *Wahid* in order to emphasize the Divine Being's Unity. In other words, *Ahadiya* denotes God's having no like and is used to reject any claim of likeness unto Him; while *Wahidiya* (Unity) is used to emphasize or confirm His Oneness or Unity.

Ahad is a word signifying a quality that belongs to a single being exclusively. There is no other word that has the same meaning. Therefore, it is an attribute particular to the Unique, Eternally-Besought-of-All. The Realm of *Ahadiya* (Uniqueness or Absolute Oneness) is the horizon of the manifestation of this Attribute. While *Wahidiya* negates the existence of any attribute that is comparable to the Attributes of the Divine Being, *Ahadiya* indicates that the Divine Being has absolute freedom or exemption from having any likeness or resemblance. In short, *Ahadiya* denotes a sacred reality which has nothing to do with multiplicity, and which encompasses all existence, contains all the truths pertaining Divinity, and is absolutely free from any restrictions of time and space.

Some assert that Absolute Oneness or Uniqueness means that God cannot be qualified with any attributes or names, or that any attribute or name is annihilated in the Divine Being. This is wrong and God is exalted above such assertions. Uniqueness or Absolute

Oneness means that we are focusing only on the Divine Being or Essence as being absolutely free from having any like or resemblance—without, however, denying Him Names or Attributes that are particular to Himself. By saying, "God is the Unique," or "God is the Absolutely One (*Ahad*)" we stress that nothing exists by itself, for everything exists only as a mirror of the absolute Divine Existence, that the Divine Being bears no resemblance to any other thing or being, and is infinitely beyond all conceptions. God's Unity (*Wahidiya*) calls to mind the fact that like a sun, the Divine Names and Attributes shine on and in everything—or that whatever exists is a result of the manifestations of those Names and Attributes.

While God's manifestation of His Unity denotes the annihilation of all existence in the light of the Divine Names and Attributes—without, however, ignoring the fact that things have an established, real essence (appointed for each by Divine Knowledge)—God's Absolute Oneness, or Uniqueness, encompasses all the Names and Attributes, without calling to mind the existence of these Names and Attributes. The Absolute Oneness, or Uniqueness, refers to the Divine Being exclusively. Those who are annihilated in the consideration of the Divine Essence close their eyes to His Names and Attributes—and since it is impossible for any created beings to perceive or comprehend the Divine Essence, they only feel wonder and amazement. Considering the Divine Essence with His Names and Attributes leads us to see that whatever exists is a mirror where those Names and Attributes are manifested or is a result of their manifestations.

The Realm of the Manifestation of Divine Uniqueness or Absolute Oneness is also the Realm where Divinity is manifested beyond all perception and all concepts of modality and comparison. In this respect, the absolutely pure, sacred Realm of the Transcendental Manifestation of Divinity is identical with the Realm of the Transcendental Manifestation of Divine Uniqueness. This Manifestation is the initial manifestation of the "All-Hidden

Treasure" (the Divine Being) with His Majesty and Grace in order to be known. For this reason, all the instances or manifestations of honor, grandeur, and power, as well as those of grace, benevolence, and particular favor, are distributed from or have their source in this realm. This is also the realm "where" the Divine Being manifests His all-sacred love for His Essence, His Acts, His Art, and His Works, and makes our spirits familiar with this love, arousing our consciences with love and yearning. In addition, this Realm is an all-comprehensive mirror to God's being the Eternally-Besought-of-All and is the first step toward the manifestation of His Unity.

The Realm of Divine Uniqueness or Absolute Oneness can also be viewed as a mysterious expression of the truths of Divinity and the mysteries of His All-Glory before the Sphere of Divine Unity. The expression of these truths of Divinity is most briefly or most succinctly embodied in, *In and with the Name of God, the All-Merciful, the All-Compassionate* and, *Say: He: He is God, the All-Unique or the Absolutely-One*. That is, as God is One with respect to His Divinity or as the Divine Being, He is also One as the Lord. In addition, He is One, or incomparable, with respect to His Attributes and Names; He is One with respect to His Essence and Existence; and He is One as the All-Merciful, the All-Compassionate, the All-Providing, and the Creator.

As is indicated by the fact that the Proper Name of the Divine Being—Allah (God)—contains all of His other Names, the Sphere or Realm of Divinity is the realm that encompasses all other realms and which contains all Divine Names and Attributes. All other realms have their source in this realm. So, Divine Uniqueness or Absolute Oneness refers to a realm that is "continuously" and infinitely expanding and designates or appoints identities, while Divine Unity signifies another realm where everything is particularized and clothed in an identity. For this reason, Divinity manifests Itself as an all-encompassing Grace that bears Itself with Majesty; Divine Uniqueness or Absolute Oneness embodies both Grace and Majesty to the same degree, while Divine Unity reveals itself as the Majesty from which Grace develops. Nevertheless, Uniqueness, or Absolute Oneness, and Unity change places in the eyes of some who see the characteristics of each in the other. This approach seems to be more compatible with the meanings expressed by the Essence, the Attribute, and the Name in the phrase, *In and with the Name of God, the All-Merciful, the All-Compassionate*.

With the consideration of the Divine Essence alone, or of the Divine Essence together with God's Names and Attributes, after the manifestation of Divine Uniqueness comes the manifestation of the Divine Names and Attributes. Divine Names and Attributes and similar titles and nominations are not considered within the Sphere or Realm of Divine Uniqueness. Since this Sphere is the meeting point of the inward and outward, it is also known as the Broadest Intermediate Realm. "The First Identification or Determination" is another title used to describe this realm, while "the Truth of Muhammad" or "the Truth of Ahmad" is the most widely used designation. (Just as Divine Uniqueness, or Absolute Oneness, and Unity change places in some eyes, so too are the Truth of Ahmad and the Truth of Muhammad used one in the place of the other by some.) As for the realm where the Names and Attributes are initially manifested, it is the starting point of the classification of the realms into the incorporeal and corporeal. In this realm, or in this second stage of the manifestation of Divine truths, there is no room for multiplicity in the face of the initial manifestation of the Divine Names and Attributes. This realm, or sphere, is also called, "the Second Identity or Archetype," while it is generally known as "the Origin of All Else save God," and it is qualified as "Holy Absorption."

God's Unity signifies that the Divine Being is absolutely free from anything or any attribute that belongs to the created, such as composition or decomposition, multiplicity, possessing a body, having a like or resemblance, or a form, or being contained in time and space. The Divine Being's manifestation of Unity is His manifesting Himself with His Names and Attributes, as well as the Source of all beauties, favors, and rewards. This can also be considered to be the perfect manifestation of Divine Majesty as Divine Grace. All instances of grace and perfection and of majesty and grandeur are then only shadows of the shadows of the manifestation of His Grace and Majesty.

Divine Uniqueness, or Absolute Oneness, refers to the Divinity of the Divine Being and His being the All-Merciful (*ar-Rahman*), though there are many who ascribe the Divinity and All-Mercifulness of the Divine Being to His Unity. So the Divine Uniqueness is beyond all perception and concepts. This is why we cannot perceive the manifestations of Divine Majesty caused by His Uniqueness, for they relate to the Divinity, All-Mercifulness, Honor, and Grandeur of the Divine Being and, therefore, they are all-comprehensive and limitless—so intense and dazzling that they cannot be comprehended. For this reason, we need another manifestation that considers our capacity of perception and experience. The noble Qur'an is such a manifestation of Divine Speech according to our horizon of understanding. The Qur'an is so compassionate that it considers all levels of understanding from the highest to the lowest, holding binoculars or lenses of comprehensibility on the most profound truths at the same time that it takes us around the layers of the universe. It enables us to see and read everything accurately, and it does not leave us in bewilderment at the incomprehensibility of that which is all-encompassing.

Divinity manifests an overwhelming majesty, and this majesty reveals itself as being surrounded by a profound grace, for the sphere of Divinity is the source of all the Attributes of Perfection and the Names of Glory. For this reason, the sphere of Divinity has grandeur and uninterrupted majesty, as well as favor and endless grace, so that all the manifestations of the Attributes and Names have their source in it. Any radiance in the stage of identification and determination, any effusion toward expansion and growth, or any manifestation in the sphere of development and extension all issue from the encompassing throne of Divinity.

The manifestation of Majesty, which is considered to be the manifestation of infinite Honor and Grandeur, is also mentioned with the title of "Absolute Identity." In order to emphasize this Grandeur and Honor, Which are indispensable to the Divine Being, the blessed word of Allah (God), the Proper Name of the Divine Being, has always been mentioned as the Word of Majesty, while God Himself is known as the One of Majesty. From another perspective, while God Almighty's manifestation with His Grace and Favor according to the capacity, merit, and need of every being is called the manifestation of Grace, His all-overwhelming, all-encompassing, and dominating manifestation of His Attributes and Names is mentioned as the manifestation of Majesty.

The Absolute Essence, whom some call the "Absolute, Pure Uniqueness," is also the source of majesty-predominating manifestations that issue from the Sphere of Divine Uniqueness or Absolute Oneness. In this Sphere, all the Names, Attributes, and Reputations are considered subordinate to the Divine Essence. This consideration causes the concept of God, the Ultimate Truth, to embrace all of existence with its all-encompassing nature and His Oneness becomes apparent with all its clarity and comprehensibility to those who are able to feel it. Those who feel His Oneness find themselves in the state of wonder and amazement that is caused by the all-overwhelming, imperceptible manifestation of Majesty. In the face of this manifestation, they cannot help but utter, "God is the All-Great in His incomparable, incomprehensible Greatness, and all glory be to Him in the morning and evening (i.e., at all times)." The All-Compassionate One's manifestations of favor, help, and observation are the manifestations of Grace, and they cause those who can feel them deeply to express their joy and thrills with the utterance, "All praise be to God forever!" The manifestations of Majesty are felt but cannot be comprehended or encompassed and therefore they cause constant wonder and utmost astonishment, while those manifestations of Grace are felt, perceived, and tasted, providing standards to interpret the mysteries that are related to the sphere of the other manifestations.

According to verifying Sufi scholars, Majesty is an overwhelming and all-encompassing Attribute of Honor and Grandeur, and it relates to His Absolute Oneness or Uniqueness—or, according to those in whose approach Uniqueness and Unity change places, to His Unity. As for the Divine Unity, it is both a title to and the realm of the manifestations of the Divine Being's Attributes and Names.

Majesty gives rise to fear, awe, respect, and reverence in hearts, and with its works and imprints causes amazement and utmost astonishment. However, with respect to consequences, the manifestations of Majesty are extraordinarily warm, gentle, and exhilarating. Just as some who have the necessary capacity can observe the imprints of Unity in Absolute Oneness or Uniqueness, so too can the breezes of Grace be experienced on the horizon of Majesty; however, everyone can perceive them according to their capacity. This can also be described by saying that Majesty changes into Grace at the highest point of its perceptibility, and when experienced in the perfect degree, Grace becomes Majesty to a certain extent.

When we mention God's Face or God's Grace, we always consider the manifestations of the all-sublime Attributes and All-Beautiful Names in the mirrors of existence, for we are unable to study and describe the Divine Essence, Essential Qualities, or Attributes. We look at the works, ponder the acts, reflect on the Names, and think about the Attributes. In other words, we try to study the mysteries, grace, harmony, and meanings that are beyond the corporeal realm in the exhibition of nature, or in the book of existence, or in the dictionary of the universe, and we are content with the messages which are intended to be experienced by our spirits, and we should endeavor to understand well and correctly. Provided we can read things and events well and accurately, we might not need to be occupied with epistemological theories, something some of us attach great importance to.

All beauties, perfections or excellences, attractions, instances of harmony, and splendor in the outer and inner dimensions of existence are the shadows of the manifestation of the Divine Beauty and Grace reflected through numerous veils. In the face of all existence, and in the countenances of human beings, in the depths of human nature, in mutual helping and solidarity among all parts of existence, and in instances of mutual love and embracing, and also in elevated characters, the standards of good morals and instances of good, altruism, and in all other merits and virtues—in all of these, which are all shadows of the manifestation of Divine Beauty and Grace, we observe dazzling beauty and harmony, perfection and extraordinariness, with which we are intoxicated and go into raptures and ecstasies. We feel elated to reach the source of all these beauties and excellences, and advance toward that source according to our degree of belief, the extent or capacity of our spirituality, and the profundity of our spiritual life. Initiation on the Sufi path is only one of the ways of such advancement. In accordance with our capacity, we understand that everything good and beautiful has its source in and depends on the Divine Attributes of Mercifulness, Compassionateness, Providing, and Creativity, as well as of Favoring, Munificence, and Benevolence. We obtain the opportunity to observe the mirrors where the Hidden Treasure is reflected with these and other Attributes from Which the Divine Names issue, and we find ourselves in the middle of exhibitions of endless, concentric spheres of beauty.

For those who see existence from this perspective and travel through it toward the sole Source of all beauties and excellences, the manifestations of Divine Absolute Oneness and Uniqueness become manifestations of Divine Unity, and Majesty becomes Grace. Just as in all acts from the creation of everything to giving it its perfect form, and in creating the most compassionate mirrors of His manifestations from clay, the name the Lord always manifests itself with grace, so too do the Names the All-Overwhelming and the All-Compelling continuously present to us bouquets of roses and clusters of fruits from the gardens and orchards of Grace in the horizon of Majesty by wiping out appearances and destroying the imagined power of physical forces in our views respectively.

All these beauties and excellences, which are reflected in the works from the First Identification or Determination through the Attributes and Names, have been considered and evaluated by people of insight as a book to be studied, an exhibition whose observation gives endless delight, and a palace that arouses in people irresistible feelings of pleasure. They provoke the thrilling desire to catch sight of their Owner. By virtue of such a view of creation or existence and life, instances of coming into the world and departure from it have gained a profound meaning, the former being considered as undertaking a sacred duty, and the latter as a discharge from this duty and union with the Beloved. Life has become a continuous journeying toward Him.

Those who make this journeying are always with Him, even while in the world. Every attempt and movement of theirs is toward Him. Although living in a world of multiplicity, their goal is unity. Despite the heavy load of corporeality they carry on their backs, they always fly toward Him in the horizon of their spiritual life.

Wherever they are, they always pronounce, "God is Unique, Absolutely One; God is the Eternally Besought of All." They fasten their heart to Him and pour themselves out only to Him. They solve the mysteries of God's Uniqueness with the lights of His Unity. In the face of the sounding blows of the manifestations of Majesty, they cool off with the breezes of Grace. They voice their wonder and astonishment with words of Divine glorification and exaltation, and the favors they receive with words of praise and thanks. They try to avoid ignorance of the Absolutely One, the Eternally Besought-of-All, changing the losses anyone might suffer into *a trade which will never perish* (35: 29), and the absolute distance from God into His continuous company by acting as described in the following lines:

O initiate! Flee the realm of multiplicity and advance;
Take your home in the shelter of the All-Independent Single,
The Unique One, and advance.
If you want to see the face of Unity amidst this multiplicity,
Purify and brighten the mirror of your heart and advance.
Some circumambulate the Ka'ba and some others, the Divine Throne,
But you prefer the privacy of Divine nearness, and advance.

Ismail Haqqi Bursavi[69]

Acting so, they continuously waft their way to the heavens of God's Absolute Oneness and Unity.

Our Lord, do not let our hearts swerve after You have guided us and bestow upon us mercy from Your Presence. Surely You are the All-Bestowing,

Our Lord, take us not to task if we forget or make mistakes.

Bestow Your blessings and peace, our Lord, on him who is himself rightly-guided and guides to the truth, our master Muhammad, and on his Family and Companions, altogether.

---

69 Ismail Haqqi Bursavi (1653–1725) is one of the great Sufi guides and writers. He spent much of his life in Bursa, Turkey. His *Ruh al-Bayan* (a four-volume commentary on the Qur'an) is very famous. *Kitab an-Natica* ("The Book on the Result") is his last work. (Tr.)

AL-AWWAL (THE FIRST), *AL-AHIR* (THE LAST) *AZ-ZAHIR* (THE ALL-OUTWARD), *AL-BATIN* (THE ALL-INWARD)

Al-Awwal (the First) means the One Who is the First of all, without having a beginning, and Who brings all other existent things and beings into existence. Meaning the Last, with no end at all, *al-Ahir* (the Last) is the One in Whom everything ends while He has no end, as described in the verses:

> *Everything is perishable (and so perishing) except His "Face" (His eternal Self).* (28: 88)

> *All that is on the earth is perishable; but there remains forever the "Face" of your Lord, the One of Majesty and Munificence.* (55: 26–27)

The One Who is the First and the Last is also the All-Outward, Whose existence is more manifest than the existence of everything else and Who causes the hearts and spirits of all existent things and/or beings to be aware of all His Attributes, while all these existent things and beings indicate themselves only to the extent of their bodily existence; and He is the All-Inward, Who cannot be comprehended because of His Honor and Grandeur and the intensity of His manifestation.

The First and the Last are mentioned in the Qur'an as contrasting Names, like day and night, Paradise and Hellfire, or believers and unbelievers. When we use the First for the Divine Being, we mean the Necessarily Existent One Who exists by Himself eternally without having a beginning and Who is infinitely independent of all things and beings. The Prophetic saying, "There was God and nothing existed besides Him,"[70] denotes God's eternal existence without a beginning. Some add to this *hadith*, "Now it is the same as it was then."[71] If, by this addition, they mean that God exists necessarily and by Himself, while the existence of all other things and/or beings depends on Him, there is no harm in it. But if they mean that only He exists and all other things are only fancied or imagined things, we cannot accept such an erroneous statement because it is a fundamental rule that "things have established realities or real essences (appointed for each by Divine Knowledge)."

The Divine Being is the First, Who exists eternally (in the past) before all other things and beings; He is the Last, Who will exist eternally, sending things from existence into non-existence and bringing "some thing that is non-existent" into existence, and in Whom everything else is bound to end; He is the All-Outward, Whose existence is the most apparent in every word of (the book of) existence; He is the All-Inward, Who is infinitely beyond all existence and on Whose Existence all things and events depend. He simultaneously is the First, the Last, the All-Outward, and the All-Inward, without being one being different from being the other. Being the First, He is eternal in the past exclusively, and being the Last, He is eternal in the future, particularly to Himself. His determinations and decrees as the First appear according to His Knowledge in His being the Last.

He is the First eternally (in the past) and the Last everlastingly. He existed when there was nothing else besides Him; He will eternally outlive all things and beings, which are bound to perish and which suffer continuous appearance and disappearance. Everything belongs to Him, coming from and ending in Him, but He is absolutely free from coming into existence or going into non-existence.

He exists eternally without coming into existence;
That is, He exists without having a beginning.

---

70 *al-Bukhari*, "Tawhid" 22; Ahmad ibn Hanbal, *al-Musnad*, 4:431. (Tr.)

71 adh-Dhahasi, *Siyar 'Alamin an-Nubala*, 18:474. (Tr.)

Nor is there an end for Him.
It is He Who creates, and by Him does everything subsist.
All of existence has been created from a light with Him;
He said, "Be!" and everything was from a pure light.

He is the First in that He creates and favors, and the Last in that He has mercy and forgiveness for His servants, preparing palaces of eternal happiness for them. He is the First in that He guides and the Last in that He rewards guidance. He is the First in that He has no beginning, is the Necessarily Existent Being, the Unique, and the One of Unity; He is the Last in that He is absolutely free from decay or going into non-existence.

Those who are favored with the manifestation of the Name "the First" dive into the depths of the past and writhe in torment about what their judgment from Destiny will be; but the Name "the All-Outward" leads them to consider God's favors of belief, submission, and excellence in action, and to come to understand that their acts of worship are, in fact, the duties of giving thanks for those and other favors, thus strengthening their hope. A heart absorbed in the manifestation of the Name "the All-Inward" feels continuous wonder and astonishment in the face of thousands of enigmatic events; through the breezes of mercy blowing in through the windows of the Name "the Last," they feel relieved of worries and find themselves in a delightful horizon of awe that opens on eternity.

All the existent worlds have a beginning on account of God's being the First, and an end on account of His being the Last. When we consider eternity in the past, we experience wonder and amazement; and when considering eternity in the future, we shudder with fear and anxiety. Supposing the Prophet Muhammad, the truthful reporter, upon him be peace and blessings, had told us nothing about the signs of the end of time, the Resurrection, Paradise, and Hell, and so on, we would have been without words for eternity, both in the past and in the future.

He is both the First and the All-Inward, and the Last and the All-Outward. With all the stages of their existence, everything belongs to Him and goes back to end in Him; with respect to its creation, being fashioned and equipped, and its subsistence, existence is in His disposal and control. He is the First because He is God and everything is a result of His manifestations.

Whatever exists and happens consists in a dot created by God;
All those stars contained in a mustard seed were fashioned by God.
Everything exists by the All-Outward and All-Inward Truth's
giving it existence;
No one truly knows what the beginning is.

Ismail Haqqi Bursavi

He is the Last; all spiritual journeys end in Him and everything goes back to Him. He is the All-Outward for the book of existence, the exhibition of things, the palace of the universe clearly expresses Him with all its signs, indications, and witnesses. He is the All-Inward, and all the ranks in existential realms of spirituality end in Him. There is nothing beyond Him, nor can the concept of beyond be in question for Him. The end of any spiritual journeying has always been marked with the truth expressed in, *So he was (so near that there was left only the distance between) the strings of two bows (put adjacent to each other), or even nearer (than that)* (53: 9).

However, He is not an Outward One whose identity we can know, nor an Inward One that is completely unknown. By contrast, as He is an Outward One beyond our sensations, conceptions, and imagination, He is also an all-transcending Inward One. If we do not consider Him as the All-Inward when we think of Him as the All-Outward, we will have to attribute all the manifestations of His Essence, Attributes, and Names to things and events themselves. If, on the other hand, we ignore all the evidence and witnesses of His Existence while thinking of Him as the All-Inward, we will deviate into the acceptance of a universal, pervasive Spirit. On account of what all things point to as well as the manifestations of His Names and Attributes, He is an All-Outward observed on the face of the book of the universe, and an all-transcending Inward beyond all sensations. He is an All-Outward One with the dazzling magnificence of His Honor and Grandeur shining through His works, and the most Inward of the inward with His imperceptible Identity; an All-Outward with His creativity, sustaining, and favoring, which we observe on the breast of existence, and an All-Inward Who causes us to disappear and die; an All-Outward with the showers of His favor and grace throughout the universe, and an All-Inward Who is impossible to see or meet. In short, He is both the First, and the Last, and the All-Outward, and the All-Inward—simultaneously.

These Names may vary in the areas of their manifestations until their points of intersection are reached. The event of the Prophet Moses and Khadr is an example of this.[72] One of these two persons is a few feet ahead of the other on account of his duty or mission, while the other is a few meters before the other because of the service he represents. When some subtle points of Divine acts came to be discovered at the end of the mysterious journey of these two men of lofty horizons, they finally agreed on the matters about which they had previously been arguing, and even though they no longer continued their journeying, it became clear that the outward and inward aspects of existence and Divine acts are never incompatible with each other.

We can approach this point from another perspective, which is as follows:

Every act and event occurs on the horizon of the Divine Name the All-Outward from the realm of the created toward the realm of the Creator, within the frame of a certain sphere. One appointed as a guide in this sphere is dutiful in training or educating people in a certain way so that they can develop their potentials and be guided toward God, the Ultimate Truth. On this horizon, the Name the All-Inward executes the judgments of Destiny independent of causality, such as causing living beings to die. Even though death occurs as the result of a physical cause, it is absolutely inevitable for every living being as a judgment of Destiny. So, from the perspective of the way he followed as a Prophet and his spiritual profundity, the

---

72 See note 15. (Tr.)

Prophet Moses, upon him be peace, is a distinguished one who has the duty of guiding people to earn Divine approval and eternal happiness, while Khadr, upon him be peace, is another distinguished one whose duty pertains, like that of the Angel of death, to the inner aspect of human life and existence, in which physical causes have only a nominal part or no part at all. One of these two great persons is a religious guide and representative, and the other seems to be a link between Destiny's judgments and whatever takes place in human life. Their missions are complementary to each other:

The outward and inward are two dimensions
of a unity, know O brother;
As are the first and last counterparts of each other.

The Names the All-Outward and the All-Inward manifest themselves primarily in the Qur'an and the Sunna, and these manifestations are observed or followed through religious life. On account of the Divine commands for life and the creation and operation of the universe, the whole universe is the language, translator, and realm of the reflection of the Name the All-Outward, while the Name the All-Inward is its spirit and meaning.

The universe is a grand book of God throughout;
Whatever letter you study, you see its meaning is God.

Recaizade Mahmud Ekrem[73]

The manifestation of the Name the All-Outward as Divine religious commandments finds its greatest representative and implementation in the political leader of Muslims, while that of the Name the All-Inward is represented by the spiritual Pole, who is the commander of the realm of spiritual truths. The outward is the manifestation of the inward in the corporeal realm, and the inward is the inner dimension of the outward. If the "All-Hidden

---

73 Recaizade Mahmud Ekrem (1847–1914) was one of the important literary figures of the declining years of the Ottoman Turkey. He was a novelist, and dramatist and a poet. (Tr.)

Treasure," which is inward, had not manifested Itself, It could not have been known, nor would all those dazzling beauties throughout the universe have been observed, nor could the meanings in the horizon of the Name the All-Inward have been read. The Treasure of the inward has breathed itself out through the outward, which has consequently become an ornate envelope for the inward. It is a multi-dimensional, splendid envelope, which is described in Imam al-Ghazzali's famous saying: "It is not probable that there is a universe more beautiful than the present one."

Despite the clarity of the matter, some deviating ideologies—which have tried to distort even matters that are so clear that there can be no different understanding or interpretation—have separated the outward from the inward and made strange, unreasonable, and religiously unacceptable interpretations of the inward, thus attempting to muddy Islamic thought. Many such distorted interpretations have their sources in ancient Greek philosophy, Indian belief and thought, Hermeticism, and the doctrines of the Sabaeans. Whether knowingly or unknowingly, many of us Muslims have been influenced by such distorted thoughts and approaches and have suffered doctrinal deviations.

Some among the Muslims have labeled with literalism and belittled the manifest commandments of the Qur'an and the Sunna and the sincere, scholarly deductions concluded from these two basic sources by the profound, righteous scholars in the early centuries of Islam. Carried away by the desire to make fantastic interpretations, they have even attempted to give different, unacceptable meanings to the fundamental, explicit rules and principles of Islam. They have regarded Prayer as the way followed by the common people to reach God and claimed that it is not necessary for those who "have followed the way of inwardness and reached God." They have also looked upon the Prescribed, Purifying Alms with the same distorted approach, considered the Pilgrimage as an attempt by the common people to be united with God, seen Fasting as meaningless suffering, viewed avoidance of the religiously forbidden things as folly, and tried to drive everyone to what is nearly a bohemian life.

Such approaches and considerations were first produced in such currents or centers as Jami'ism, Adhamism, Haydarism, Babaism, Shamsism, Qarmatism, and certain schools of Ismailism,[74] and then transported, to some extent, into some Sufi lodges and madrasas. They have interpreted the Qur'an and Prophetic Traditions arbitrarily, considering even the explicit verses of the Qur'an and Prophetic Traditions as symbolic expressions, interpreting them like interpreting dreams. Such movements of dissent and corruption, which began with Ibn Saba',[75] were continued in increasing dimensions by Maymun of Ahwaz,[76] and grew into flames with Barqai; they became so great a problem that they shook Islamic life at its foundations with Hasan Sabbah.[77] Finally, everything ended in complete freedom from religious responsibilities.

---

[74] Jami'ism, Adhamism, and Shamsism were certain deviating sects that in order to gain following, attributed themselves to important saints Mawlana 'Abdu'r-Rahman ibn Ahmad al-Jami' (1414–1492), Ibrahim ibn Adham (d. 782), and Shams at-Tabrizi, who had a great influence on Jalalu'd-Din ar-Rumi, respectively. Haydarism is a branch of Nusayrism following Shaykh Haydar 'Ali, who lived in the fourteenth century. They deified 'Ali, the Fourth Caliph, and son-in-law of the Prophet Muhammad, upon him be peace and blessings. Babaism appeared in the thirteenth century in central Anatolia and was founded by Baba Ishaq and Baba Ilyas, who claimed Divine Messengership. They caused a great revolt against the Anatolian Seljuk State. Qarmatism was the deviating *Batini* (esoteric) sect founded by Hamdan Qirmit or Qarmat. They caused revolts and shed much blood during the second half of the ninth century and the first quarter of the tenth century. They were even able to found a short-lived state in Bahrain. Ismailism was another esoteric sect which claimed the imamate of Ismail, the eldest son of Imam Ja'far as-Sadiq, whom the Shi'a Imamiyya accepted as their sixth Imam. Muslim theologians and historians point out that the followers of some of those and similar other sects such as Qarmatism were in fact materialists and atheists and defended and pursued a hedonistic life. (Tr.)

[75] 'Abdullah ibn Saba' was a hypocrite from Yemen. He caused great dissent among the Muslims during the caliphate of 'Ali, the Fourth Caliph. He went so far as to claim 'Ali's divinity. (Tr.)

[76] Maymun ibn Daysan al-Qaddah al-Ahwazi lived in the eighth century. He was one of the founders of the movement of Batiniyya (Esotericism). (Tr.)

[77] Hasan (ibn) Sabbah (d. 1122) was one of the most famous figures of the Batiniyya sect. He made the Alamut castle, situated in a precipice between Tehran and Qazvin in western Iran, his base in 1090. They spread great terror and assassinated many important religious and political figures in the Muslim world. Finally, the Mongol armies destroyed them and their castle. (Tr.)

According to such approaches, the explicit meanings of the Qur'anic verses and Prophetic Traditions are not valid and should never be followed. Continuing with this argument, what we must regard and follow are the inner, esoteric meanings, and only those who are specialists in the esoteric dimension of the Religion can know them. They also claim that believing that God has Attributes means accepting as many gods as the number of Attributes that have been ascribed to Him. *All-Glorified He is, and absolutely exalted, immeasurably high above all that they say* (17: 43). They also claim—God forbid such claims!—that God is powerful not because He has Power but because He gives others power—I do not even know what they mean by such assertions. They consider other of His Attributes from this viewpoint.

Like other false beliefs and thoughts which have been inherited from ancient philosophers, the so-called "Doctrine of Ten Intellects" is one of their false doctrines. According to this, God first created a First Intellect, and then, through this, a First Soul. When the Soul demanded the perfection of the Intellect, it needed an action, which, in turn, caused the generation of celestial spheres. The movement of these spheres generated coldness, heat, moisture, and dryness. These "four basic elements" caused the coming about of three earthly classes of existent things and/or beings, namely inanimate objects, vegetation, and animals. According to this view, this process continued until humankind came into existence. We seek refuge in God from such corrupt thoughts.

Referring existence to a First Intellect and substituting the Prophets for what some call the Perfect or Universal Men is something that is common to all false systems of beliefs and thoughts. We should add to these two assertions their fully esoteric interpretation of the Qur'an and the Sunna. Furthermore, some other assertions, or doctrines, or practices, such as giving letters meanings that are incompatible with the Shari'a or sound reason, pursuing wonder through abstruse or ambiguous expressions, giving a sense of mystery to whatever they do with ceremonies resembling those of some secret societies, and pretending to do all such things for the sake of the Religion and religious life have deceived the masses, who are unaware of the essential reality of the Religion and religious life.

Their incorrect interpretation of religious worship and obedience and their attitudes giving the impression that they are encouraging sin and immorality have made many people indifferent to good moral standards and religious rules, finally leading to anarchy. Since such approaches corrupt hearts and spirits gradually, those who are unaware of the spirit of the Religion have fallen into this accursed net unawares, and have not been able to recover. What follows are some indications of this dangerous process:

- *Recognition and choice*: Recognizing and choosing the targeted person well as far as their capacity for understanding is concerned. Simple-minded ones who have no correct knowledge of the Religion and are able to be deceived are chosen.
- *Gradual education and training*: Conquering the hearts of the audience through gradual education and training.
- *Throwing into doubt*: Causing the audience to doubt the truths and cardinal beliefs of the Religion, and directing them to rituals other than the worship of God.
- *Dependence*: Making the acceptance of candidates dependent on certain conditions.
- *Holding one's tongue*: Getting candidates to promise that they will never tell their secrets.
- *Persuasion*: Persuading candidates that whatever they hear from the leader is a Divine inspiration.
- *Separation*: Causing those who are believed to be fully aware of the "esoteric dimension" of the Religion to ignore the apparent meanings of the Qur'an and to abandon the daily religious practices.
- *Complete freedom*: Leading candidates to a belief in complete freedom from religious responsibilities.

The truth is that, like creation, the Religion has both outward and inward dimensions for the Unique, All-Absolute One is both the All-Outward and the All-Inward. Nothing in and concerning existence is unknown to Him, because He is the All-Outward; He is also the All-Inward, therefore He has full knowledge of whatever concerns humans during their whole lives, decreeing good for the good, righteous ones, and punishment for the evil, sinful ones as declared in: (*The will of) God came upon them from where they had not reckoned (it could come*) (59: 2).

As mentioned above, the Religion of Islam has both outward and inward dimensions based on its two basic sources, the Qur'an and the Sunna, and on the principles deduced from them by eminent scholars in the early ages of Islam. The Shari'a has rules and principles for perfect spiritual education, and it disciplines people with respect to their feelings, thoughts, attitudes, and actions. In addition, it contains necessary knowledge for the entire life of humans with all its aspects. For example, it provides sufficient rules for human religious responsibilities, such as physical purification, the Prayer, fasting, the Prescribed Purifying Alms, Pilgrimage, and *jihad* (striving in God's cause); in addition, daily acts or transactions, such as buying and selling, employment, commerce, business, building and running companies, and administration are covered by the Shari'a, as well as penalties, whether those established by God Himself in the Qur'an, or by the Messenger in the Sunna, or by scholars based on the unchanging principles laid down by the Qur'an and the Sunna. These constitute the outward aspect of the Shari'a. The Shari'a also has rules and principles for the mental and spiritual education and perfection of humans, expressed in certain concepts such as confirmation, belief, certainty, sincerity, knowledge of God, love of God, submission to God, placing one's trust and reliance in God, commitment and resignation to God, recitations, repentance, penitence, and contrition for errors, reverence and fear of God, patience, contentment, nearness to God, intense love for God, ecstasy, immersion in God, modesty, exaltation and glorification of God. These constitute the inward aspect of the Shari'a. There is no and can never be conflict between the outward and inward aspects of the Shari'a. Rather, the two are dimensions of a single reality and they complement each other.

On the Sufi way, initiates ignore their existence with respect to their egos or annihilate their egos in God's Existence. They are content with God's decrees and faithful to their promises, paying no attention to anything other than God and inwardly burning with the yearning to observe the Divine "Face" in the other world. Nothing here is contrary to the principles that have been established by the Qur'an and the Sunna. On the contrary, these are the rules that ought to be observed so that we can lead a life at the level of the heart and spirit. They are originally based on the Qur'an and the Sunna.

In short, a religious life is incumbent upon every responsible being, and it is only possible by following the Shari'a. Metaphysical discoveries and spiritual pleasures are favors that come in return for the sincerity of initiates without their demand. Following the Shari'a and reaching a certain level of spiritual life or spiritual profundity are not mutually exclusive; rather, they complement one another as two dimensions of the same reality.

What an initiate first feels of the inward is certain manifestations of the Divine Names and Attributes. This has been called "the inward relative." So long as an initiate advances toward the end of this spiritual journey, manifestations from the Realm of Divine Essence begin to invade their conscience. This state has been called "the most inward within the inward." There are many who reach the horizon of the inward, but few can go deep into "the most inward of the inward" and, therefore, few have knowledge of the mysteries of Divinity.

Let us put an end to this highly subtle, ambiguous matter with the comprehensive approach of Bediüzzaman Said Nursi. According to him, the outward dimension of creation is called the *mulk* (the corporeal dimension of the Divine kingdom), while its inner dimension is the *malakut* (the absolute, incorporeal dimension of the

Divine kingdom). The relationship between a human being and his or her heart is an example of these two aspects or dimensions of existence or the Divine kingdom. With respect to the corporeal dimension, a human being is an envelope and the heart is its contents. With respect to the absolute, incorporeal dimension, the heart is an envelope while the human being is the contents. This same relationship also exists between the Supreme Divine Throne and the universe. The Supreme Divine Throne is a combination of the manifestations of the Divine Names the First, the Last, the All-Outward, and the All-Inward. With respect to the Divine Name the All-Outward, the Supreme Divine Throne represents the *mulk* and is the envelope of creation, while with respect to the Name the All-Inward, It is the *malakut* or the heart or contents of creation, and the universe is the *mulk* or the envelope. Considering the Divine Name the First, the Supreme Divine Throne is indicated by *His Supreme Throne was upon the water* (11: 7), which points to the beginning of existence. In respect of the Divine Name the Last, the ceiling of Paradise is the Supreme Throne of the All-Merciful, which alludes to the finality of everything. As a result, being the combination of the manifestations or the all-encompassing mirror of the Divine Names the First, the Last, the All-Outward, and the All-Inward, the Supreme Divine Throne encompasses the whole universe.

> *O God, the Lord of the seven heavens and the Lord of the Supreme Throne, our Lord and the Lord of everything; the One Who sent down the Torah, the Gospel, and the Qur'an; the Splitter of the grain and fruit stone—there is no deity but You! I seek refuge in You from the evil of everything, which You hold by its forelock.*
>
> *You are the First, without any preceding You; You are the Last, there is none to succeed You. You are the All-Outward, with none being above You; and You are the All-Inward, with nothing more penetrating than You. Forgive us whatever evil we have done, so that You may not call us to account for anything. Surely You are powerful over everything, and ever responsive to calls. And bestow blessings and peace upon our master Muhammad and his Family and Companions, altogether.*

WAHDA AND *KASRA* (UNITY AND MULTIPLICITY)

Like the Divine Names the First and the Last, and the All-Outward and the All-Inward, the concepts of unity and multiplicity are, with respect to their literal meanings, opposite to one another, but in reality, they complement and are associated with one another.

As a concept, *wahda* (unity) means that initiates attribute all things and events to God in origin and creation; they observe His Attributes like His Knowledge, Power, and Will in every thing, state, or movement in the universe; they see and perceive the manifestations of the Divine Names behind the entire realm of acts; in short, they are always aware of Him and they always feel Him, they turn to Him and attain His company in spirit. Moreover, they desire Him and pursue His good pleasure alone, living a life in strict accordance with His commandments and decrees. These are, in fact, the actions that true believers must carry out in their relationship with God, the Ultimate Truth.

When used in relation with God Almighty, unity means that God is One, Unique, and absolutely free of having any partners, likes, and helpers. It also denotes that while every thing and every being is in constant need of Him, He is absolutely independent of all, and He is the Sacred Being Who has such Attributes of perfection as absolute Knowledge, absolute Power, absolute Dominion, and absolute Rule; this also denotes that He is called by the All-Beautiful Names He possesses. Although all the occurrences, changes, colorings, forms, and states in the universe finally end in

Him in origin and creation, He is absolutely free of any of these qualities which are peculiar to the created.

As for multiplicity, it denotes all existent things and events on which there is the stamp or seal of an all-encompassing Knowledge, an all-overwhelming Power, and all-dominating Will. It also signifies the entire book of the universe, on the face of each letter, word, sentence, paragraph, and part of which initiates observe the All-Manifesting by One by reading and evaluating the Divine laws of the creation and operation of things and events correctly but each according to their horizon of belief and knowledge of God.

We Muslims understand and deal with the subjects of unity and the way of unity, and of multiplicity and the way of multiplicity from the above points. All travelers who follow the way to God in the light of Prophethood have understood them to be the same. For this reason, their attribution of every thing and event to God Almighty with respect to their origin, creation, and administration, and their consideration of them in relation to Him, should never be confused with the thoughts or approaches of some philosophers. Such philosophers regard our view of Divine Unity as monotheism; the view of unity that is based on the affirmation that everything comes from and is dependent on Him as monism; and our consideration of multiplicity as pluralism. This view is completely incompatible with and different from the considerations and approaches of Muslim Sufis.

With the two basic sources of Islam, the Qur'an and the Sunna, and the branches of religious knowledge such as Theology, Jurisprudence, and Sufism, which are founded upon these two sources, Islam accepts that it is God Who eternally knows, destines, and creates everything and Who sustains everything; it accepts that all acts of coming into and departing from this world are by His command, creation, rule, and administration. Again it is He Who will eternally maintain those whom He judges to subsist eternally in another world. Islam judges considerations that are contrary to these basic doctrines to be deviant and heretical. The doctrine of the Unity of Being, maintained by a very few among the Sufi saints—which is in essence an assertion expressed in spiritual intoxication and immersion or absorption—was discussed before. This doctrine, confused with pantheism and monism, is the exact opposite of these two philosophical assertions. For while the latter two assertions deny God on behalf of the universe, the doctrine of the Unity of Being ignores the universe on behalf of God's Existence. All the leading scholars of the basic religious sciences and Sufism absolutely believe that God is the Creator, Administrator, and Sustainer of everything. Considerations such as those wherein creatures are from or included in the Essence of the Creator, or that all the universe existed in the Essence of the Creator and has come into existence as the materialization of this Essence, or that existence is nothing but the materialization of the Divine Essence are all assertions of pantheists, who have no knowledge of the truth about the Divine Attributes, the characteristics of the Divine Names, or the nature of the Divine acts. In terms of the emanation or the material manifestation of the Divine Being, these ideas date back as far as Heraclitus and Parmenides, and even as far back as Plato and Plotinus, and the philosophies of the Ten Intellects.

There may be some Sufis who confuse the All-Manifesting with the manifestation, the All-Original with the shadow, and the Self-Subsisting with the sustained and maintained; others, due to insufficient words to express themselves, may have to use the same phrases as the pantheists and monists use. These should never be taken for the philosophical assertions mentioned above. While the philosophers who defend monism, pantheism, and similar views are unaware of the Divine truths, and they are those who try to look at the transcendental truths that can only be seen in the light of the Divine Revelation with the dim light of their reason, the Muslim Sufis who maintain the Unity of Being are modest ones who try to live in strict obedience to the Divine commandments, and in profound devotion to the Almighty, spiritually absorbed and intoxicated with the manifestations of His Existence and other Attributes. The map of their beliefs and spiritual experiences shows that the relationship between God and all other existent things and beings is the relationship of the Creator and the created, as well as that of the Self-Subsisting and Sustainer and the sustained; whatever they say in sobriety is essentially based on the Qur'an, the Sunna, and on the knowledge given by scholars of basic religious sciences.

From another perspective, multiplicity is the assembly of the manifestations of the Divine Names in the mirrors of different natures according to the forms given by Destiny. That is to say, everything has been and is created dependent on the united manifestations of the Divine Names, and the whole of existence, composed of innumerable mirrors, expresses the same meaning with the essential characteristics of unity, solidarity, harmony, and mutual assistance it displays, as well as with its different sounds, melodies, and songs. As all things and events announce His Unity and Oneness or his Uniqueness with their positions, so too, being a relative mirror to the Divine Being—as God Himself says: "Time is My relative mirror"—time clearly indicates the Unique One of Unity in the uninterrupted chains of mirrors of multiplicity.

Travelers on the way to God gaze upon all things and events with these considerations, and see and feel the absolutely Unique One on the face of everything, whether corporeal or incorporeal, material or spiritual; they are exhilarated by the designs, colors, and languages, all of which are interrelated and interconnected with one another and therefore indicate unity; and they go into raptures with the observation of the works of His Knowledge, Will, and Power in every thing and event. As if standing at every moment on a new platform or ramp, prepared to leap to meet with the All-Beloved, they utter,

One who wishes to see Your All-Beautiful Face
Through innumerable faces,
Should split into numerous parts like broken mirrors.

and feel that they stand just before the door of beholding Him, with the exhilarating hope that a new start will be given to a never-ending observation.

God is absolutely One and Unique; there is none who resembles Him in any way. The mirrors that reflect His different Attributes and Names, with the distinctive features of each, are countless. These mirrors, although countless, display a unity in multiplicity and therefore indicate the One of absolute Unity. All the scenes and sounds that belong to or are exhibited by multiplicity express Him, show and speak about Him, and present messages from Him. The multiplicity of the mirrors in this world of formation and dissolution displays differences and causes different views to arise in minds; however, they never contradict the Unity of the Original Source. Every thing, with its every state, is connected with Him, moving dependent on His Will, and following the way that is bound to end in Him. Because of this, we can describe multiplicity as the manifestation of the unfolding of the Unique, All-Hidden Treasure.

All these considerations are not for those who remain distant from Him despite His infinite nearness to everything; they are for those who have been able to build sound relationships with Him in the awareness of their being His created servants and His being their Creator and Lord. An ascetic says:

He is nearer to you than your own self;
so never remain distant from Him;
Give up multiplicity, find unity,
and look through knowledge of Him in your heart.

For those who have reached a life at the level of the heart and spirit, and who have set up their thrones at the peaks where spirit beings fly, and who have escaped from the restrictions of time and space, and day and night, neither multiplicity nor unity constitutes a problem. For them, both multiplicity and unity are only mere conceptions that have certain, important meanings.

Even though the darkness of human nature surrounds humanity's horizon of perception, the light of truth and unity removes this darkness. Those who rise high enough to go beyond the atmosphere of their corporeality and to remove the veil from their eyes so that they can see the realms beyond become familiar with the lights of the realm of unity; they find themselves in showers of surprises through their perceptions, sensations, and observations. However, if the initiates who are favored with such showers cannot preserve the harmony of religious faith, thought, and life, but fall away from the basic principles of the Religion, they may lose out on the way to cycles of attainment. Just as the Names the All-Outward and All-Inward are two dimensions of the same, single truth, so too, is it vitally important to observe the balance between the rules of multiplicity and unity.

It is because of the inability to preserve this balance that those who consider only the inward dimension of both their own and the universe's existence and are based on their observations and spiritual discoveries during their spiritual journeying feel compelled to express the Divine Unity and the unity in multiplicity that emanates from this Unity by saying, "There is no existent being save He." On the other hand, those who restrict themselves to the outward dimension of existence are usually immured in naturalism and drown in different ways of associating partners with God. There are still others who, although they consider the Inward and the Outward and their manifestations together, have given priority to the Inward and His manifestations under the influence of their spiritual state and pleasures, and basing the true, perfect concept of Unity on their own observations, have limited their horizon of belief despite the limitless profundity of belief in the Unseen, by saying, "There is nothing witnessed (or observed) save He." As for those who base their considerations on the Divine Attributes and Names, and look at existence from this perspective, they never restrict their considerations of Unity to any specific dimension of existence or to the manifestations of only one or some certain Divine Names. Without confusing the manifestations and principles of the Inward and the Outward with one another, and considering the differences between the observations of the states of "awareness" and "immersion" or "absorption,"[78] they have proclaimed the true nature of the Divine Unity and unity in multiplicity coming from this Unity by saying, "There is no object of worship, truly besought and desired, save He." This concept of Unity is based on the Qur'an and the Sunna, and it is free of any confusion or misunderstanding. It preserves balance between the Inward and the Outward with the manifestations of each, and it stresses both the Unity of the Divine Essence and the Unity of Divine Attributes. That is, God is One, both in His Essence in the sense that there is no Divine Being save He, and He is One in His Attributes in the sense that He has all the attributes of perfection and is absolutely free from any defect, and in that all the positive attributes shared by creation belong to Him to an infinite, perfect degree.

Unity in the inward dimension of existence can be seen as a seed, and unity in its outward dimension is the tree that grows from it. The former is felt by conscience, while the latter is reached, observed, and experienced by studying the realm of multiplicity—the realm of corporeal existence. This difference of perception and perspective causes some other differences. For example, when we mention the Absolutely One, Eternally-Besought-of-All in view of our relationship with multiplicity through our external senses, and when we want to draw attention to these relationships—as during the *Hajj* and the Prayers of the religious festive days—we mention Him out loud. But when we mention Him from the perspective of the sensations of our conscience or inner faculties, or with respect to our innermost relationship with Him, we mention Him silently in the secrecy of our hearts.

When we inwardly call ourselves to account for whatever we say and do and for our inner relationship with Him, be it in our individual recitations and supplications in the privacy of our houses or in houses of worship, we try to remain devoted to the horizon of the heart and other inner senses or faculties. But especially

78 For these conceptions see, M. Fethullah Gülen, *Emerald Hills of the Heart – Key Concepts in the Practice of Sufism,* The Light, NJ, 2004, vol. 2, pp. 199–209. (Tr.)

during the *Hajj* and the congregational Prayers on Fridays and religious festive days, where we should proclaim the public symbols or marks of Islam, we mention Him in a loud, enthusiastic voice. We both try to give voice to some truths concerning Him on our account and try to make them heard by the conscious beings that travel between the heavens and earth. Without being entangled in His mirrors, we penetrate through the atmosphere of multiplicity far into immaterial realms, and show that we always turn to and pursue unity. This manner of mentioning Him means both observation of the rules that must be observed at the beginning and end of the journeying toward Him, and using the tongue of our inner experiences together with our external sensations.

To explain this point more, everything is given an immaterial nature and form—I use the words "nature" and "form" because we lack the exact words in this material world to express the truths that belong to the immaterial dimension of existence, particularly those concerning the Divine Being—while it exists only in the Divine Knowledge. The Divine Destiny appoints these forms, that are dependent on the Most Sacred Effusions, through the Sacred Effusions, and the Divine Power clothes them in external existence or bodies. That is to say, according to the dictates of the all-encompassing Knowledge, every thing and being receives a particular identity and becomes a particular mirror. Explaining the matter with a simple comparison, every thing or being, in its initial existence in the Divine Knowledge, is like the essence or spirit of the letters that form words and sentences. In the same way that they indicate certain meanings when they form words, things or beings take on different identities and forms. Their silhouettes on the immaterial tablets of the World of Representations or "Ideal" Forms can be likened to the verses of the Qur'an, while their physical forms, particular to each, are like its chapters.

With respect to its inner aspect, everything transcends the horizon of the perception of most of us; it is transparent and displays unity. Causality has a part of its own in its coming into external existence, which exhibits multiplicity. In the same way that the Qur'anic chapters are composed of verses, and verses are formed of words, and words of letters, and letters of points and lines—the whole of existence, animate or inanimate, constitutes the sentences, paragraphs, booklets, and books that the Divine Will and Power create from "ideal" tablets according to the eternal program of Destiny. The "ideal" tablets are formed of non-physical words which are in turn composed of the letters that exist in Divine Knowledge. Those who are distinguished with knowledge of God and perceive this reality always observe unity beyond multiplicity, and God's Unity manifested by the whole of existence beyond the manifestations of His Uniqueness or Absolute Oneness exhibited by each existential entity. They experience deeply the awe-inspiring manifestations of Divine Majesty through the observatories of His Grace. All types or acts of worship, including primarily the Prayer, are extraordinarily important in that they define their responsibilities to those talented with the capacity to experience such manifestations, and warn them about performing these responsibilities carefully.

Those who cannot look at existence with all its dimensions through the lens of Divine Uniqueness, with the illuminating torches of Divine Grace, have been entrapped in the veils of causality, and live in longing for light, despite innumerable sources of light. Just as those who cannot go beyond the voices and melodies while reciting the Qur'an consume their lives with logical and philosophical chatter in the name of its interpretation, so too, those who are unable to read the book of the universe correctly and are entangled in apparent means and causes have never been able to get into its concentric levels of meaning; they live devoid of the illuminating lights of the Divine Revelation and are dragged hither and thither through the unsparing waves of multiplicity without ever reaching the shore of unity.

* * *

The reason why the Prophet Adam, upon him be peace, was favored with vicegerency was his comprehension of the Divine Names, and the fact that he was able to "read" the things that were the results of the manifestations of those Names. He proceeded to the All-Holy One Who is called by these Names, and perceived everything's true nature and reality. He "read" the names taught to him, together with the things and beings that are called by them, and comprehended these things and beings with the particular characteristics of each. Thus, observing the reality of unity on the face of everything—on each and every member or part of multiplicity—he was saved from the turbulence of multiplicity, and advanced to the Divine Being in the light and guidance of the All-Hidden Treasure in his heart. In other words, he correctly read the mysteries of Divinity on the face of the operations of God's commands of creation and absolute control of things and events, and in awareness of the fact that things have established realities or real essences, proclaimed the effects of the Divine Knowledge and Existence. In the face of his capacity, the angels, who are the gorgeous beings of the spiritual realms, could not help but declare to God Almighty: "*All-Glorified are You! We have no knowledge save what You have taught us. Surely You are the All-Knowing, the All-Wise*" (2:32). This declaration meant that God might have servants more noble and virtuous than His noble, virtuous servants—the angels—thus emphasizing the vicegerency of humanity.

Although the faculty of reason may make it seem possible to have glimpses of unity in multiplicity, like having glimpses of the All-Inward in the outward aspect of existence, actually it is not within the capacity of everyone to perceive and experience it in its true reality or profundity. The Prophet Adam, the first human being on earth, lived in the world of multiplicity. As he was able to comprehend multiplicity, he was also the first guide who summoned people to the highest point of the perception of unity. Without being dazzled by the almost unlimited extensiveness, variance, and mixture of multiplicity, he always saw the manifestations of the beauty and grace of Divine Uniqueness amidst the manifestations of His Unity. By observing the concentrated manifestations of certain, particular Divine Names on each entity, which we call the manifestations of

Divine Uniqueness or Absolute Oneness, he perceived God's special favors on himself as a representative of humanity, and by fully opening the doors of his heart to the All-Holy Being, he read the stamp of unity on the face of everything with the eyes of his heart, through the lights coming from Him. He fully comprehended that everything owes to Him whatever it was favored with, and observed that everything was fully controlled and directed by the Divine Power, and proclaimed with a deep conviction that He has neither a partner nor a helper in His Divinity and Lordship. Having used his full capacity in the correct way, he outdid the angels and left the door open for every talented one to arrive at the same achievement.

This door is open to everyone who sincerely intends and resolves to follow the way of unity. Insightful souls who always close and open their eyes in reflective thought, whose hearts continuously beat with compassion, and who make their innate weakness and helplessness a dynamic for reaching His Power, and their poverty and destitution a means for arriving at His infinite Wealth can observe unity in multiplicity, and God's Unity in the mirrors of multiplicity; they feel His existence through the rays of the light of His Existence manifested on every face; they are cooled with the breezes of the manifestations of His Grace even in the face of the all-overwhelming showers of the manifestations of His Majesty; and they sip the pleasures of being in His company beyond all concepts of modality.

It has occasionally been observed that those who have reached this point have not been able to save themselves from confusion or choose words well in expressing their states; or as they have been overwhelmed by the breezes of the manifestations of His "Face," they have made utterances which might be interpreted as Incarnation or Union. But this has happened only occasionally, and in particular those who make their journeys in the light of the Prophethood of the Master of creation, upon him be perfect blessings, have never been and, in fact, will never be witnessed to do so.

This is the station where a full light is perceived or a voice is echoed from the manifestations of the Necessarily Existent Being's declaration, *Whose is the absolute Sovereignty on that Day? It is God's, the One, the All-Overwhelming* (40: 16), in the hearts of the travelers on the way to the Ultimate Truth. In other words, it is observed in this station that the Unity of the Divine Being, which lies in the essence and origin of all existence, has completely surrounded multiplicity, which is accidental or contingent, and colored everything with unity. Therefore, those lost in spirituality and living in "immersion" may be excused for the utterances incompatible with the essentials of the Islamic creed. This station is also where initiates who have reached a certain point of nearness to the Divine Being feel overwhelmed by the manifestations of the All-Beautiful Names, catch "glimpses" of the All-Holy Being, Who is called by these Names with all their faculties, and sense the manifestations of His Attributes with their hearts, which begin beating with contemplations of the One Who is qualified with these Attributes. Heroes of spirituality who are invaded by such degrees of feeling and sensation experience with joy the manifestations of Unity that devastate everything. So they should not be expected to act like those who live in sobriety.

Some describe the degree of the expansion of the heart as the body being engulfed by the heart to its very depth, while others see it as the human spirit's attainment of its essential power that emanates from its being a Divine "breath." Heroes of spirituality, who have attained this rank wherein they have gone beyond the limits of their existence, no longer feel the difference between the earth and the heavens, or this world and the worlds beyond. They are in the worlds beyond the heavens with their hearts and "secrets" at the same time as they are in this world with their bodies—and they are in the highest realms with their spirits while they are in this realm with their physical existence.

Since they always live on the horizon of life at the level of the heart and spirit, they constantly experience the manifestations of Divine Uniqueness—the manifestations of Grace—within the manifestations of Divine Unity—the manifestations of Majesty. They continuously observe the manifestations of Unity through the windows of their inner senses, and are no longer aware of anything other than the One of Unity and Uniqueness. As mentioned before, when they reach this horizon, overwhelmed by the All-Encompassing One's Majesty and Magnificence, and observing the complete disappearance of the encompassed realms under the devastating manifestations of Majesty and Magnificence, they may endure excusable confusions and say, "I see nothing other than Him," or "What you see is but an illusion."

Thinking that something exists or does not exist is partly dependent on the perception of the thing by the inner senses. Especially when things and events are viewed through the windows of those senses that have attained the utmost refinement, the scope of outer existence becomes extremely narrowed. It can even completely disappear in the sight of the travelers who are on the way to the Ultimate Truth and able to view everything with their innermost senses. Even if some pictures of multiplicity sometimes attract the attention of such people, they have no effect on the feeling of Unity that has developed in the bosom of knowledge of God and become a dimension of the experiences of the heart. For this reason, heroes of spirituality, who observe existence from this horizon, may sometimes utter, "I am the Ultimate Truth," under the overpowering influence of their inner sensations, when actually they should say instead, "I am a servant, and You are the Ultimate Truth." Perhaps they may state, "Glory be to me! How grand I am in respect of my essential qualities!" instead of saying, "All-Glorified is God, the Supreme!"

Such utterances and considerations are not only incompatible with modesty and humility, which are the essence and requirements of servanthood and religious life, but they are also contrary to the doctrine of Divine Unity which was taught by Prophets. If they are uttered by those who do not live immersed in the overwhelming manifestations of Divine Unity and intoxicated with His love, they are completely opposed to the basic principles of Islamic faith and represent a deviation from the Straight Path. Similarly, utterances that express Incarnation and Union are also incompatible with the spirit of Islam.

Those who follow the Prophet's way strictly have always observed unity amidst multiplicity, and considered the Divine Being from the perspective of His Attributes and All-Beautiful Names, while approaching the whole of creation within the framework of its own characteristics. They have always admitted that the Ultimate Truth is an all-transcendental Being, and all other beings, whose realities issue from His being the Absolute, Ultimate Truth or Reality, owe their existence to His Creativity and their subsistence to His Self-Subsistence and Maintenance. In addition, in order to always avoid confusion in concepts, thought, reasoning, and belief, they have never made utterances that are incompatible with the truth of Divinity. Seeing all the relative truths as originating from and being dependent on an essential, absolute truth, they have always stressed that things have established realities or real essences, even though they are shadows of the shadow of the light of the Ultimate Truth's Existence.

In conclusion, all the things we see with our eyes and experience with our hearts are an exhibition brought into existence by God's Will and Power; the earth with whatever is in it is a vast, magnificent palace that has been made on the loom of His Knowledge, Will, and Power, and presented to the view of observers; and humanity is an official charged with observing all things to know them with their meanings and the essential purpose of existence. We see the undulation of multiplicity throughout the universe, and we feel and experience the spirit of unity in the essence of every thing and event. Wakeful souls have always had this conviction and followed the way that leads to the Ultimate Truth, while those who have gone to extremes have fallen halfway.

O God! Show us the truth as truth and enable us to observe it, and show us falsehood as falsehood and enable us to avoid it. And bestow Your blessings and peace upon the leader of the Prophets and the commander of the cavalry of Messengers, and on his pure Family and Companions, altogether!

THE SPIRIT AND WHAT FOLLOWS

Based on *al-Milal wa'n-Nihal* ("The True and False Ways of Belief and Thought") by ash-Shahristani,[79] *Tahafut al-Falasifa* ("The Incoherence of the Philosophers") by Imam al-Ghazzali,[80] *Mawqif al-'Aql wa'l-'Ilm wa'l-'Alam* ("The Place of Reason, Science, and the Created World") by Mustafa Sabri Efendi,[81] *Falsafa-i 'Ula* ("The Ancient Philosophy") by Şemseddin Günaltay,[82] and *al-Ba'th wa'l-Khulud* ("The Resurrection and Eternity") by Ali Arslan,[83] I deem it useful to take a short journey around the Sufi concept of spirit in the "*Emerald Hills of the Heart.*" I seek refuge in my Lord from and implore forgiveness for any mistake I may make and any disregard of the truths that lie in the essence of the matter that I may unwittingly show. I also seek His

---

79 Abu'l-Fath Muhammad ibn Abdu'l-Karim ash-Shahristani (1079–1153) was perhaps the most famous of medieval Muslim writers on the trends of thought and religious sects. He lived in eastern Iran. *Al-Milal wa'n-Nihal* ("The True and False Ways of Belief and Thought") is his most famous work. (Tr.)

80 Imam Abu Hamid Muhammad al-Ghazzali (1058–1111): A major theologian, jurist, and sage who was considered a reviver (of Islam's purity and vitality) during his time. Known in Europe as Algazel, he was the architect of Islam's later development. He wrote many books, the most famous being *Ihyau 'Ulumi'd-Din* ("Reviving the Religious Sciences"). (Tr.)

81 Mustafa Sabri Efendi (1869–1954) was a Turkish scholar and Shaykhu'l-Islam. He lived in Turkey and Egypt. *Mawqif al-'Aql wa'l-'Ilm* is among his most well-known works. (Tr.)

82 Şemseddin Günaltay (1883–1961) was the eighteenth prime minister of the Republic of Turkey. He studied natural science, Turkish history, and Muslim peoples. *Zulmetten Nura* ("From Darkness to Light"), *Hurafattan Hakikata* ("From Superstitions to the Truth"), *and Islam Dini Tarihi* ("The History of the Religion of Islam") are his most famous works. (Tr.)

83 Ali Arslan Aydın is a contemporary Turkish scholar. *Islam İnançları ve Felsefesi* ("The Beliefs and Philosophy of Islam") is his most well-known book. (Tr.)

forgiveness if I confuse pure, simple minds, and throw them into any ungrounded suspicion.

In the Qur'an, the Qur'an itself—the Divine Revelation—and the angel who brought the Revelation are both called *ar-Ruh* (the Spirit). However, the spirit which we will study here is the non-material essence of human existence, motion, perception, feelings, and intellectual and "spiritual" development. Throughout human history many have discussed this matter, from philosophers to the sacred Scriptures, and from primitive societies to civilized ones; numerous volumes have been published about it. I think this is partly because humans have a tendency to go into detail without being content with the summarized information given, and partly because of confusing the essence or essential nature of the spirit with its functions. It may also be due to the fact that the horizon of people is usually restricted to the scientific level of the age in which they live. The essential nature of the spirit was taught to humanity via the Prophets in a summarized form, but people have not been content with that and have tended to go into detail. Therefore, the matter has been elaborated. However, both religions and philosophical approaches have generally agreed on the fact that the spirit is the sole source of life, motion, perception, feelings, and consciousness.

From the very beginning of its existence, humanity has been concerned with the existence and nature of the spirit, the existence of which it has felt in dreams and certain other experiences, and has tried to understand its real nature. However, not being satisfied with the information given by the Prophets, it has ramified the matter with subjective approaches and considerations, mainly from the perspective of different names—such as "the intellect," "the soul," "the speaking soul," and "the ego"—which it has given to this non-material essence, and it has only made it more confused and incomprehensible.

As God has bestowed a spirit on all living creatures as a manifestation of His Attribute of Life, He has also breathed into the Prophet Adam, who was the first human being on earth, as well as into each of his descendants, a conscious spirit from the Realm of (the Initial Manifestation of) His Commands. This is what the Qur'an and the established Prophetic Traditions say about the spirit. That is, the only information the Qur'an and the established Prophetic Traditions give about the spirit is that it is something breathed into humans by God from the Realm of (the Initial Manifestation of) His Commands. This information has been developed by some philosophers and Sufis to the extent that it has come to cover innumerable volumes. These philosophers and Sufis have attempted to know and describe it in respect of both its essential nature and its functions and its relations with the body.

We will approach the matter from the viewpoint of what the Sufis mean by the spirit and spiritual life. However, since the matter of the spirit has been a matter of lengthy debates, we will summarize how it has been dealt with in different cultures, philosophies, and religious traditions in order to provide the reader with an opportunity to make comparisons. So, let us examine how different trends of philosophy, religious traditions, intellectuals, and scholars from different religious sciences have elaborated on a matter about which the All-Sublime Creator has given only a small piece of information.

Even in the earliest centuries of history, humanity thought and spoke about the spirit, including its origin, nature, and functions. Although it sometimes approached the matter in the light of the guidance brought by Prophets, it frequently erred and suffered contradictions, without being able to understand or correctly explain why or how we come into the world, and why we stay here for some time, and then depart. But it always affirmed the existence of an immaterial or metaphysical power, which is living, conscious, perceiving, and which causes motion.

Some have called this metaphysical power, a power that all agree is a living, conscious, immaterial thing independent of the body, by names that mean soul, psyche, air, life, or liveliness. Sanskrit-speaking people call it Atman, the Greeks, Psyche, the Latin people, Animus, the French, Esprit, the Goths, Saivala, and the Persians, Rawan.

People from different cultures and religious traditions have generally not only agreed on the spirit's being an immaterial essence independent of the body as the source of life, perception, and motion, but have also shared similar views about its future. The majority have believed that after spirits depart from the world, they continue to live in another realm in accordance with how their owners lived in this world. The spirits of those who have lived a righteous life will receive a hospitable welcome and be rewarded, while the spirits of those who have contaminated them with evil will be punished.

Even in the earliest centuries of history, humans perceived a duality in human existence, but when they tried to work out the details of the nature of what we call the spirit, they came up with many fallacies. We come across some of them in the chapters about animism in books concerned with the history of religions. One of these fallacies is undoubtedly the doctrine of reincarnation in the sense of the rebirth of a spirit in another body or the transmigration of spirits. In order to satisfy their inborn feeling or need for eternity and to lessen the suffering that comes from anxiety about going into eternal non-existence, some have sheltered in a doctrine that is based on the continuous migration of spirits from one body to another.

Reincarnation proposes that bodies are like forms or matrices which the spirits enter to breathe life into them and cause their motion. When one form or matrix of a spirit decays, the spirit simply enters another one. If the body which a spirit enters belongs to a human being, the spirit adds to it also perception, consciousness, and will.

Edward Tylor (1832–1917) dates the origin of the doctrine of reincarnation to the earliest periods of human history, and gives various examples. According to many religious historians, this false belief was born in ancient Egypt as an invention of Hermes Trismegistus and was carried to ancient Greece by Pythagoras. However, the historian Herodotus recorded that reincarnation had been known in Greece before Pythagoras.

Over time, the fantasy of reincarnation came to be adopted by some followers of certain Divine religions. They cited as examples of reincarnation Niobe's turning into a stone and the Prophet Lot's wife, into a pillar of salt (*Genesis*, 19:26). However, neither of these examples is compatible with the theory of reincarnation or continuous transmigration of souls.

We also come across the traces of reincarnation in ancient Hindu texts. We can see some vague references to it in some supplications found in the *Vedas*. The Vaiseshika School or Philosophy holds that the spirits or souls which are contaminated by evils will live a completely miserable, lower level of life. *Vedanta* maintains that spirits suffer and move about agitatedly in many bodies until they attain sacred or ultimate knowledge (of the essential non-difference between Brahman and Atman).

Charles Fourier (1772–1837), a French utopian socialist philosopher, basing his work on the information given above and similar other approaches, embellished the matter with many fantasies and made unimaginable predictions. Unfortunately, some religious people adopted some of his predictions, attempting to support them with some true, religious elements, and propagated the doctrine explicitly or tacitly.

Except for some extremist Shi'as and Hurufis,[84] Muslims have been influenced the least by the fallacy of reincarnation. For if reincarnation is a doctrine founded upon or in pursuit of wisdom, justice, reward, and punishment as a response to the greatest need of humanity for eternity and a remedy for its worries of eternal

84 The Hurufis are the followers of Hurufism, an esoteric heterodox trend—religion, according to some—which attributes sacredness to letters, claims that each letter of the Arabic alphabet has a numerical value, and deduces histories and predictions from the Qur'an based on the numerical values of letters. It was founded by Fadlullah Hurufi (1340–1394), who lived in Iran, and claimed that he was an incarnation of God. (Tr.)

non-existence—there are many who assert that it is such—then Islam promises humanity, created for and bound to go to eternity, an eternal life after an overall resurrection after a temporary separation; thus it removes all the worries of eternal separation and non-existence of humanity. It promises its followers the eternal happiness of Paradise, for an hour of which thousands of years of worldly happy life cannot be a substitute, and a vision of God Almighty and being honored by His good pleasure, which will provide happiness thousands of times greater than the happiness of Paradise. Thus, there is no need in Islam to search for alternative means of attaining happiness.

Both the Sunnite and Shi'ite scholars categorically reject the kind of reincarnation that is adopted by the extremist Shi'as and Hurufis, which was partly borrowed from Mazdakism and Brahmanism, and which had similarities with the false doctrines of Union and Incarnation. As for the words of some Sufis, which imply incarnation, except for the fallacies of Shaykh Bedreddin,[85] they are either due to the lack of proper words to express the state of "absorption" that some achieved, or were misunderstood and misinterpreted utterances. The words of some Sufis like Muhyi'd-Din ibn al-'Arabi, who are known to belong to the School of the (Transcendental) Unity of Being, which some interpret as suggesting reincarnation, relate to the assertion of "appearance in another's form." That is, they are concerned with the fact that some perfect guides communicate their inspirations into purified, capable spirits and raise them to their horizons, that they reflect their inspirations in the spiritual mirrors of their capable followers. The assertion of "appearance in another's form" also means that an initiate who follows a perfect guide may sometimes be mistaken for that guide. This is merely confusion, even though it has sometimes caused

85 Shaykh Bedreddin Simawi was born in Simavna town in today's Greece. He is generally known for his materialistic views of existence. He was sentenced to death because of his participation in revolts in the political scene in the Period of Interregnum (1402–1413). His *Waridat* is famous. (Tr.)

some imperfect souls to claim to be the Messiah or Mahdi. However, it can never be reconciled with reincarnation, which means that a spirit or soul which has not been able to be perfected enough to complete its earthly journey in a body is reborn and continues to live in another body or a lower or higher level of life.

Now, let us mention what those who have talked about the spirit with its nature and functions have said.

The information of the earliest thinkers and philosophers about the spirit was quite simple, much like their information about and opinions on existence and things. According to them, the earth was flat, the sky was a dome over it, and the sun, the moon and stars were lamps that hung from it. Existence was formed of what they called "the four elements," namely earth, water, air, and fire. So, the spirit must have been some substance that was more refined than these elements.

Ionia

Thales (624–546 BCE), one of the earliest philosophers of Ionia, thought the spirit to be some fluid substance that brought about life in the body. According to Anaximander (610–546 BCE), who succeeded Thales as the second master of the Milesian school, spirit was some boundless substance that was different from the above-mentioned four elements. His pupil Anaximenes (585–525 BCE) perceived the spirit as having a relationship with air, as he held that air was the source of all things. Belonging to the same school, Heraclitus (535–475 BCE) considered the spirit to be something like fire that is separate from the body.

We can consider all the Ionian philosophers as hylozoists—philosophers who maintain that the essence of life is inseparable from matter. However, although according to some historians of philosophy, he belonged to the Ionian School of philosophy, Anaxagoras (500–428 BCE) was the first to assert that the spirit, which he called the "universal intellect" was an independent entity, and emphasized the duality of matter and force, and the spirit and body. He clearly described an independent, subtle agent that was possessed of all knowledge and power which caused motion, moving the original form of existence and eventually creating the known universe, and which rules all forms of life. But unfortunately, the thoughts of that genius were misunderstood and misinterpreted, and it was claimed that he regarded the spirit as a subtle, material entity.

The first serious blow to the Ionian philosophers' considerations of spirit came from Pythagoras (580/572–500/490 BCE), who was born in Samos, one of the eastern Aegean islands; as a young man Pythagoras left for Croton in southern Italy. He saw the "ideas," images that existed or formed in the mind, as the basis of existence. Pythagoras and his followers destroyed the school of Sensualism and substituted it with what we can call some sort of idealism. The idealism which Pythagoras and his pupil Empedocles (490–430 BCE) laid the foundations to, and which was later elaborated by Plato (428/427–348/347 BCE), entered Muslim thought in later centuries. However, since that idealism lacked a sound doctrine of afterlife, was open to reincarnation, and asserted that individual spirits were the manifestations of what they called the universal spirit, Muslim theologians criticized it severely.

Unlike Pythagoras, who always preserved his line of thought, Empedocles was not consistent in his considerations of the spirit, but wavered between naturalism, skepticism, and mysticism. In the face of the enthusiastic welcome of some people, he even became so arrogant as to claim divinity, and say, "I am an immortal God, I am no longer mortal!" As a result, his ideas lost respect, including those concerning the spirit.

Before passing on to the ideas of Socratic and post-Socratic philosophers about the spirit, the pantheism of the Eleatic school, founded by Parmenides (early fifth century BCE), including particularly Zeno's (490–430 BCE) philosophy of the immortality of the spirit, and the atomism of Democritus (455–370 BCE) are worth mentioning.

Socrates (470-399 BCE)

The matter of spirit entered a new phase with Socrates, who proved to be a turning point in ancient Greek philosophy. Socrates freed the spirit from the narrow frame of matter and physicality, and adopted a much wider approach to it. His pupil Plato explains the views of his master in his book *Phaidon* as follows:

> God is the source of wisdom Who encompasses all things, and the Spirit and Intellect of the whole universe. The human body is composed of material elements, while the spirit is an individual manifestation of the Universal Spirit. The spirit controls the body in a way similar to God, being invisible, and ruling the whole universe. When one day the body decomposes, the spirit remains eternally.

God alone knows whether these considerations totally belong to Socrates or if Plato added his ideas to them.

Plato (428/427–348/347 BCE)

Although it was Anaxagoras who, being a spiritualist philosopher, discussed the physical and metaphysical dimensions of human existence under the titles of the spirit, intellect, and carnal soul for the first time in the history of philosophy, Socrates and his pupil Plato developed this philosophy and made it known worldwide. Their works were translated into many languages, including Arabic, and came to be known by Muslim scholars at a very early period in the history of Islam, being widely discussed among Muslim philosophers and theologians. Therefore, based partly on Shahristani and partly on Şemseddin Günaltay, a twentieth-century Turkish researcher, I will provide a summary of Plato's considerations concerning the spirit, which in fact are a developed amalgamation of the ideas of Anaxagoras, Pythagoras, and Socrates.

Plato mentions a third soul, which he calls "the speaking soul," in addition to "the soul of lusts" and "the soul of anger." He regards the soul of lusts as the source of carnal desires and appetites, and the soul of anger as that of the feelings and attitudes like wrath, violence, and aggression. As for the speaking soul, which Plato also calls the spirit, it is the origin or center of perception, reasoning, and understanding. Being a simple, invisible, and indivisible substance which causes movement, it has been created directly by God Almighty, and inserted in the mold of the body. Since it is from God, it does not die or cease to exist. Having been created before the creation of the body, it continues to exist after its death. The intellect and intelligence are thus two profound dimensions of the spirit, which itself is the source of the body's movement.

According to what Shahristani writes, Plato divided the universe into two worlds: (1) the world of ideas, which comprises "ideas" or metaphysical entities, and (2) the sensed world of bodies. Before coming to this sensed, corporeal world, humans were honored with the observation of truths in the world of ideas. When humans were sent to this narrow world of physical bodies, they were engulfed in the darkness of corporeality.

We can summarize Plato's considerations of the speaking soul as follows:

- The spirit is an immaterial, immortal element of perception and reflection. It thinks, reflects, perceives, judges, and decides.
- The spirit sets the body into motion and it was created before the body.
- The spirit is the source of all good and virtues. Its worst enemy is moral corruption, which extinguishes it.

Neo-Platonism, which appeared in later centuries, would be based on these thoughts of Plato's.

Aristotle (384–322 bce)

Aristotle is the most renowned figure of ancient philosophy after Plato and Socrates. He continued, and still continues, to be connected to the Peripatetic School, which he founded based on deductive and inductive thought. Unlike his master Plato, he followed the way of deducing conclusions from premises and analogy. With this rationalism, he both secured a long life for his philosophy and struck great blows at mechanistic and helical thoughts. According to Aristotle, life depends on the spirit. If life is a movement, it is the spirit that sets it in motion. The spirit is neither of the same essence and nature as the body nor completely separate from it. The body is something akin to an instrument of the spirit, and life develops based on the spirit.

Like his teacher Plato, Aristotle places the spirit in different categories. However, according to him, the spirit is created with the body and returns to its origin after the death of the body. It experiences a process of perfection during the life of the body, and on reaching perfection, it gains resemblance to the Divine Being, continuing to live in pleasures that are particular to itself.

With such thoughts, Aristotle gave both Muslim scholars and Christian thinkers much to occupy themselves with over long centuries. But today he is no more than a subject of philosophical study.

After Aristotle, neither Epicurus (341–270 BCE) nor Zeno of Citium (333–264 BCE) were able to offer considerable thoughts about the spirit. Following Democritus' way of thought, Epicurus confined himself within the narrow frame of sensations, while Zeno, who founded the School of Stoic Pantheism, spent his life approaching everything through the window of some sort of skepticism and repeating the thoughts of his predecessors. He asserted that it was the duty of researchers and people of knowledge to study things and events, and they should keep themselves within this frame, not imagining that they can arrive at the absolute truth by merely reading. Thus, he blocked the way of research to some extent.

Philo (20 BCE–50 CE)

Alexandria's repertoire of the spirit, like that of the Greeks, is very rich. While the early philosophers of the Alexandrian school usually

the spirit and claimed that what we call the spirit was the name we gave to the activities of some bodily organs, while others asserted that existence essentially consisted of the spirit and all that we sensed was its manifestations; others regarded the spirit as something like matter, and still others maintained that it was a substance separate from the body. Except for a few materialists, they accepted the existence of the spirit and expressed their views about its nature and functions. Thus, numerous volumes consisting of ideas about the spirit took their places in libraries.

Materialists see existence as consisting of matter, and thus regard the human being as a body formed of bones, flesh, a nervous system, and a brain, attributing all human intellectual activities, feelings, and emotions to the brain. Tutil claimed that we have risen through the brain to the rank of animate beings from inanimate ones; Carl Foht compared the relationship between the brain and thought to that between liver and bile, as reflected in the famous formula of Moleschott: "The brain secretes thought as the liver secretes bile." Büchner asserted that human intellectual activities were impressions of events and movements in nature on the human nervous system. He attributed everything to matter and the human organism, and denied the existence and functions of the spirit.

Materialists based their claims on theories and concepts such as transformism, Darwinism, evolution, mutation, coincidence, and necessity, and so on. Within the scope of this book, I will discuss neither their claims nor these theories and concepts.

The way adopted by the idealists from the beginning is contrary to that of the materialists. While matter is the sole source of existence for materialists, idealists base all their theories on ideas. Descartes' famous adage, "I think, therefore I am," can be considered to be the summary and basis of this trend of thought.

The basic assertions of idealism have also not been found to be sound. George Berkeley (1685–1753) summarizes one of these assertions as follows: "There is nothing substantial other than the thinking soul. Things exist because souls think that they exist; we do not know the existence of things in a dark room. Without thinking or ideas in our minds, we cannot assert the existence of things. This can be described as things and events being identical with the mental concepts of them."

Another approach of ideals can be summarized as follows: The things we assert that we see and feel are nothing more than mental images. If there is a world around us, it is a mental world. Materialists, who reduce everything to matter and physical activities of the brain, and idealists, who see existence as consisting of mental objects, are agreed about the non-existence of the spirit or the "speaking soul."

Henri Bergson (1859–1941)

Bergson's philosophy is based on indeterminism. That is, according to determinism, the state of things at any given moment is the necessary result of its state just prior to that moment. What this signifies is that the same things or causes in the universe always produce the same results. Bergson rejects this attitude and asserts that there is no certain necessity in the universe. His approach to the matter of the spirit is similar to that of Berkeley. He maintains that something material cannot be the real origin of our feelings; the source can only be the soul. According to Bergson, being existent means perceiving, therefore, something that has no perception cannot be regarded as existing. What perceives is the spirit, which is always active and effective. What the spirit perceives are ideas. Therefore, it is only the spirit and ideas that really exist. Like idealists, Bergson also sees things as consisting of mental images. While materialists attribute "mental images" or thoughts to the activities of the brain and, therefore, see them as posterior to it, Bergson considers mental activities to be the results of mental images, which are, according to him, the real motives or motors of these activities.

Pantheism and/or Monism

The approach of pantheists to the spirit is different from the approaches that have so far been discussed. Despite some minor differences of viewpoint among them, pantheists maintain that the spirit and body are the same entity, both being a single manifestation. Being one of the foremost representatives of this trend, Spinoza claims that the Divine Being is identical with the universe—God is absolutely exalted above all that they assert! There is nothing of substantial reality other than the Self-Existing and Self-Subsisting One. The real existence is infinite and eternal, having infinite attributes and forms or reflections. This is the reality of what we call existence. The spirit and body are a combination that forms the absolute essence or being.

This view of Spinoza's superficially resembles some of the utterances which certain Muslim Sufis asserted about the Unity of Being while in a state of spiritual absorption or intoxication. But these two approaches are radically different from one another. Asserting the unity of existence or claiming that the Divine Being is identical with the universe is one thing, while absorption in the Existence of the Divine Being in utter neglect of the universe is yet another. Monism, particularly Hegelian monism, never considers the metaphysical dimension of existence but accepts bodily existence as being identical with spiritual manifestations. According to Hegel, God is contained in the external, observable world—God forbid such a thought! Our spirit is a part of what he calls the universal spirit, and our bodily existence is an inseparable part of God's Existence. Matter and force are no more than the manifestations of the same substance. In short, like materialists, Hegel gives priority to matter and attributes the functions of the spirit to it.

Spiritualism

Spiritualism accepts the existence of both the body and the spirit, and while attributing all physiological activities to the body, perceives that the functions of the soul are under the control and disposition of the spirit. According to spiritualists, it is the substance which is called the spirit and on which ideas are based. This substance, which we call "*ana* (the ego)," has a separate, independent existence from the body. Compared to others schools, spiritualists are clearer in their consideration of the spirit. Plato stressed the existence and permanence of the spirit, although his words are associated with reincarnation; Aristotle regarded the spirit as the most essential element of human existence, that which separates humankind from other kinds of beings. Even though they use different concepts or descriptions, Descartes, Berkeley, and Leibniz expressed almost the same considerations. All of them admitted the existence of a substance in human existence which is other than the body and which thinks, wills, and perceives.

Humans undergo constant physical changes from the time they come into the world, but every person remains himself or herself. Therefore, there must be an essence in every human being which determines his or her identity and nature, and this is what we call the spirit. Malebranche adds to this consideration: The spirit and the body have interactive relations and reciprocal effects upon each other. In accordance with the laws God has established, when the spirit manifests will or wills something, some movements occur in the body; any movement in the body produces effects on the spirit. The real or ultimate cause of both interactions is the Divine Will (this seems to have been inspired by the approach of the Muslim Ash'aris[86]). The apparent interactions of the spirit and body are normal human activities which occur within the framework of the Divine unchanging laws of life and which never ignore human free will. Since both the spirit and body act in accordance with these Divine laws, there is an exact order and harmony in human "natural" existence and life or in the activities of the spirit and body.

86 'Ash'aris constitute one of the two main branches of Ahl al-Sunna wa'l-Jama'a. The founder of this branch is Abu'l-Hasan al-'Ash'ari (d. 936). Although they accept the role of human free will in human actions, the free will consists of an inner tendency. It is God Who creates all human actions. They also maintain that things do not have attributes essential to and originating in them. For example, fire does not burn as an indispensable attribute; rather, God always creates the attribute of burning in fire so long as He wills it to burn, and if He does not will it to burn, fire cannot burn. Therefore, the universe, with whatever is in it, is under God's direct disposal and control. (Tr.)

APPROACHES FROM THE MUSLIM WORLD

Now, let us see how Muslim sages and scholars have approached the matter of spirit.

We do not have exact knowledge about how God informed the previous Prophets of the identity of the spirit. However, the Qur'an contains a specific declaration concerning it: *They ask you about the spirit. Say: "The spirit is of my Lord's Command"* (17: 85). That is, the spirit is a conscious entity that issues from the Realm of Pure Divine Commands or the Realm of the Transcendental Manifestation of Divine Commands.[87]

The earliest Muslim scholars were content with the information given in the Qur'an and avoided going into details concerning the identity of the spirit. The considerations of such Western thinkers as Claude Bernard (1813–1878), Raymond, Spencer, and Hamilton are similar to that declaration from the Qur'an.

The attitudes of the earliest Muslim scholars were free from taking any risks. Just as with the spirit, they did not attempt to make any comments on other allegorical statements of the Qur'an. However, when the legacy of ancient philosophy began to be translated into Arabic and found its way into Muslim minds, "the scholars of later periods"—as they are called in Muslim sources—felt obliged to make explanations and interpretations concerning these statements, including the existence, nature, and functions of the spirit, and what awaits it after the death of its owner in the grave and Hereafter. They tried to correct the wrong concepts that originate from the legacy of ancient philosophy and other trends of thought and religions.

There were differences of views among those Muslim scholars concerning the spirit. A few approached it from the viewpoint of the

---

87 Said Nursi writes in explaining this: "The spirit resembles laws (for example, the law of growth in a tree). Both issue from the Realm of Pure Divine Commands and Divine Will. If the law had had consciousness, it would have become a spirit; if the spirit had been without consciousness, it would have become a law." *The Letters*, "Epigrams or Seeds of the Truth," The Light, New Jersey, 2007, p. 447.

atomism of Democritus (455–370 BCE), and there were some among them who thought like hylozoists. Some dealt with the matter like modern physiologists, while others discussed the existence of three souls and three varieties of soul, namely the animal (vital or natural) soul, the vegetable soul, and the human soul, seeming to be followers of Aristotle. There were some theologians who thought that the spirit was a fundamental dimension of the human form; while physicians regarded it, like Galen (129–200/216), as the manifestation of the balance of the four elements or fluids—blood, bile, phlegm, and black bile. Yet others considered it to be a "subtle entity" which is related to the body, like the relation of oil to olives, or the rose oil in roses; some avoided making any comparison or explanation and were content with describing it as "a sensitive, perceiving substance."

However, the overwhelming majority of Muslim theologians and Sufis have regarded the spirit as a basic, immaterial substance of human existence and nature, attributing human value to its perfection and stressing that while the body decomposes and rots away after death, the spirit remains alive and awaits the Resurrection, to meet either eternal happiness or punishment after the Resurrection. Thus, they have adopted a unique way, different from that of materialists, spiritualists, monists, and followers of reincarnation.

Except for a few who were influenced by Platonic thought, Muslim scholars believe that the spirit was created in time. But there is a difference of views concerning whether the spirit of every person is created before they come into the world, or whether it is created at the time when life is breathed into the embryo in the mother's womb. This difference of opinion has caused some to argue about whether the Resurrection will be only spiritual or both spiritual and bodily. Despite these differences, all Muslim scholars, philosophers, and Sufis agree on the existence of the spirit, and that it will remain alive after the death of the person by God's Self-Subsistence causing it to subsist.

Despite following different schools of thought in Islam, philosophers and thinkers such as al-Kindi,[88] Ibn Sina,[89] Ibn Bajja,[90] Ibn Rushd,[91] and Nasiru'd-Din at-Tusi,[92] and verifying scholars such as Raghib al-Isfahani,[93] Sadr ash-Shirazi,[94] Abu Zayd ad-Dabusi,[95]

---

88 Yaqub ibn Ishak al-Kindi (800–873 CE), also known in the West by the Latinized version of his name, Alkindus, was a Muslim Arab philosopher, mathematician, physician, astronomer and musician. He was regarded as the first Muslim peripatetic philosopher, and is particularly known for his efforts to introduce Greek philosophy to the Arab world. (Tr.)

89 Abu 'Ali Ibn Sina (980–1037 CE) was a Muslim Persian physician, astronomer, logician, mathematician, metaphysician, philosopher, physicist, scientist, and theologian, known in the West as Avicenna, and the author of some 450 books on a wide range of subjects, many of which concentrated on philosophy and medicine. (Tr.)

90 Ibn Bajja, Abu Bakr Muhammad ibn Yahya (1095–1138 CE) was an Andalusian-Muslim astronomer, logician, musician, philosopher, physician, physicist, psychologist, poet and scientist. He was known in the West by his Latinized name, Avempace. He died in Morocco. (Tr.)

91 Ibn Rushd, Muhammad ibn Ahmad (1126–1198 CE) was a master of early Islamic philosophy, Islamic theology, Maliki law and jurisprudence, logic, psychology, Arabic music theory, and the sciences of medicine, astronomy, geography, mathematics and physics. He lived in Spain, and died in Morocco. He was known in the West by his Latinized name, Averroes. He has been described as the founding father of secular thought in Western Europe. He wrote about seventy works in different fields of science. (Tr.)

92 Muhammad ibn Muhammad ibn al-Hasan Nasiru'd-Din at-Tusi (1201–1274 CE) was born in Tus, in eastern Iran, and died in Baghdad. He was a prolific writer: an astronomer, biologist, chemist, mathematician, philosopher, physician, physicist, scientist, and theologian. (Tr.)

93 Abul-Qasim Husayn ibn Muhammad ar-Raghib al-Isfahani (d. 1109 CE) was one of the most renowned linguists who appeared during the 'Abbasid period. He made contributions to Qur'anic commentary, ethics, theology, and Sufism. His fame rests, however, on his *Mufradat alfaz al-Qur'an*, which reflects his exceptional aptitude for subtle semantic analysis and marks an advance in the systematic studies of the Qur'an. (Tr.)

94 Sadrud-Din Muhammad ibn Ibrahim ash-Shirazi, known as Mulla Sadra (1571–1640 CE) may be regarded as the most important philosopher in the Muslim world in the last four centuries. The author of over forty works, he revived philosophy in Iran. He constructed a critical philosophy which combined Peripatetic, Illuminationist and gnostic philosophy along with Shi'ite theology within the compass of what he termed a "metaphilosophy." (Tr.)

95 'Ubaydullah Ibn 'Umar Abu Zayd ad-Dabusi (978–1039 CE) was one of the most renowned jurists of his time. He lived in present-day Uzbekistan. He had exceptional knowledge about the different views and approaches among the Muslim schools of law. He also wrote on worship, morality, knowledge of God, and training of the self or the soul. (Tr.)

Imam al-Haramayn Juwayni,[96] Imam al-Ghazzali, Fakhru'd-Din ar-Razi,[97] Ibn Qayyim al-Jawziyya, Sa'du'd-Din at-Taftazani,[98] Jalalu'd-Din ad-Dawwani,[99] and Imam Sharani unanimously accept that the spirit is the essence of human existence. Now let us examine the ideas of the spirit of the most famous among these thinkers.

Ibn Sina (Avicenna) (980–1037 CE)

Being one of the most famous Muslim philosophers and scientists, Abu 'Ali ibn Sina influenced almost all thinkers and Sufis who came after him. With his great genius, extraordinary love of science, resolution, and endeavor, he understood ancient philosophers well, and he had sufficient knowledge of the thoughts of such philosophers as al-Kindi and al-Farabi.[100] In his works, he quoted from the philoso-

---

96 'Abdu'l-Malik ibn 'Abdullah ibn Yusuf, known as Imam al-Haramayn al-Juwayni (1028–1065 CE) was al-Ghazzali's teacher, jurist, scholar of the methodology of jurisprudence, and expert in theology. He was born and lived in Naysabur, eastern Iran, and stayed for some four or five years in Makka and Madina. His authority gained him the titles such as "the Glory of Islam," and "Imam of Imams." He was the main figure in the Ash'ari school in his time. (Tr.)

97 Abu 'Abdullah Muhammad ibn 'Umar ibn al-Husayn Fakhru'd-Din ar-Razi (1149–1209 CE) was a very famous Muslim theologian, philosopher, and a commentator on the Qur'an. He was born in Ray, now a district of modern Tehran. He died in Herat, in modern Afghanistan. He also wrote on Islamic law, medicine, physics, astrology, literature, and history. His most famous work is *at-Tafsiru'l-Kabir* ("The Great Commentary on the Qur'an") known as *Mafatihu'l-Ghayb* ("Keys to the Unseen"). (Tr.)

98 Sa'dud-Din at-Taftazani (d. 1390 CE) was a famous scholar of logic, rhetoric, grammar, theology, and jurisprudence of Samarqand during the rule of Timur. His *Sharh al-'Aqaid an-Nasafiyya* ("A Commentary on the Islamic Creed by an-Nasafi") is among the basic works of Islamic theology. (Tr.)

99 Jalalu'd-Din Muhammad ibn As'ad ad-Dawwani (1426–1502 CE) was a prominent philosopher and theologian from Shiraz. He combined elements of Illuminationist and Peripatetic philosophy and possibly also interests in Ibn al-'Arabi. His *Lawami' al-Ishraq fi Makarim al-Akhlaq* ("Lustres of Illumination on the Noble Virtues") is famous. (Tr.)

100 Abu Nasr Muhammad ibn al-Farakh al-Farabi (872–950 CE) was one of the greatest scientists and philosophers of the Islamic world in his time. He was also a cosmologist, logician, musician, psychologist and sociologist. He was born in Farab, mod-

phers of Ionian, Italy, and Elea, and made references to the thoughts of al-Kindi and al-Farabi as well. Therefore, knowing his ideas also means having knowledge of those of these two philosophers.

According to Ibn Sina, life is the result of feeling, motion, and the spirit. All activities related to consciousness and perception originate in the spirit and life. Nevertheless, the continuous and healthy manifestation of life requires the healthy operation of the physical system or mechanism.

Ibn Sina also discusses three souls or three varieties of the soul. They are the vegetable, animal, and human souls. The vegetable soul has two powers: the power of nourishment and the power of growth. There is also another power which he calls "the power of reproduction," which serves the continuation of every species. The animal soul has the powers of motion and perception, or the powers that cause motion and perception. The power of motion has sub-powers of cause and agent. We can describe these as the power that causes something to happen and the power of doing it. The power of cause has two faculties: the faculty of desire, or of attractive and repulsive passions, and the faculty of anger, or of defensive passions. He sees the power of the agent, or the power that performs an action, as the origin of physical movements under the influence of the faculties of desire and anger.

Ibn Sina also mentions certain internal senses in addition to the five external ones. They are the *common sense* (*sensus communis*: the mental sense or faculty of general perception),[101] which he calls "bantasya," as well as the powers of supposition, imagination, rec-

---

ern Uzbekistan, and traveled to Baghdad to pursue higher learning. As a philosopher, al-Farabi was a founder of his own school of early Islamic philosophy known as "Farabism" or "Alfarabism." Although he introduced Plato and Aristotle to Muslim philosophy, his school of philosophy moved from metaphysics to methodology, a move that anticipates modernity. He also wrote on politics. (Tr.)

101 The phrase "common sense" was derived from a wrong interpretation of this concept. However, while common sense means the ability to behave in a sensible way, *common sense* in psychology or *sensus communis* is the faculty which initially receives and comprehends the perceptions of the five external senses.

ollection, and conceptualization. He offers detailed explanations concerning the duties and activities of these senses.

Ibn Sina assigns the most important place to the power of reason or intellect in his explanations of the soul. According to him, the human soul is not something material, nor does it subsist through the subsistence of the body. It is something immaterial and essentially independent of the body, but it needs the body in the fulfillment of its functions. It is a single substance, but it has many powers or faculties. These powers or faculties serve as means in the soul's relationship with the body. In addition to these, each human being has two other powers, namely the power of knowing and the power of acting. The latter is related to the lower realms and makes them subservient to it, while the former builds relationships with the higher realms and tries to realize true humanity. In one respect, the power of knowing in Ibn Sina's thought can be considered to be human reason or intellect, and the power of acting is the origin of human secondary or physical actions.

The power of reason has categories or abilities. It has the capacity or ability to reason and reflect; it can perceive self-evident facts and realities and indispensable truths which are necessary to know; and it has the rank of deduction in theoretical matters; and more particularly, in certain exceptional people, there is a level of extraordinary perception and reasoning. According to Ibn Sina, this last level of human reason or intellect is a sacred power endowed with the capacity to make contact with the Spirit of Holiness. Prophets have this power at the highest level, and then there are those who succeed them in continuing their mission, (but they do not receive Revelation). Ibn Sina accepts both Prophethood and the contact of the Prophets with the highest realms, and, unlike al-Farabi, acknowledges that the Prophets were endowed with the capacity to have some knowledge of the Unseen.

Ibn Sina maintains that the Prophets, who are those most knowledgeable of Divine truths, are able to make a powerful contact with the Active Intellect due to the full purification of their hearts, and to gain a sacred power through which they obtain knowledge of the metaphysical realm and truths. Knowledge pours into their hearts, either directly or through some means. If this knowledge comes not only as a meaning but also in the form of words, it is a manifest Revelation. But if it comes only as a meaning and its wording or expression is left to the Prophet himself, it is a Revelation that is not manifest. Ibn Sina also affirms that a soul which has attained this level of perfection can exert an influence on things. Therefore, he believes in both the miracles of the Prophets and the wonder-working of saints. He offers powerful arguments to prove these acts, many of which He based on the Qur'anic verse, *God is the Light of the heavens and earth. The example of His Light is like a niche wherein is a lamp....* (24: 35). Following him, many other scholars such as Imam al-Ghazzali and Elmalılı Hamdi Yazır[102] primarily, have made extensive interpretations of this profound source (the verse mentioned).

Ibn Sina stresses the spiritual nature of the speaking soul, and in his works titled *an-Najat* ("Salvation") and *al-Ishara* ("The Indication"), he offers many arguments to support his idea, some of which are as follows:

1. The speaking soul is aware of its existence without needing any external means or causes. It never doubts its existence, and is always conscious of it even during sleep or while in a state of intoxication or spiritual absorption. More than that, even at times when there is no contact with the outer world, the soul is aware of its existence. So, such a substance, the existence and functions of which everyone feels in himself or herself, and which perceives itself as itself, cannot be of a material nature, nor can it be the brain or nervous system. This sensitive, perceiving power, which is the cause of motion, is the spirit or the speaking soul. It is such a

---

102 Elmalılı Muhammed Hamdi Yazır (1878–1942) was one of the most celebrated scholars of the last period of the Ottoman State, as well as of modern Turkey. He had expert knowledge of *Fiqh* (Muslim jurisprudence) and Qur'anic commentary. His monumental commentary on the Qur'an, *Hak Dini Kur'an Dili* ("The Qur'an, the Language of the Religion of Truth") is among the best-sellers in Turkey. (Tr.)

substance that, like a tree being related to its entire environment, through which it expands with its roots and branches, it affects all the organs and limbs of the human being.

2. According to Ibn Sina, the human soul, which we call the spirit, is created together with the body. But it does not perish when the body dies; rather, it continues to live in another realm after death. The body is a system or mechanism employed by the spirit. When its period of employment ends, it is destroyed; but the human soul, which is a spiritual entity, continues to live eternally in another realm.

3. The relation of the spirit with the body, and its control of it, is not of the nature of incarnation or union. It is a relationship of direction and administration, whether through the direct contact or not. As the existence of the spirit does not depend on the body, it does not perish through the death of the body. The spirit is a simple, indivisible entity and is not composed of atomic particles. Therefore, the spirit, which leaves the body through death—these are also Plato's opinions about the spirit, but we are told that Plato explains the spirit's further, permanent life as a cycle of transmigrations—continues its life in another realm, either in indescribable pleasure or in pain and suffering. The spirit which believed and did good, righteous deeds while in the world will live an eternal, happy life, while the other which spent its worldly life in unbelief and dissipation will suffer eternal misery. Although some claim that Ibn Sina, whose belief in the other, eternal world is indisputable, did not believe in the bodily resurrection, this might have come from a misunderstanding of his assertion that the bodily resurrection cannot be rationally proven.

Imam al-Ghazzali (1058–1111 CE)

As with many other subjects, Imam al-Ghazzali fundamentally shook the opinions of both ancient philosophers and renowned Muslim philosophers such as al-Kindi, al-Farabi and Ibn Sina, and the

Mu'tazilite thinkers, all of whom may be regarded as students of ancient philosophy, about the spirit as well, and opened a brand new field of study for the Ahl al-Sunna wa'l-Jama'a along the way of the Ash'aris. While he expounded his objections to and counter-arguments against all the ancient and new thoughts and philosophies which he saw as erroneous in *Nafhu'r-Ruh wa't-Taswiya* ("The Breathing of the Spirit and the Full Formation"), *al-Madnun bih 'ala Ahlih* ("Addressing the Specialists"), *Usulu'l-Arba'in* ("Forty Principles"), and *Tahafutu'l-Falasifa* ("The Incoherence of the Philosophers"), he explained the way of the Ahl al-Sunna wa'l-Jama'a in *Ihyau 'Ulumi'd-Din* ("Reviving the Religious Sciences") in the style of his time. In this last work of his, rather than theoretical matters, the Imam concentrates on religious life, worship, sincerity, avoidance of forbidden things, the purification of the soul, and the refinement of the heart.

In the works mentioned, Imam al-Ghazzali assigns extensive room to psychology under the title of "The Science of the Spirit." Based on the verses, *We will show them Our manifest signs (proofs) in the horizons of the universe and within their own selves, until it will become manifest to them that it (the Qur'an or the truths it preaches) is indeed the truth* (41: 53); and, *On the earth there are (clear) signs (of God's Oneness as Lord and Sovereign) for those who seek certainty, and also in your own selves. Will you then not see (the truth)*? (51: 20–21), and on relevant Prophetic Traditions, he draws attention to the human soul and makes extensive explanations concerning it.

The Imam is an important advocate of the Sunni scholars regarding their views of the spirit. He frequently reminds his audience that human nature contains a spirit separate from the body. Though he refers to it sometimes as "the speaking soul," sometimes as "the spirit," sometimes as "the soul," and sometimes as "the heart," he points out the nuances among these, and he emphasizes the spirit as the essential reality of humanity.

Due to the views which he put forward when he discussed the duality of the spirit and the body, those who lack sufficient knowledge of Imam al-Ghazzali may suppose that he thinks like the spiritualists. While others, who primarily consider his reiterations on the body as having no essential value, but that we should rather concentrate on "the essence of humanity," may think that he is a pantheist. The truth is that the illustrious Imam is neither a spiritualist nor a pantheist. He affirms that the spirit is a substance separate from the body but one which controls it. While doing so, he also insistently emphasizes that the spirit is not something material or corporeal, and that its relationship with the body is not of a nature of either incarnation or separation, but of control and direction. In his *al-Madnun bihi 'ala Ghayr-i Ahlihi* ("Addressing the Non-Specialists"), the Imam stresses that the spirit is neither a part of the body nor detached from it. For joining or attachment, and detachment are actions peculiar to material things. The spirit is not something material. As for its effect on and control of the body, we should only point out that it is a mystery known only to God. Its explanation in human language may cause confusion in minds such that particularly common people may liken it to God's control of things and events. The Imam also points out that we may make similar mistakes and cause confusions in dealing with the spirit's relationship with time and space, and is very careful about God's having no resemblance at all to the created.

According to al-Ghazzali, the spirit is something created, and therefore it has no eternity in the past. Its being brought into existence is like an effusion or diffusion from a limitless source into the frame of the body. God sometimes forms a body out of clay and endows it with the capacity to receive a spirit as in the case of the Prophet Adam, upon him be peace; sometimes He creates a body out of a human seed—a few drops of fluid coming from a male and female—and causes it to develop so that it can receive the spirit. We should not understand the effusion mentioned as a part detaching from a whole. In accordance with the rule, if we should present Divine truths using parables, we should present them with the most sublime parables—this effusion can be likened to reflections in mirrors. We should point out here that although the Imam, like others who discuss spiritual matters, cannot avoid using comparisons and parables associated with corporeality, the spirit is from the Immaterial Realm of (the Initial Manifestation of) Divine Commands, and it is therefore almost impossible to explain it in terms of corporeality.

Imam al-Ghazzali also discusses the permanence of the spirit after the death of the body. Based on the Qur'anic verses concerning life after death, such as: *Do not think at all of those killed in God's cause as dead. Rather, they are alive; with their Lord they have their sustenance* (3: 169), and the Prophetic Traditions that mention life in the grave and beyond, he emphasizes life in the grave and rejects any considerations that oppose this. Saying, "A human being is human due to their spirit, not their body," the Imam considers the other-worldly existence as a new creation and existence.

Fakhru'd-Din ar-Razi (1149–1209 CE)

Fakhru'd-Din ar-Razi, one of the great interpreters of the Qur'an, holds the same opinions about the spirit as other Sunni scholars. However, when he goes into detail, he can be seen to have different, individual views. Even though some think that Imam ar-Razi, like Imam al-Haramayn al-Juwayni, and Imam an-Nawawi,[103] maintains that the spirit is a refined, transparent substance, like the rose oil in roses, he actually always avoids describing the spirit as something corporeal, no matter how refined and transparent it is, and he stresses its freedom from corporeality. In *Ma'alimu Usuli'd-Din* ("The Sciences of Religious Methodology") and *Mafatihu'l-Ghayb* ("Keys of the Unseen"), he, like Imam al-Ghazzali, emphatically

103 Abu Zakariya Muhyi'd-Din Yahya ibn Sharaf an-Nawawi (1234–1278 CE), popularly known as Imam an-Nawawi, was a Sunni Muslim scholar of *Fiqh* (jurisprudence) and *Hadith*. He was born and died at Nawa near Damascus, Syria. During his short life of only forty-five years, he wrote many books on Islamic studies and other topics. He was especially famous for his *Forty Hadiths*, composed of the *hadiths* he collected and sourced back to one of the Companions of the Prophet Muhammad, peace and blessings be upon him. (Tr.)

argues that the spirit is the essential reality of humanity, opposing those who claim that the reality of humanity lies in its corporeal existence; he criticizes materialists, spiritualists, and some theologians who were not able to find a proper style in expressing the truths. Razi's arguments can be summarized as follows:

1. Despite continuous change in the body, the individual nature and identity remain unchanged. Although the body, like a military barracks, is continuously filled, emptied, and refilled, and the particles or atoms that leave it are replaced with new ones, thus undergoing a constant change and renewal, the individuals remain as themselves and, at every instant, perceive themselves as they have always been. This clearly demonstrates that the essential reality of humanity lies in something other than the body, and which does not change through bodily changes.

2. Like Ibn Sina and Imam al-Ghazzali, Imam Fakhru'd-Din ar-Razi argues that even at times when people are lost in something, or completely indifferent to or oblivious of their bodies, they never become oblivious of their identity. This state is described as "something known being different from what is unknown." This is a self-evident reality, demonstrating that the essential reality of humanity lies in the spirit, not the body.

3. Humanity involves the existence of learning and knowing. Knowledge can neither be obtained nor preserved by the body. Therefore, it is the spirit which forms the essence of humanity.

4. The Qur'an and Prophetic sayings declare that the essence of humanity is the spirit. In the holy Qur'an, God declares, "*O you soul at rest! Return to your Lord, well-pleased (with Him and His treatment of you), and well-pleasing to Him!*" (89: 27–28), and reminds us that human identity does not consist of only the body. For the address "Return!" is made to the soul at rest, which is dying. This shows that the human identity has an essential element which can receive the Divine address and will return to God after the death of the body.

5. We also read in the Clear Criterion (the Qur'an): *He is the All-Omnipotent over His servants; and He sends to you (angel) guard-*

ians (who watch over and keep a record of whatever you do). When death finally approaches any of you, Our envoys (the angels assigned to this duty) take his soul, and they do not neglect (any part of their tasks) (6: 61). This means that every person has an essential substance which will be taken and submitted to God following death.

Based on these and other verses, such as *Do not think at all of those killed in God's cause as dead. Rather, they are alive; with their Lord they have their sustenance* (3: 161), which is about the martyrs, and *The Fire: they are exposed to it morning and evening* (40: 46), which describes the state of the Clan of Pharaoh in the intermediate world of the grave, as well as Prophetic declarations like "*The Prophets do not really die; they are transferred from one realm to another*,"[104] and "*The grave is either a garden from among the gardens of Paradise, or a pit from among the pits of Hell*,"[105] Fakhru'd-Din ar-Razi, like earlier scholars who were of the same opinion, confirms both the existence of the spirit and the truth of the life of the grave. According to him, the intermediate realm of the grave is like a waiting room on the way to the Hereafter.

Stressing, like all other Muslim scholars, the existence and immaterial nature of the spirit, ar-Razi is severely opposed to the notion of reincarnation, something which all leading Muslim scholars decisively reject. He regards the arguments of Ibn Sina in its refutation to be insufficient and sets forth new arguments.

Again, like the overwhelming majority of Muslim scholars, ar-Razi believes in the bodily resurrection. That is, all human beings will be resurrected in body and soul in the Hereafter. The following quotation from his illustrious, voluminous commentary on the Qur'an, entitled *Mafatihu'l-Ghayb* ("Keys of the Unseen"), clearly shows his view:

> God Almighty has equipped humankind with an intellect that is able to distinguish good from evil and the willpower to

---

104 *Abu Dawud*, "Salah" 201; *an-Nasa'i*, "Jumu'a" 5. (Tr.)

105 *al-Bukhari*, "Jana'iz" 68; Muslim, "Janna" 70. (Tr.)

choose between them. He also has warned humankind, which He has created with this nature because of His Justice and Wisdom, against heresy, unbelief, and misguidance. He calls on them to refrain from harming the Prophets, saints, and indeed, all existent beings, and encourages them to do good deeds and attain virtues. A warning and encouragement can be fruitful with the promise of rewards for good deeds and the threat of punishment for evil. However, virtues and good deeds cannot receive their full reward in the world, nor can sins and evils be punished adequately and justly. This concludes that there must be, and is, another realm for the just, sufficient reward and punishment. That realm is the Hereafter.

The human carnal soul continuously drives human beings to satisfy their lusts and desires. This causes a constant conflict between human intellect or reason and the carnal soul. Reason or intellect should be supported in this conflict. Only the Divine promise of reward and the threat of punishment can lead human beings to give such support. But this promise of reward or threat is not completely fulfilled in this world. Therefore, there must be another realm where this Divine pledge will be completely fulfilled. In fact, the Divine pledge is essentially made with respect to that other realm, which is the Hereafter.

Both human reason and the Wisdom of God, the All-Wise, perceive it as necessary for good and evil to be treated differently. However, we cannot observe that this different treatment is fully made in this world. Many an evil person lives happily and comfortably, while numerous virtuous people suffer great hardship and deprivation. The Justice and Wisdom of God, the All-Just and All-Wise, require that there must be another realm where good and evil will receive their due fully. This realm is the Hereafter. It is also a requirement of Divine Justice and Wisdom that the right of the oppressed must be restored from oppressors and rights must be established. However, many oppressors depart from this world without their oppression being punished. Therefore, there must be, and is, another realm where everyone will get their just deserts. This realm is the other world, of which the Qur'an frequently reminds us.

But for the other world, human beings would be more wretched and miserable than animals. Animals have no consciousness or conception of definite time divisions, so therefore they suffer neither pains that arise from past misfortunes nor

> anxiety for the future. They live only for the moment. If they can find or are offered food, they eat and go; if they cannot find it, they continue to search for it or are content with the amount they have found. But humanity experiences the pains that come from past and present misfortunes, as well as anxieties about the future, all intermingled. Particularly if one's belief and degree of submission are not strong enough to struggle against these pains and anxieties, one writhes with constant, unbearable suffering. Therefore, there must be another realm where humanity, which has been favored with feelings, consciousness, and the faculty of perception, will find absolute, eternal happiness. Otherwise, its faculties, such as reason and consciousness, on account of which it has been given a rank superior to other existent beings, would each be a source of torment for it.

Fakhru'd-Din ar-Razi sets forth other arguments for the other, eternal world, thus emphasizing the particular end which awaits humanity. He also provides answers based on the Qur'an to the human desire for eternity, and severely and categorically rejects considering good and evil, and the idea of reward and punishment in connection with the false notion of reincarnation. The bodily resurrection is absolutely certain to take place, and there is no reason to drive the souls to different adventures in our imaginations. Just as God Almighty created the world in the beginning, returning or restoring it after its destruction is easier in the view of reason, a fact which the Qur'an emphasizes. More than that, God is absolutely able to create from nothing, so why can He not restore creation? Thinking and asserting otherwise means attributing a limit to His infinite Power. In addition, if God were not to create the other world, this would mean His breaking His promise to reward and punish. God Almighty is absolutely above being powerless and not fulfilling His promise.

The Considerations of the Scholars of Sufism about the Spirit

The scholars of Sufism regard the considerations of philosophers and some theologians about the spirit to be a futile exercise. However, we see the traces of the doctrine of the Unity of Being in many Sufis' views of the spirit.

The respectable scholar, Mustafa Sabri Efendi, quoting from Sa'du'd-Din at-Taftazani, divides the scholars of Sufism into two categories with respect to their views on existence. This division gives us distinct knowledge about the difference between their views on the spirit. For this reason, it would be useful to summarize the two different approaches of the Sufis to the matter of existence before proceeding to give their views on the spirit.

According to Sa'du'd-Din at-Taftazani, the scholars of Sufism are divided into two groups with respect to their views on existence: the Sufis and those who pretend to be Sufis. In their approach to the matter of existence, the Sufis are grounded in the fact that things have essential, established realities. Just as there is more than one existent thing, so too is existence multiple. That is, God's Existence is different from the existence of other existent things and beings. However, when some initiates reach the rank of what they call "annihilation in and subsistence with or by God," in which they are utterly absorbed, they are surrounded by the waves of the manifestations of Divine Oneness. They feel their beings are lost in the Being or Existence of God, and their attributes are absorbed in the light of His Attributes. They no longer feel anything other than the Divine Being, or His Existence. A perfected initiate who has reached this point of what they call "annihilation in God's Oneness" may sometimes utter words that are apparently incompatible with the Shari'a, and thus cause confusion, such as, "I did not know myself to be so," or "I wonder whether I am Him or He is me." But the true successors of the cause of Prophethood never utter such things. Even if there may appear some who utter such phrases, they correct them according to the basic commandments of the Shari'a when they recover sobriety.

As for those who pretend to be Sufis, they adopt the doctrine of the Unity of Being as a philosophy. They affirm and defend it. According to them, there is a single existent being. This consideration of the Muslim pretenders of Sufism is, as Mustafa Sabri Efendi points out, based on the thought that God's Attribute of Existence is identical with the Divine Being Himself. It is the Divine Being Who exists, and the whole universe is something imaginary or an illusion, or, according to some among them, is a manifestation or reflection of the Divine Being.

Even if the Unity of Being voiced by the Sufis is an inner experience or an instance of absorption or spiritual intoxication, the philosophical Unity of Being defended by the pretenders cannot be regarded as such. Verifying scholars consider Khallaj al-Mansur, Ibn al-Farid,[106] as-Suhrawardi, Jalalu'd-Din ad-Dawwani, Muhyi'd-Din ibn al-'Arabi, and Mulla Jami'[107] to be among the genuine Sufis. Although there are some who include Shaykh Bedreddin, who said that the archetypes had not experienced the scent of existence, nor would they, to be in the same category, his main book, *al-Waridat* ("The Divine Gifts") makes it impossible to regard him as such.

The considerations of the pretenders about the spirit are in line with their views on existence. According to them, like existence, the spirit is a manifestation or reflection. Just as humanity does not really exist, neither is the spirit something that exists independently. It is a manifestation or reflection of the All-Holy Creator or the Universal Spirit. The concepts of "the vegetable spirit," "the animal spirit," "the human spirit," and "the speaking soul," which philosophers and some scholars mention, are only designations given by humanity to

---

106 Umar ibn 'Ali ibn al-Farid (1181–1235 CE) was a Muslim Sufi Arab poet. He was born in Cairo, lived for some time in Makka and died in Cairo. He is regarded as the greatest Sufi poet of the Arab Muslims and called the Prince of Poets. Some of his poems are said to have been written in ecstasies. His most famous works are *Hamriyya* ("The Wine Ode"), which is on the "wine" of Divine love and spiritual bliss, and *Nazmu's-Suluk* ("The Poem of Following the Sufi Path"). (Tr.)

107 Mawlana Nuru'd-Din 'Abdu'r-Rahman ibn Ahmad al-Jami' (1414–1492 CE), commonly called Mulla Jami', is regarded as the last great classical poet of Persia, and a saint. He composed numerous lyrics and idylls, as well as many works in prose. His *Salaman and Absal* is an allegory of profane and sacred love. Some of his other works include *Haft Awrang*, *Tuhfatu'l-Ahrar*, *Layla wu Majnun*, *Fatihat ash-Shabab*, and *Lawa'ih*. (Tr.)

certain shadows of this reflection. However, Muhyi'd-Din ibn al-'Arabi has a somewhat different consideration about the matter with respect to the Hereafter. According to him, the final destruction of the world will not be a complete destruction or annihilation. This destruction and the Resurrection that follows will be a different picture of the same reality. When God takes a person to Him through death, He makes a new form for his or her spirit and human identity, which is different from his or her worldly body. This new form will be of the same sort as or suited to the station to which the dead will be transferred. In other words, a person will respectively take on a new form and nature in the intermediate world of the grave, the Place of Supreme Gathering, and Paradise or Hell that is in keeping with their spiritual state and each of these places.

Some among the scholars of Sufism have adopted the Sufis' views on the spirit, while some others have accepted that of the pretenders. There are also many among them who think like theologians; in turn, among these there are some who use a language similar to that of philosophers, following the line of the asserters of the Unity of Being, and those who, like the earliest, righteous scholars, are content with the concise knowledge the Qur'an gives about the spirit and do not go into detail. However, the majority of those scholars strictly follow the Qur'an and the Sunna in their considerations.

Bediuzzaman Said Nursi's views on the Spirit

Before proceeding to conclude this long discussion with the views of the Sufis of sobriety and wakefulness, I should present the considerations of Bediüzzaman Said Nursi, who is regarded as one of the most outstanding and effective minds of the modern age.

In several of his treatises, Bediüzzaman Said Nursi emphasizes the meaning and importance of life, and expresses what should be expressed concerning the spirit according to the Qur'an and the Sunna. He also deals with the matter of the spirit together with the existence of angels and other spirit beings, and voices the Sunni line of thought and belief by explaining the future of the spirit after death with the reality of revival after death (the Resurrection). He discusses the satisfaction of the perennial aspirations of humanity, which has been created for eternity and therefore passionately aspires to eternal happiness—but not searching for that satisfaction in the consolations sought in theories of a drop's returning to the sea from which it has departed, nor in difficult journeys offered by the false assumption of reincarnation or transmigrations of the soul. He breathes relief into hearts provided by the Divine promise of both bodily and spiritual eternal happiness, and shows those who are in hopeful expectation to the eternal happiness that shines on the horizon of the Qur'an and the Sunna.

Bediüzzaman makes frequent references to life. According to him, just as life is a gift of God Almighty as a direct operation of His Names the All-Living and the Giver of Life, so too does the human spirit, which is something that has been "breathed" by God, originate in the same source. Let me summarize his considerations:

> Life is the most important aim pursued in the creation of the universe, and its greatest result, it is its most radiant light, its most delicate essence, its distilled extract, its most perfect fruit, its most sublime perfection, its finest beauty and its most brilliant adornment. In addition, life is the axis of the unity of existence, the source of its perfection—and in regard to art and nature, it is its most wonderful aspect endowed with spirit and its miraculous reality which makes the minutest creature like the universe itself. Also, life is a miracle of the Divine Power, which makes each living being an index or sample of the whole universe in relationship with most other creatures. Again, life is a work of Divine Art, which makes a tiny part as great or comprehensive as the huge whole, and an individual living entity as encompassing as the universal one which contains it. With regard to the Lordship of God, life demonstrates that the universe is an indivisible and inseparable whole. Moreover, it is the most decisive and perfect of the proofs in the universe for the absolutely necessary existence of the All-Living, Self-Subsisting Being; it is the most subtle and yet the most apparent of the

> Divine artifacts, the most valuable yet the most abundant and the purest, most radiant, and most meaningful of them.[108]

After these definitions of life, Bediüzzaman explains life's relationship with the six pillars of belief, and he concludes his remarks with a discussion of servanthood to God. His explanations about the spirit, which he regards as the pure essence of life, or even as life itself, are original. He says:

> The spirit is a law with consciousness and has a real, sensible existence. Like the enduring laws of creation, the spirit also issues from the World of (the Initial Manifestation of) Divine Commands and the Divine Attribute of Will. Divine Power clothes it in an energetic envelope within a body of sensory organs. This spirit, which exists in each human being, is a counterpart of the laws of nature. Both are unchanging and permanent, and come from the World of (the Initial Manifestation of) Divine Commands. If Eternal Power had clothed laws with external existence, each would have been a spirit; if the human spirit were stripped of consciousness, it would become an immaterial law.[109]

In another work where he discusses the spirit and life together, Bediüzzaman writes as follows:

> The perfection of existence is through life. Life is the real basis and light of existence. Consciousness, in turn, is the light of life. Life constitutes the foundation of everything and appropriates everything for each living thing. Only through life can a living creature claim that everything belongs to it, that the world is its home, and that the universe is its property, conferred by the Owner. Just as light causes (concrete) things to be seen and, according to one theory, is the real cause of color, life unveils creation. Life causes qualities to be realized and archetypes to gain material existence. It makes the particular universal and the universal concentrated in a particular. Life is the manifestation of oneness in multiplicity, the reflection of

---

[108] Bediüzzaman Said Nursi, *Sözler* ("The Words"), "The Twenty-Ninth Word", p., 527; *Lemalar* ("The Gleams"), "The Thirtieth Gleam." (Tr.)

[109] Bediüzzaman Said Nursi, *Mektubat* ("The Letters"), "Hakikat Çekirdekleri (The Epigrams or Seeds of Truth)," p. 447. (Tr.)

> unity in plurality. See how lonely even a mountain-sized object is without life. Its interactions are restricted to its location, and all that exists in the universe means nothing to it, for it is unconscious of other existents. But as such a minute living being as a honeybee can have close interactions with the universe, particularly with plants and flowers, it can say, "The earth is my garden, my marketplace where I do business."[110]

Where he expresses his considerations about the physical and metaphysical dimensions, Bediüzzaman remarks, "The corporeal world is only a lace veil over the World of Spirits and the World (Realm) of the Transcendental Manifestation of Divine Commands."[111] Further, he makes the following explanations about the spirit and life:

> Matter is not the essence of existence, so that existence should be restricted to it. Rather, matter exists and subsists through something immaterial, which is life and the spirit. Matter is also not something served so that everything should depend on it; rather, it serves the perfection of something substantial, which is life. And the spirit is the essence of life. Again, matter is not something dominating, so that things should be referred to it; rather, it is something dominated, subject to the decree of something which has a fundamental place in existence. That thing is life, the spirit, and consciousness.[112]

Elsewhere, after offering many rational and reported proofs—those based on the Qur'an and the Sunna—concerning the existence of angels and other spirit beings, Bediüzzaman draws the following conclusion:

> Since the people of wisdom and religion and philosophers and religious scholars are agreed that existence is not restricted to the

[110] Bediüzzaman Said Nursi, *Sözler* ("The Words"), "The Twenty-Ninth Word," pp. 526–527. (Tr.)

[111] Bediüzzaman Said Nursi, *Sözler* ("The Words"), "The Twenty-Ninth Word," p. 530; *Mektubat* ("The Letters"), "Hakikat Çekirdekleri (The Epigrams or Seeds of Truth)," p. 446. (Tr.)

[112] Bediüzzaman Said Nursi, *Sözler* ("The Words"), "The Twenty-Ninth Word," p. 529. (Tr.)

> witnessed, corporeal realm, and since this apparent, corporeal realm has been inhabited by innumerable beings that possess spirit, although it is material and not suitable for the origination of spirits, for sure, existence cannot be restricted to it. Rather, there should be many other realms of existence in relation to which the witnessed, corporeal realm is an embroidered veil.[113]

Bediüzzaman also emphasizes the existence of angels and other kinds of spiritual beings, and whenever occasion appears, he stresses the permanence of the spirit. In "The Treatise of Resurrection" (The Tenth Word) and "The Second Aim" of The Twenty-Ninth Word, he convincingly proves the bodily resurrection based on many reported and rational arguments and by referring to Divine Attributes and Names. Afterwards, Bediüzzaman draws attention to the benefits of belief in the revival after death for human individual and social life. He offers readers highly significant clues in line with Sunni belief and thought about the reality of life, the spirit and its permanence, and the reward and punishment that await us in the other world.

The Sufis and the Spirit

The Sufis have defined the spirit as a manifestation or shadow of Divine life, and an immaterial substance; God Almighty has not enabled anybody to have perfect knowledge about its exact identity. While philosophers tend to call it "the speaking soul," the Sufis prefer designating it as "the spirit breathed," based on God's declaration in the Qur'an, "*I have breathed into it (the body) out of My Spirit*" (15:29). According to them, in addition to the spirit's being the essence of human existence and nature, the perfection of humanity is possible through spiritual perfection, which one can realize by journeying in the heart on the way to God. The spirit is also an important means for the human relationship with God. It is only through the spirit that a human being can travel toward and through the metaphysical realms, feel a relationship with God Almighty, and

---

113 Bediüzzaman Said Nursi, *Sözler* ("The Words"), "The Twenty-Ninth Word," p. 530. (Tr.)

observe on the horizon of the heart and other inner faculties numerous marvels which are impossible for the body to observe.

The body is the mount of the spirit, and the physical heart is the base of what we call the (spiritual) heart. A person knows and perceives through the spirit, and it is also through the spirit that they become aware of and experience themselves. In sleep or other similar situations, for example, when one is unconscious, the spirit partially cuts its relationship with the body and begins traveling in its own horizon. When death comes, the spirit departs from the body completely, and lives a transitional form of life between this world and the next until the new creation in the other world. It never suffers complete annihilation.

The spirit essentially belongs to the Realm of the Transcendental Manifestation of Divine Commands. The Qur'an declares, *All that is on the earth is perishable* (55: 26). The "death" of the spirit is of a relative nature and must be in the form of absorption. Humans enter and live in the intermediate world of the grave with their spirits still living, and during their long journey, with the "ups" and "downs" after the grave, their spirits command their bodies. As all their eternal physical and spiritual pleasures in the other world depend on living in this world at the level of the spirit, so too, all sufferings and torments will arise from leading a worldly life at the level of animal appetites. A person enters Paradise in the "patronage" of their developed "spirit breathed," and the completely refined and illuminated body shares this favor. Such a favor may be enjoyed by God's chosen, best servants in the world as a miracle. The Ascension of the Master of creation, upon him be peace and blessings, is the brilliant example of such a favor.

The spirit has no need to dwell in a body, but the body is its dwelling place in the world. As a Divine reward for its refinement, the spirit has no need to be in a specific place. But this does not mean that it is like the Divine Being, absolutely above being contained in time or space. The body is a mechanism for the spirit to execute its control over, or an instrument with which it voices its feelings. It is not a part of the body, attached to or contained by it. With its roots in the Realm of (the Initial Manifestation of) Divine Commands, its branches and leaves at its worldly address, and in a certain type of relationship with the body that is unknown to us, it speaks, thinks, loves, pities, and if submitted to God, continuously does good deeds, advancing toward Paradise. But if it is made subservient to the body, then whatever a person does, says, and thinks becomes like a growl or a snarl.

The spirit is a subtle, refined being that resembles the angels. It commands all the physical and immaterial senses and faculties of a person. The mind, which materialists and materialist physiologists see as the source of all human "mental" activities, is like a telephone exchange between the spirit and physical organism, a reservoir for the produce of the faculties that are dependent upon the spirit, the center of connection between the sense organs, a library of the intellect and soul that contains worlds, a set of switches for feelings, motions, and activities of perception, and a laboratory to study, distinguish, analyze, and synthesize Divine gifts. It is a dynamic element of the spirit.

According to the majority of Sufis, the spirit is something created, even though it comes from the Realm of (the Initial Manifestation of) Divine Commands. It is the most subtle, purest, and most refined of creatures. It is a mirror for the reflection of Divine Attributes and Names, one that is able to penetrate the densest of things. It reminds us of the Divine Being. Those equipped with the capacity to see and hear the things unseen and unheard by ordinary humans see and hear by means of either the (spiritual) heart or secret (an innermost faculty more subtle and refined than the heart), which is under its control and guidance. The people who have knowledge of the truths that lie in the essence of existence and the Religion rise to the peaks of (spiritual) discoveries and observations on the wings of the spirit. While we can only see the outer dimension of things with the physical sense of sight, the spirit is honored with penetrating the inner dimension through the windows of the (spiritual) heart, and with the observation of what lies behind the manifestations of Divine Attributes and Names through the windows of the secret. Although all believers will be honored with this favor in the other world, the one who has the greatest capacity to receive it is the Master of creation, upon him be the most perfect of blessings and peace, who says, "The thing which God created first is my light."[114]

Being a breath from the Realm of (the Initial Manifestation of) Divine Commands, the spirit takes on a form according to each individual. It has an energetic or astral envelope and can appear in the form of the double of the individual to whom it belongs. It departs from its body at death, and by God's will and leave, it keeps waiting for the union.

Life is a manifestation of the Divine Names the All-Living and One Who Gives Life. With respect to humans, it manifests itself as the spirit that is breathed and which displays multifarious activities in the body into which it has been breathed. In its relation with humans, the spirit is an entity created within time, and it can be said that it is breathed every moment in an ever-renewed cycle through the constant, ever new manifestations of the Divine Names the All-Living, the One Who Gives Life, and the One Self-Subsisting and Causing to Subsist. Those who cannot see this reality behind life either attribute the spirit to the physical composition of the body or to the mind or brain, or in heedlessness of the points or inner senses or faculties of support and seeking help on which it is dependent, regard it as eternal (in the past) and independently self-subsisting. However, it is neither valueless, to be attributed to a decaying physical composition or other material causes, nor too arrogant to claim self-eternality and self-subsistence. It exists because God has made it exist, and subsists because He is the One Self-Subsisting and Causing to Subsist. The Prophetic declaration, "The thing which God created first is my spirit (according to another narration, "my light)," indicates to this fact.

---

114 al-'Ajluni, *Kashfu'l-Khafa'*, 1:311. (Tr.)

In respect of its body and carnal soul being related to the Physical Realm of Creation, of its spirit relating to the Realm of the Initial Manifestation of Divine Commands, of its (spiritual) heart that is open to the Realm of the Transcendental Manifestation of Divine Commands, and of its secret (its innermost faculty more subtle and refined than the heart) turning toward the Realm of the Transcendental Manifestation of Divine Attributes and Names, humanity—this noble being—is a peerless, most comprehensive copy of creation. However, despite or due to this elevated nature, it has both the qualities of excellence and the attributes of carnality. (This division is made by those who regard the spirit and soul as separate entities.) The effects of both the qualities of excellence and the attributes of carnality relate to the materialization of human acts. Belief, intention, resolution, discipline, determination, and first and foremost, turning to God in faith and obedience, or turning away from Him in disobedience, are each like a seed from which good or evil grows and develops, so that a person either rises to the highest of the high, or falls to the lowest of the low.

Those who regard the soul and the spirit as separate entities see the former as the center of human evil attributes and the latter as the source of praiseworthy qualities and values. They consider reason or intellect to be the tongue of the spirit, and insight its translator. According to this approach, reason is connected with the spirit, not with the soul. According to such thinkers, the spirit is the basis of the mechanism of learning, discernment, inspiration, and conscience, and it is the essence of humanity. It is the spirit which in a healthy body sees with the eyes, tastes with the tongue, hears with the ears, touches with the skin, and smells with the nose.

The spirit has a deep, intimate connection with the body beyond consciousness. This connection is of a nature that the spirit experiences by means of the body itself, all bodily attributes and activities, each of which principally originates in a different manifestation of Divine Names, and is able to penetrate the nature of matter with certainty.

However, some Sufis use the spirit and the soul interchangeably. They categorize the spirit as the vegetable soul or spirit, the animal soul or spirit, and the human soul or spirit. They also categorize the soul according to its degree of spiritual evolution as the carnal, evil-commanding soul, the self-accusing soul, the soul receiving inspiration, and the soul at rest, and so on. According to the majority of scholarly Sufis, a soul that has reached the rank of being at rest avoids all evil and makes doing good, praiseworthy deeds a dimension of its nature. Taking another step upwards, it keeps even involuntary occurrences in its mind under control. Angelic qualities and holiness are observed in a hero of truth who has reached this point, and then the doors of the knowledge of the Unseen are slightly opened onto him or her. Over time, such a soul becomes a pure spirit, and its carnality is totally transformed into spirituality.

This point needs further elaboration, as follows: According to the Sufis, as long as the spirit is supported and strengthened through ever deepening belief, good deeds, the avoidance of sins, and true learning and reflection, the soul begins to display the traces of straightforwardness. When this continues with constant purification of the soul and the "refinement" of the body through regular worship, both the soul and the body can receive the gifts of turning to God Almighty under the guidance of the spirit.

We can also approach this matter from another perspective, as follows: If the animal soul is so powerful as to dominate the body, this causes the "death" of the spirit, while leading a life at the level of the heart and the strengthening of the spirit results in either the "death" or submission of the soul, or even in acquiring an angelic nature in some people of superior spirituality. Seeing the good side of everything, positive thought, sound belief, regular worship, orderly recurring supplications and recitations, and continuous imploring for forgiveness of sins constitute the securest way of strengthening the spirit and compelling the soul into submission. Those who follow this way sincerely have never been witnessed to fall halfway. Far from falling halfway, those who never give up self-supervision on this way and who are always careful of their relationship with God Almighty, continuously advance toward the highest of the high. The scholarly Sufis call them "the people with illuminated and illuminating spirits." But those who always see the evil side of things and events, who suffer deviances in thought, who spend their lives on worldly ambitions and daydreams, who have never been able to attain truth in belief, who are heedless of worship, who do not strengthen their inclination toward good through prayer, and who cannot overcome their tendency toward evil and sins through asking God for forgiveness inevitably fall to the lowest of the low. Such are called "the bodies of darkness."

The spirit becomes like a "pigeon" or angel, flying toward the heights of the Hereafter; this is to such an extent that people restrain their carnal desires, fill their heart with knowledge and love of God, and live a life according to the religious rules. If, by contrast, a person lives in dependence on carnal or bodily appetites, then the spirit weakens, the heart fades, feelings become polluted, and the "secret" is silenced. In brief, the dominion of carnality always results in the paralysis of spirituality, and the strengthening of the spirit leads to the submission and purification of the soul. To express this point, some saints say, "Those who care about their bodies cannot care about their spirits, and those who care about their spirits cannot remain as those who care about their bodies." These saints teach people how to discover their spirits.

An unpurified soul tends to carnality and pursues the satisfaction of bodily desires. Until it becomes a soul at rest and becomes almost identical with the spirit, it displays this characteristic to some extent. But when the spirit reaches the rank of being pleased with God and being pleasing to Him, by God's help, it begins speaking like the spirit. When a person attains this character, the reason, which is a curious, inquisitive faculty, rises to the horizon of being an analyzer of the proofs and essentials of religious commandments, taking on the "color" of the heart, and begins observing metaphysical realms from the observatory of the *spiritual intellect*. The *heart* lies in ambush to hunt the mysteries that pertain to the Realm of the Transcendental Manifestation of Divine Attributes and Names, and the *secret* breathes with yearning for the Divine Being.

The heart and the secret are like two eyes of the spirit with which we can look on eternity. Along the spiritual journey, the spiritual intellect beats with the dreams of the Realm of the Transcendental Manifestation of Divine Attributes and Names, and the secret with a yearning for the Realm of the Transcendental Manifestation of Divinity. When they have obtained what they are enamored of, each becomes intoxicated with what it observes in its horizon in great amazement. When Divine gifts, flowing from the secret to the heart and taking on the color of the Realm of the Transcendental Manifestation of Divine Commands in the receptors of the heart, are transferred to the spirit in the tongue of the heart, they begin to give voice with angelic accent. This may be analogous—even though imperfect and limited—to the conveyance of Divine mysteries to the Prophets by the angels, whom we may liken to spirits with the depth of their secrets and hearts. Indeed, in the verse, *He conveys the Spirit (the life-giving Revelation, from the immaterial realm) of His command to whom He wills of His servants* (40: 15), the Qur'an sometimes uses the Revelation in the meaning of the spirit. Just as the spirit is the essence of life in the body, so too, the Revelation is the essence and most important means of spiritual life and vitality. The spirit is a Divine breath, direct or indirect, and the Revelation is also a breath issuing from His Attribute of Speech. The most loyal trustees of this Divine secret are the perfect or universal men.[115] The spirit, which the greatest of universal men, the Master of creation, upon him be peace and blessings, received and breathed into his community is the Divine Revelation itself, and the gifts and inspirations that come to relatively universal men following in his footsteps are a means of mercy for the Muslim Community, provided these gifts and inspirations are tested and verified according to the basic standards that are established by the Revelation.

---

115 For the "Universal Man" see, M. Fethullah Gülen, *Emerald Hills of the Heart – Key Concepts in the Practice of Sufism,* The Light, NJ, 2004, vol., 2, pp., 289–305. (Tr.)

Both of these spirits—the spirit and the Revelation—are of vital importance for humanity. In the same way that the growth, health, and survival of the human body are possible through the spirit, the life and survival of all the worlds depend on the "spirit" that is breathed by the universal man. Before the creation of the first universal man—Adam, the first human being and also a Prophet who would read creation and illuminate reasons and hearts with the breath he conveyed—the world was dark. Especially through the light which the Greatest Spirit and the Spirit of Holiness diffused, the middle part of its history was illuminated. If one day this light disappears, leaving the world in darkness, and things and events begin to be interpreted as playthings of chance, a new way will appear before humanity. That is, like the alternation of night and day, the world, which will have been darkened, will be replaced by the illuminated world of eternity. Let us once more listen to Bediüzzaman:

> Just as life is a pure extract distilled from the universe, just as consciousness and sense perception are extracts distilled from life… and just as the spirit is the pure essence of life—indeed, it is life itself stable and autonomous— so too is the physical and spiritual life of the Prophet Muhammad, upon him be peace and blessings, the most refined extract distilled from the sense perception, consciousness, and intelligence of the universe. The Messengership of Muhammad, upon him be peace and blessings, is the purest extract distilled from the sense perception, consciousness, and intelligence of the universe. Indeed, as testified to by his works, accomplishments, and legacy, the physical and spiritual life of Muhammad, upon him be peace and blessings, the very life of the universe's life, and his Messengership are the light and very consciousness of the universe's consciousness.
>
> It is truly so. If the light of Prophet Muhammad's Messengership departs from the world, the universe will die. If the Qur'an deserts the universe, the universe will go mad. It will lose its mind and cause the destruction of the world by striking its head on a star.[116]

---

[116] Bediüzzaman Said Nursi, *Lemalar* ("The Gleams"), "The Thirtieth Gleam, The Fifth Part, the Fourth Sign." (Tr.)

The spirit breathed into a human being potentially means the same as what Islam, the Prophet, and the Qur'an mean for existence, each as a universal spirit which encompasses the universe, and as its consciousness, life, and light. However, in order to manifest itself in the corporeal realm, the spirit needs a system or a mechanism. Whether transparent or dense, all things are receptors of the universal laws that issue from the Realm of the Initial Manifestation of Divine Commands and which are appointed for their creation and operation or life. All living beings, including humans, with their particular composition and capacities, and the universal men with their distinguished nature and the particular favors accorded to them, are where the spirit particular to each rises.

With respect to humanity, the spirit has some stages of rising or birth, as follows:

1. Its rise during the initial determination of natures. This stage of its rise has a relation to the truth of Muhammad as Ahmad—his archetypal existence before his coming into the world as Muhammad. This is the view of those who maintain that spirits were created before the bodily existence of humanity.
2. Its rise during the creation of Adam—and indeed of every person—which is expressed in, *I have breathed into him out of My Spirit* (15: 29).
3. The rise of the breathed spirit in the horizon of the heart and the secret. This rise also describes humanity's actual undertaking of the high status of vicegerency. The one who is the perfect representative of this status is the universal man. The body of the universal man, even if it is inferior to the spirit as a corporeal entity, has spiritual refinement. The Ascension of the Master of creation, upon him be peace and blessings, during which his blessed body accompanied his spirit—which he made with his spirit and body together—is an example of this. Even in its everyday activities and states, such a body manifests the Divine Being's Attributes of

Majesty and Perfection, as stated concerning the Prophet Muhammad, upon him be peace and blessings: "When he is seen, God is remembered and mentioned."[117]

A universal man displays certain distinctions. He is born with the distinctions particular to him, and lives in awareness of them. He tries to fulfill whatever these distinctions require him to do. He advances into the other world in the way he lives. Even his body enjoys its share in his distinctions. For example, the bodies of the Prophets do not decompose or rot in the earth.[118]

The spirit of the Core of Prophethood, upon him be peace and blessings, was the first to be determined and specified at the beginning of creation. However, he was transferred into material existence in the world as the rhyme of the verse of Prophethood, the fruit of the Tree of Creation, the sun of the sky of Divine Messengership, and the conveyor of the final, decisive judgment in all matters, whose advent had been awaited for centuries with great excitement and joy.

He is both the fruit and the seed; both the first signal and the last sign. He has both the secrets of the *Basmala*[119] (as the beginning of everything), and the mysteries of the *Fatiha* (the Opening Chapter of the Qur'an). He can also be regarded as the forerunner coming from behind. He describes himself and his Companions, saying, "We are those who have come the last, but who have outstripped the others."[120] As the community of every Prophet will follow its Prophet on Judgment Day, it must be a most glad tiding for us regarding the station or rank which will be bestowed on those who follow that Greatest Spirit, upon him be peace and blessings. He is the Greatest Spirit, and his community is the happiest, most fortunate community.

---

117 al-Munawi, *Faydu'l-Qadir*, 2:528; at-Tabari, *Jami'u'l-Bayan*, 11:132. (Tr.)

118 *Abu Dawud*, "Salah" 201; *an-Nasa'i*, "Jumu'a" 5. (Tr.)

119 *Basmala* is the phrase, "In the Name of God, the All-Merciful, the All-Compassionate," and mentioned at the beginning of every good, religiously lawful deed. (Tr.)

120 *al-Bukhari*, "Wudu'" 68; *Muslim*, "Jumu'a" 19, 21. (Tr.)

In Sufi terminology, the term the Greatest Spirit is generally used in the meaning of the Truth of Ahmad—the meaning or truth that the Prophet Muhammad, upon him be peace and blessings, represented before his coming into the world as Muhammad. Since that most illustrious being is the most polished, purest mirror of Divine Attributes and Names, He is the most radiant "face," the most resplendent "stature," of the Visible or Corporeal World and the (invisible) Realm of the Transcendental Manifestation of Divine Commands. By means of the lights he diffused, all things and events have come to be understood as a thoroughly meaningful book to study, and humankind has clearly learned from where it comes and where it goes, while the human spirit, enamored of eternity, has been re-born and saved from the veils of the darkness of corporeality through his promises of eternal happiness.

However, some regard the Greatest Spirit as the manifestation of universal life, some as the universal manifestation of Divine Majesty, and some, based on the Qur'anic verse, *The angels and the Spirit descend in it (the Night of Power and Destiny) by the permission of their Lord with His decrees for every affair* (97: 4), as the Greatest, Universal Spirit Who descends on a blessed day or night as a means of spiritual expansion and elation for believers. There are still others who consider it to be the most comprehensive representation of spiritual journeying toward God from the beginning to the end, while yet others call Him the First Intellect or the Universal Soul. As a matter of fact, like the Spirit of Holiness, who is the unperceivable being regarded as the source of the radiations of the Prophets, the Greatest, Universal Spirit is unknown to us in His real identity.

The spirit of everyone is in fact open to the Realm of the Transcendental Manifestation of Divine Commands, and has a connection with it. Those having expert knowledge of the matter describe the spiritual discernment and perception through this connection as "the near conquest," the intuitions and impression of a heart open to and connected with the Divine Attributes and the Realm of the Transcendental Manifestation of Divine Attributes and

Names, as "the manifest conquest," and the observations of the secret turning toward the Realm of the Transcendental Manifestation of Divinity, as "the absolute conquest."

A human being is a candidate for both Paradise and eternity, and for both the "observation" of God in Paradise and gaining His good pleasure, with his or her inner faculties such as the spirit, heart and secret. Since all the favors to be accorded in the other world primarily relate to these faculties, and we are therefore unable to perceive them in our corporeality, they will come as surprises: "*I have prepared for My righteous servants things that no eyes have ever seen, no ears have ever heard of, and that have never occurred to the heart of anyone*."[121] Certainly, the Divine favors to come in the Hereafter are impossible to perceive by "worldly reason" or "the reason of worldly life"—the reason busied with worldly affairs only. Who knows what surprises the One Who gives the answer, *Therein will be for them everything that they desire, and in Our Presence, there is yet more* (50: 35), to those who ask, "Is there yet more?" in pursuit of more knowledge and love of God, will bestow from the source of the promise, *For those who do good, aware that God is seeing them, is the best (of the rewards), and still more* (10: 26). We think that the infinite Mercy of the One Who has made the contract with humanity, *Whoever is for God, God is for him,* requires it to be so.

To summarize, life is everything in the universe and it is directly connected to Him, the All-Living and Self- Subsisting (by Whom all subsist). The life of God Almighty is Life Itself, essential to His Being, and eternal in the past and future. His Life is by Itself, not dependent on any spirit. But the spirit of every living being is an immaterial substance and the cause of the life of that being. Being refined, pure bodies, angels continue to exist by means of their spirits, which are almost identical with their lives due to their purity and refinement. For this reason, some scholars maintain that the death of angels is not like the death of corporeal living beings, but

---

121 *al-Bukhari*, "Bad'u'l-Khalq" 8; *Muslim*, "Iman" 312; *at-Tirmidhi*, "Janna" 15. (Tr.)

like fainting or absorption. According to these scholars, the death of the spirits will be like the death of angels. Since, in their view, the spirits are simple, living, and conscious Divine laws issuing from the Realm of the Initial Manifestation of Divine Commands, they will not decompose or rot like compound or composed entities. However, as declared in the verse, *The Trumpet will be blown, and so all who are in the heavens and all who are on the earth will fall dead* (39: 68), they have also been destined to pass over the bridge of death, even in the form of absorption or fainting.

According to the Sufis, like the three separate but interdependent faculties of a complete entity, the spirit is an immaterial entity that has three dimensions as the object of three separate Divine favors. They are as follows:

The first is what they call "the spirit itself." It is the first manifestation of the all-encompassing Divine Mercy in the name of bringing the spirit into existence. It appears to be subsisting as the result of the mutual, interdependent relations and positions of the elements that form a living being.

The second is the "spirit breathed." It is what they call "the speaking soul," which is favored with reason, willpower, spiritual intellect, certain inner senses, and consciousness, and with the capacity for developing through learning and belief. It is a living, conscious Divine law or command breathed into the embryo in a certain stage of its development in the womb of mother. A *hadith* says that it is breathed by means of an angel. This spirit was breathed into Adam by God Almighty Himself, as stated in, *I have breathed into him out of My Spirit* (15: 29); and into the Prophet Jesus, upon him be peace, by means of Archangel Gabriel. These spirits of human beings are called "the spirits particular." The spirit of every individual human being has particularities of its own that emanate from particular manifestations of Divine Compassion, and is related to his or her own particular nature, character, and capacity. These spirits may be likened to the different reflections of the sun in earthly objects, varying from one another in nature, capacity, and particularities. The almost limitless diversity and multiplicity of the objects are not contrary to the oneness of the sun that is reflected in them. Each receives a reflection according to its particular capacity, nature, and features from a single sun, which has all of the reflections. Without ignoring the inadequacy of the comparison, we can say that just as all the instances of light, heat, and some other features shared by all the objects on the earth and even other planets, are reflections of the sun's light, heat, and other features, the spirits having particularities according to each human being are reflections of the Life of the One Who has Attributes of Majesty and Grace, and manifestations of His Names the All-Living and the One Who Gives Life. It is for this reason that as some Sufis living in absorption of Divine Existence and who always consider the Real, Essential Existence even while looking on the shadowy existence, and experience annihilation under the lights of the burning manifestations of the Divine "Face," state that they feel no existence but Him. Some ecstatics among them go so far as to see existence as if it were the dead reflection of a human being in a mirror, and view it as something imaginary.

In fact, this is confusion that arises from being overwhelmed by spiritual intoxication and absorption. Therefore, such considerations of Muslim Sufi ecstatics should not be confused with the philosophical views of pantheists. Even though there seems to be a similarity between the two views or considerations, while Muslim Sufis have concentrated on Divine Existence as the real existence, and have been annihilated in It, regarding contingent existence as something imagined, the others concentrate on the corporeal existence, either ignoring the Divine Existence or viewing the former as the incarnation of the latter.

The third dimension of the spirit is the "biological spirit," which the Muslim Sufis call the "animal spirit." It is an element of connection between the breathed spirit or the speaking soul and the body. This may also be regarded as a veil of the spirit's subtlety, purity, and dignity that is related to the Divine Name the All-Outward.

The spirit breathed by God is an abstract, non-biological substance. The tides of humans between guidance and straying, good and evil, and happiness and misery, occur in relation to the animal spirit. If it were possible to listen to the spirit breathed, we would always hear it singing tunes of happiness. The sufferings and pains of the animal spirit in those whom the real human spirit dominates are means of perfection for the spirit breathed. If, by contrast, they are weak in respect of their spirit breathed—those who are not alive in respect of their conscience, who are dead in their relationship with God—they gain nothing in return for their sufferings and pains. The most important mechanism of the spirit is the conscience, which is an observatory for the "observation" of God.

O God! Show us the truth as the truth, and enable us to observe it, and show us falsehood as falsehood, and enable us to avoid it. Make us die as Muslims and include us among the righteous.

Bestow Your blessings and peace on the Light which rose from the Unseen into existence, having the reality of all existence, and subsisting by You for You in the Realm of the Transcendental Manifestation of Divinity, and which was equipped with Your standards of conduct in the Realm of the Transcendental Manifestation of Divine Attributes and Names, and on his Family and Companions, who represent all that the Prophet brought into the Realm of Corporeal Existence.

WIJDAN (CONSCIENCE)

Literally meaning the essence of human existence and a person's perception of themselves, *wijdan* (conscience) is a spiritual mechanism composed of the willpower, which chooses between good and evil, the spiritual intellect (*fuad*), which is the inner, most essential dimension of the heart, the inner power of perceptiveness (sensation or feeling), and consciousness. It is a mechanism through which a person perceives themselves, and feels or experiences and interprets existence and its relationship with God, providing for humans a window opening on belief, knowledge and love of God, and yearning for Him in proportion with the vitality of the above-mentioned four pillars. In this mechanism, which has various metaphysical depths, we can sense the voice of willpower, the discernments and observations of the spiritual intellect, the mind's acquired knowledge, fed or filtered by consciousness, and the sensations of the power of perceptiveness and the gifts of Divine knowledge that flow into it.

The conscience is also a conscious observer and interpreter in the sense that being aware of the innate powerlessness, poverty, and neediness of humanity, it feels the necessity of applying to and relying on a power that can satisfy humans in respect of these basic shortcomings in them. Consequently, the conscience takes refuge in the Divine Being with belief, submission, and reliance, and turns to Him with knowledge and love of Him and yearning for Him. In addition to studying, reflecting on, analyzing, and synthesizing the messages of all things and events in the name of knowledge and knowledge of God, the conscience has such a subtle, transcending power of expression based on its own dynamics and pillars that those who can hear its voice and judgments do not need anything else to understand the meaning of the messages of existence.

In thus speaking, I in no way mean that there is no need for rational knowledge, or that scientific research, experimental knowledge, or information acquired as a result of centuries-old experiences are insignificant. On the contrary, I would like to emphasize that, in addition to the assessment and benefit that we can derive from conclusions reached through reason, the results of experiences, and the perceptions of the five external senses, each according to their own value, there is another source of knowledge, which is based on inner experiences and intuitions and which can be attained without any means. This source, which leads humans to true knowledge through personal inner experiences without needing any means to discover or establish the truth, is the conscience. Even though such knowledge may sometimes be regarded as subjective, it is as important for those who are open to life at the level of the heart and spirit as the kind of knowledge acquired through known means of learning. Therefore, there have always been many who accept the conscience as a source of knowledge. According to these people, since the conscience leads us directly to the truth itself, rather than presenting to us its map or diagram, it is more significant and reliable as a source of knowledge. Even though the observation and study of things and events and the process of analyzing and synthesizing them enable us to observe the truth from afar and approach it to a certain extent, it cannot provide exact knowledge of it in its true nature and identity. However, the conscience perceives the truth without any means, examines it, and draws a decisive conclusion about it. Those who approach things and events from outside cannot go farther than studying or having some knowledge of these things according to their limited horizon of knowledge, their scope of observation, and personal viewpoints. Therefore, their conclusions are only of a relative value. But the conscience comprehends these regarding what and how they are in their true identity and nature. It transcends matter, is saved from the confines of space, and can grasp the truth itself in proportion to its purity and profundity.

In some of his treatises, Bediüzzaman draws a somewhat different picture of conscience and attributes important functions to it. According to him, the conscience is a conscious, innate mechanism of the same kind as Divine laws of "nature." Resembling the law of growth in seeds, the laws of creation in sperms or eggs, and the freezing and expansion of certain fluids, the conscience is a conscious law equipped with willpower which issues from the Divine Will, the spiritual intellect, consciousness, and the power of perceptiveness. It is an important tongue that sees, judges, and speaks correctly in proportion to the vitality of such pillars. Even though reason may err in its views, reflections, or judgments, the conscience always proclaims the existence of God in the language of its nature and pillars; it breathes with its vision of Him, contemplates and feels Him; and like a sunflower, driven by a sense of reliance and seeking help which is ingrained in it, it always fixes its eyes on Him. Its intuition always calls on it to remain wakeful; inspiration constantly illuminates its horizon; yearning, which can be regarded as accumulated knowledge of God, continuously indicates Him; and burning Divine love and the zeal to meet Him uninterruptedly invite it to the observation of the All-Known One with His Attributes, Names, and acts, whispering to it the fascinating aspects of life beyond carnality.

Now, let us take an overview of the spiritual intellect, willpower, and consciousness, and the power of perceptiveness, which are the pillars of conscience.

The Spiritual Intellect

Each of the pillars mentioned has an inner and outer dimension that relates to the Realm of the Transcendental Manifestation of Divine Commands and the Corporeal Realm, respectively. What we call "the bosom," which is the outer, corporeal dimension of the spiritual intellect, is a covering of the inner depths of conscience and its aspects that relate to the Realm of the Transcendental Manifestation of Divine Attributes and Names. The bosom is like a picture of the meaning or spirituality of matter. The heart, which is within the bosom, is a house for the Transcendental Manifestation of Divinity, which receives the Divine gifts or radiations that emanate on different wavelengths; the spiritual intellect (*fuad*) is a polished mirror that has the potential to reflect the Divine Attributes and Names, and is a special observer of the Realm in which they are transcendently manifested in proportion to the degree of its expansion. The spiritual intellect is also where the light of belief and conviction manifests itself and where the moon of knowledge of God rises. It receives inspirations and transmits Divine gifts and radiance. Due to its position and mission, the spiritual intellect has a furnace-like depth in which it produces flames of love for God and yearning for His reunion. As for what is called "the secret," with its incomprehensible dimensions, it is a telescope or a polished mirror that rests on the shoulder of the spiritual intellect, and which is directed toward the Realm of the Transcendental Manifestation of Divinity. The "secret" has always been regarded as a palace in the human heart for God to "visit." So long as it remains purified, it can always entertain its "Guest." In order for this visit to be continuous, the faculties of consciousness, perception, and receptiveness should be purified of all pollution of carnality. How beautiful the following couplet by Nabi is:

> Purify your mirror of perception of whatever is other than Him;
> Be ashamed of any pollution, for the Monarch does not
> come to a dirty house.

We read the same consideration in the following couplet by Ibrahim Haqqi of Erzurum, who emphasizes the importance of nighttime for such visits:

> The heart is a house of God, purify it of whatever
> there is other than Him,
> So that the All-Merciful may descend into His palace at night!

He invites his audience to remain awake at nights, because nights are more appropriate for turning toward the immaterial Realms of Divine manifestations.

Humans have more even subtle faculties than the heart and the secret. They are "the private," and "the more private." These faculties always turn toward a horizon, the identity of which is impossible to perceive, and are absorbed in their instances of turning; each is a ball of mysteries—a source of amazement and astonishment. Together with "the secret" and the spiritual intellect, these faculties are honored with special manifestations of God.

The spiritual intellect is like the pupil in the eye, the center of sight in the brain, the living room in a house, the core in a seed, the wick in a lamp, and the Ka'ba on the earth. Belief diffuses its light from the horizon of this faculty, and the fundamentals of journeying toward knowledge of God such as reverence, piety, love, resignation, certainty, reliance, composure or self-possession, wakefulness, fear, and expectation grow on its slopes. The spiritual intellect is such a mystery of Divine Oneness in His particular manifestations that its light shines in the hands of the willpower stretched toward Him, the comprehensions of the power of perceptiveness, and the position of consciousness before Him. When the spiritual intellect's connection with God is severed, then its light is extinguished, and it loses its real identity. The spiritual intellect preserves its identity so long as it remains connected with Him through belief, conviction, righteous deeds, and knowledge of Him, with its light shining brightly; and it becomes a mechanism to observe His Essential Attributes, or it acts as an observer of them. The spiritual intellect is an element that distinguishes between our feelings, sensations, and impressions; it is a mine of knowledge of God and the spirit's source of light and vitality. Due to its nature, we can regard the spiritual intellect to be unrestricted in space. It is the "touchstone" of our knowledge, the most vital depository of our perceptions, and so long as it is not paralyzed or killed through unbelief or other types of misguidance, it is the focus of attention of God Almighty, or the pavilion of His manifestations.

With the eyes of this faculty, which the Sufis call "insight," people see everything just as it is, interpreting all they see correctly, and draw correct conclusions. Under its light, they rise to the horizon of spiritual discovery and observation, and penetrating beyond "the secret," they begin to imagine the peaks of "the private" and "the more private." But if this faculty—the spiritual intellect—is contaminated with sins and exposed to any kind of misguidance, including unbelief, then as declared in the Qur'anic verse, *But what they themselves have earned has rusted upon their hearts* (83: 14), all of its horizons are darkened, and it begins to perceive white as black and vice versa, and God seals it, as indicated in the verse, *God has set a seal upon their hearts* (2: 7). It becomes extremely difficult, even impossible, for it to recover its initial purity. While established belief and regular worship and doing righteous deeds are favored with endurance or steadfastness, sins, so long as they are not eliminated through repentance, penitence, and contrition, cause people to suffer swerves in the heart. Each sin is a door to unbelief.

Both the spiritual intellect and the Supreme Preserved Tablet are each a mirror to God, according to their own capacities. With its contents, the Supreme Preserved Tablet remains unchanged. But the spiritual intellect can always display changes of color, shape, and design under the influence of different failures. Therefore, those who are aware of this apply to the Divine Court many times a day, entreating, "*Our Lord, do not let our hearts swerve after You have guided us!*" (3: 8)

So long as it remains intact and is preserved from deviations, the spiritual intellect is an excellent student of Divine Attributes, a polished mirror of Divine favors, an important stimulant to knowledge and love of God and yearning for Him, as well as to feeling an attraction toward and being attracted by Him. With the eyes of this faculty, people can observe the realms beyond; with its ears, they can listen to mysterious sermons that are given without words or voices, and guide others to the holiest manifestations by means of it. They can do all these as long as they can preserve this faculty with its primordial purity and decorate it with belief, knowledge, and love of God. Let us put an end to the discussion of this faculty with the following couplet of Hanifi:

> Come O Sufi, purify the inside of your heart to attain love,
> For one who desires the Guest should certainly decorate his palace.

Willpower According to the Basic Principles of the Islamic Creed

Four ways of thought and belief have come into existence regarding the view of this human faculty:

1. Those who deny it and therefore consider humans to be devoid of any free will like inanimate objects that have no say in their actions. This way is known as fatalism, or absolute determinism (*jabr mutlaq*).
2. Those who accept that, although humans have some degree of free will and power, their will and power play no part in their actions. Whenever they display an inclination to perform an action, God creates the power and capacity in them to do it. This is known as relative fatalism (*jabr mutawassit*).
3. Those who attribute all human actions to human free will and power and claim that humans are the creators of their actions. According to them, God has delegated His creativity to humans themselves with respect to their actions. This way is called absolute delegation (*tafwiz mutlaq*).
4. Those who reject both absolute fatalism and delegation and affirm that it is humans themselves who will and perform their actions, while it is God Who creates their actions. According to these people, doing and creating are different things, and humans are responsible for their actions as agents or doers. This is clear in the verse, *In its favor is what-*

ever (good) a soul earns, and against it whatever (evil) it merits (2: 286). This is the way of the Maturidis.[122]

Humans have both a certain degree of free will and power to execute their will. They show a tendency to do something and have a capacity to put it into action. Although God is, in principle, never obliged to give existence in the physical realm to whatever humans will or do, He creates the human deeds that are performed as a result of their tendency or free will. For humans are responsible for their will and deeds. If God did not create their will, actions or deeds, human responsibility would have been meaningless.

According to the Maturidis, along with whatever we have, including our free will and power, we are created beings. However, both human power and free will are of two kinds:

1. The universal will
2. The particular will

The "universal will" is a potential power of will or choice, created together with ourselves and inculcated in our being. It is an established pillar of the mechanism of conscience, whether we use it or not, and it is ready to use. Our use of this potential power for any activity is described as the "particular will." We can also call using our potential willpower for a particular activity our "intention," "tendency," "resolution," or "choice."

The perfect, requiring, or essential reason (*raison d'être*) for the occurrence of any action is the execution of human intention or inclination by the Divine Will and Power. Both Will and Power are essential to the Divine Being and beyond our capacity for comprehension; both the human universal will and particular will are each only a particular manifestation of Divine Will, the former

---

122 Maturidis are the Muslims who follow Muhammad ibn Muhammad Abu Mansur al-Maturidi (d. 944), who was born in Samarqand, in present day Uzbekistan, and studied theology, jurisprudence, and Qur'anic commentary. The Maturidis and Ash'aris, belonging to Sunni Islam, have always made up the overwhelming majority of Muslims. Maturidis assert that humans have free will and are doers of their actions, while it is God Who creates both their will and actions. (Tr.)

being created by Divine Power and the latter having only the nominal existence that was endowed on humanity by its Creator.

From the earliest times of human existence, many people have supposed their partial will to have a certain creative power like Divine Will and Power; therefore, they have regarded themselves as free and powerful enough to be able to do whatever they wish. This has caused them to deviate into ways of misguidance as far as associating partners with God. Many an arrogant man, many a tyrant, and many a lord of power have come into and departed from this world, leaving behind some cursed traces in people's memories. However, there have been many others who, although belittled by others, have comprehended and admitted their innate powerlessness and poverty, and thus have relied on Divine Power; these people have been favored with extraordinary accomplishments. They continue to live in our hearts as people of blessed memory, encouraging us to put our present plans into action and energizing our hopes and expectations for the future.

What this historical fact teaches us is that it is the Divine Power Which both brings us and our actions into existence, and equips us with certain special capacities. That infinite Power is not, as some assert, an inactive Power Which created the universe with whatever is in it and then entrusted its operation and maintenance to certain laws or forces. Rather, it is the Power Which does whatever It wills, Which existed eternally before all else came into existence, and Which will continue to exist eternally after the death of everything. It is also this self-existing and self-sustaining Power Which maintains everything else. While some of those who are unable to comprehend this essential truth or follow it, being partly under the influence of the deterministic-seeming operation of the universe and their innate powerlessness and neediness, have swerved into fatalism, others, intoxicated with a favorable turn of events and their apparent accomplishments, have been so arrogant as to suppose themselves to be the creators of their actions and therefore have attributed all of their accomplishments to their own supposed powers and abilities. However, humankind stands at the junction of the body and the spirit, the heart and reason, capacity and favor, the observation of necessary rules and the fulfillment of requirements and belief in and full reliance on the Creator of those rules and requirements, and free will and dependence. Humankind is different from all other creatures, being both effective and affected, free and compelled, and a possessor of heart and reason, yet in need of mercy and help. Humans need Divine illumination, and when they turn to God to be illuminated, they are illuminated. With their very being, humans are restricted, never being able to transcend the limits that have been placed on them. For this reason, those who are immured in fatalism are attributing wrongdoing and injustice to God, knowingly or unknowingly; while others who suppose humans to have absolute free will and power to be able to do whatever they will are deifying humanity. The people of the middle, straight way neither accept fatalism nor regard humans as having sufficient absolute freedom or power to do whatever they will. On the contrary, they perceive human innate powerlessness and poverty as a truth-speaking witness of the One of infinite Power, and regard their wishes and will as favors of mercy from the Divine Will. Ever conscious of their restrictions, they are representations of constraint and neediness, but thanks to Divine Mercy they have a certain degree of free will and power. The people of the middle way believe that all favors and accomplishments are from God. However, they also believe that in order to be able to receive these favors and be honored with accomplishments, they must do whatever falls to their share as responsible beings. Such people never forget that they will be treated by God according to their tendencies, choices, and actions.

We always try to follow this way of thought, creed, and action, and regard ourselves as the doers of our actions, called "the actions related to human free will," deeming it harmless to say, "We have eaten; we have drunk; we have slept; we have sat down; and we have stood up; and son on." Nevertheless, we also believe that the essential or primary cause and creator of all our actions is the sole Creator of everything. Like all other secondary causes, we are also a veil before His acts. It is our creed that matter is inactive, all secondary causes are unconscious, we are beings desiring and doing, and God is the sole Creator. Those who regard their free will and tendencies or wishes as the origin and primary cause of their actions have always suffered deviations of thought and creed. When they see that their wishes and demands are not fulfilled, they are not able to save themselves from going to the opposite extreme, thus drowning in fatalism and despair. It is absolutely true that God Almighty is the All-Compelling and the All-Overwhelming, Who can absolutely do and have others do whatever He wills. But this does not mean that He does not consider the free will He has bestowed on humanity. In addition to being the All-Compelling and the All-Overwhelming, He is also the All-Merciful, the All-Compassionate, the All-Just, and the All-Wise.

The people of sainthood have perceived human free will or willpower along with inclination, intention, and resolution in the attainment of such virtues as truthfulness, trustworthiness, purity of intention or sincerity in faith, performing religious deeds, being pleasing to God, and striving to exalt the Religion. They have always considered it in relation with the commandments and deeds that pertain to the other world. They have regarded a life of deviation, in which one pursues worldly gains in return for religious deeds, spends one's life in worldly expectations, and contaminates one's projects and endeavors with ostentation, hypocrisy, and even by associating partners with God, as forms of disrespect toward the willpower endowed on humanity and insolence toward God Who has given it.

Those endowed with knowledge of God are grounded in rational proofs at the beginning of their spiritual journey; they always follow the Divine Speech—the Qur'an—strictly at every step, and try to attain knowledge of God. These are considered to be the initial attempts required by being endowed with willpower. One who is able to maintain these inclinations in this direction is called "the one willing," or "the willing one." As a result of continuing in this direction, God opens the willing one's eye of the heart to look toward Him. This is the stage where "the willing one" becomes "the willed one." That is to say, an initiate who tries to "find" the True, Ever-Constant One in this degree of endeavor is loved and desired by the residents of the heavens, and becomes a focus of God's attention.

In the same way that willpower is a tendency, endeavor, and resolution, it is also an important means for reaching God when it is honored by a feeling of attraction toward God and a feeling of being attracted by Him. Through the value attached to willpower by God Almighty, a person lives in the world as if living in the Hereafter aided by resolution, endeavor, and steadfastness. Without expecting or aspiring to any pleasures, be they material or spiritual, he or she transcends normal human dimensions, being one who has renounced all else other than God. Once a person is intent on the true goal—this is what he or she can do—in the first step the spirit is freed from heedlessness by God's will and help, and reaches the horizon of wakefulness. He or she spreads "his or her prayer rug" on the ground of repentance, penitence, and contrition; begins breathing piety, righteousness, and abstinence; inhales truthfulness, and sincerity; acts with self-criticism and self-supervision, and finally advances toward the peaks of reliance, surrender, and commitment.

Using willpower in this way means committing oneself and all one's deeds and plans to God Almighty in full submission to Him. An initiate submits their will first to the will of their guide, and in the words of the Master of creation, upon him be peace and blessings, experiences "revival after death." While engulfed in temporary annihilation in the rays emanating from this horizon, they find themselves in a deep experience of absolute annihilation under the intense manifestation of Divine Will. If we call this state "annihilation in respect of will," the following experience of self-transformation may be called "subsistence through willpower." In the view of an initiate who has reached this point, everything created, which the theologians call "realities of contingency," seems non-existent, and the person observes nothing but "the Truth of All Truths." The words, "O God! Renouncing all my desires and aspirations, I only seek whatever You will and are pleased with," is what those who pursue this horizon utter frequently.

These are the Divine favors that come in return for directing willpower to endeavor, faithfulness, and sincerity. Those who are still at the beginning of the journey cannot experience them. Awareness of willpower as an important means to reach God is the first step or mansion on the way to God. An initiate in this mansion is usually occupied with gaining knowledge and pursuing proofs of Him. In the second step, initiates combine theoretical knowledge about and proofs of Him with spiritually experienced knowledge of Him and they begin to feel light pouring down into their eyes and hearts. At the third step, they are exhilarated with the observation of their hearts in the horizon of Divine Attributes. If they are able to take a further step, they direct their telescope of "secret" to the horizon of Divinity and start to experience "amazement" and "passion"[123] according to their capacity.

Some Sufi scholarly guides who view willpower only from the perspective of endeavor and resolution maintain that first the heart turns toward the All-Sought One with faithfulness and sincerity. This requires steadfastness in using willpower in the right direction—regular worship, doing righteous deeds, and avoiding all evil and sins. While the initiate is advancing in this way, they begin to feel attraction toward and are attracted by God. This is the point where the initiate begins to suffer no hardship in fulfilling their duties. When the breezes of nearness to God begin stroking the spirit, the initiate finds themselves enveloped by unbearable feelings of love and yearning. Without being able to resist any longer their exuberant desire to meet Him, they sigh with utterances at every breath: "My liver has been roasted; / Is there no cure for my

---

123 For the "amazement" and "passion," see, M. Fethullah Gülen, *Emerald Hills of the Heart – Key Concepts in the Practice of Sufism,* The Light, NJ, 2004, vol. 2, pp. 39–44, 52–55, respectively. (Tr.)

suffering?" Such a hero, who has fulfilled all the requirements of having willpower to the greatest degree possible, even forgets love, and begins living in absorption. Even if they are together with the Beloved, they dream about Him and burn with longing for Him. One who has not tasted does not know; one who has not experienced does not understand; those who have tasted do not relate their experiences, and even if those who have tasted it do say something, people do not believe what they say.

The Mind

The mind is the faculty for learning and remembering, a pool or library of the activities of consciousness. Acquisitions through conscious and subconscious activities flow onto the diskette of the mind, pour into the memory, and are recorded as ready to remember and use.

Consciousness is an important element of the mind. As it studies and evaluates other things, it is also aware of itself. Consciousness has equipment to form both simple and compound or composite sensations, impressions, and perceptions. Since it is aware of its content and has a connection with reason, some also regard it as a faculty open to the world of inner and outer sensations, sentiments, and feelings.

However, there are some Muslim scholars who see consciousness as the opposite of negligence and forgetfulness. According to them, consciousness is, as the first step of perception, the first impression that is received through initial contact with things or the source of the knowledge which has not yet been absorbed by reason or memory. From this viewpoint, we can regard consciousness as the first bridge of the spirit to reach the meaning or essence of things. This can also be explained by the following process: If the spirit has had contact with something in its true nature, this is "conception." If these first impressions are recorded and kept ready to study and evaluate, this is "memorization." If these acquisitions can be remembered for evaluation, this is "recollection."

In one respect, consciousness is the first and weakest stage of knowledge. Until it is established in the mind, it cannot be fully evaluated. Consciousness is like a seed in comparison with a tree, or a sperm in comparison with a living being. Although of weak nature, it has a capacity to gain stability, and is an important pillar of conscience. In one respect, it is based on the outer senses and external impressions, feeding the mind with its acquisitions.

There is another matter that should be mentioned concerning consciousness. The Sufi scholars also speak of a soul's being aware of itself, which is called "the inner perceptiveness." It is in fact this dimension or form of consciousness which is one of the important pillars of conscience. It is ready to be recollected, evaluated, studied, reflected, and reasoned out. This is no longer a matter of simple consciousness, but rather a multi-dimensional consciousness that is suitable for analyzing and synthesizing. Analyzed and synthesized, this degree of consciousness takes on a mental shape in memory, becoming employable by reason. It is after this step that knowledge begins to be formed. Reason always begins to work through the stimulation of consciousness, thus triggering the power of thinking and reflection. This activates the faculties or powers of conception, reasoning, and reflection, with the result that the information waiting in the consciousness begins flowing to the filters of analysis and synthesis in the laboratories of the mind. This is followed by the emergence of new compositions, which take on the color of the spiritual intellect and the design of willpower.

The mind is always fed through the channels of consciousness. It records the information it gains and prepares it for various faculties to use. In turn, consciousness has an important source of information: it is the power of perceptiveness.

The Power of Perceptiveness

The power of perceptiveness is the power with which people sense, feel, or perceive the things around them. A person has two powers or faculties of perceptiveness, namely the outer power of perceptiveness and the inner power of perceptiveness.

In addition to the external five senses or powers of sight, touch (feeling), hearing, smell, and taste, a person also has certain inner senses or powers such as the faculties or powers of imagination, will, conception or conceptualization, manipulation, understanding, supposition, and recollection. All of these faculties are in close coordination with the other pillars of the conscience, and each faculty gives its color to the acts related to itself and, if it preserves its vitality, directs them to the purpose of its creation.

If the things perceived through either the external senses or the inner faculties have a perceptible existence, then this perception is an "objective" sensation, and it is in this sensation that the scientific, objective value of consciousness lies. But if we cannot help but feel a tendency toward something under the influence of an indefinable drive which we call "the sense of impelling" or "a drive," or if we rejoice or feel stimulated because of something unknown under the direction of what we call "the sense of enthusing" or "enthusiasm," this is an inner, subjective sensation and therefore it does not have much scientific value. If, like the occurrence of a joyful event, or the body's shivering because of cold, or becoming sweaty due to heat, or the appearance of a light in the darkness, or a sound striking the ears, there is a concrete reason for any feeling, it is an objective sensation related to the consciousness. However, we can perceive only the outer, corporeal sphere of existence with our external senses. The metaphysical realms are beyond our sensations. The Prophet Moses' desire to see God was answered with, *"You will never be able to see Me!"* (7: 143). But there are many who accept that during his Ascension, the Prophet Muhammad, the Master of creation, upon him be peace and blessings, was honored with a "vision" of God, according to the capacity of the mirror of his spirit. This happened when he reached the rank of being as near to God as the nearness of *"two bow-lengths adjacent to each other,"* (53: 9) which is the rank where the external sensations disappear and the body becomes nearly as refined as the spirit, being a polished mirror to the realms beyond. A Muslim saint expressed this experience of the Prophet Muhammad, upon him be the most perfect of blessings, as follows:

O Messenger of God, your face became a mirror to God,
Where the holy, pure secret of Divine Essence manifested Itself.
Your body is the book of our Lord's secrets throughout;
Where the signs (verses) of God are read in the sura of your appearance.

Each human external or internal power, or faculty, of perception has both sensations and inner experiences. Objective sensations provide the material for scientific knowledge, while inner experiences are of a subjective nature, differing from one person and state to another. The Sufis categorize sensations or "objective" perceptions and inner experiences or "subjective" perceptions as follows:

The initiates who are yet at the beginning of the spiritual journey have contact with the corporeal and incorporeal realms with the superficial perceptions of their powers of sense.

The relationships of those who have been distinguished with a certain degree of nearness to God with both the corporeal and incorporeal realms exist through their intellectual and spiritual faculties. They are candidates for a vision of what lies beyond the "observable horizons."

As for those who are most advanced in knowledge of and nearness to God, who live at the level of the heart and spirit, they are honored with the particular favor of having relations with God through the telescope of their spiritual intellects and "secrets." Those veiled by the perceptions of their external senses are restricted by the Divine declaration, "*You will never be able to see Me*!" (7: 143), in the sense that they will never be able to have a "vision" of Him.[124] While those with refined, illumined spirits—those who have taken

---

[124] The Prophet Moses, upon him be peace, certainly was not veiled by the perceptions of his external senses. Like everybody else, he was only prevented from physically seeing God while in the world. (Tr.)

off on the wings of the inner senses of perception or inner experience—receive the glad tidings of "You will see Me!"[125]

Let us end this important topic with a meaningful, concise consideration by Beidüzzaman Said Nursi:

> The human conscious nature, which we call conscience, and which distinguishes between what is good and evil, which feels pleasure and exhilaration in what is good, and suffers from and is grieved by what is evil, consists of four basic elements, namely the spiritual intellect, willpower, the mind, and the power of perceptiveness. These four elements are also regarded as the senses of the spirit. In addition to their different duties and functions, each of these senses has an ultimate purpose for its existence. The ultimate purpose for willpower is worshipping God; for the mind, it is having knowledge of God; for the power of perceptiveness, it is love of God; and for the spiritual intellect, it is vision of God. What we call *taqwa* (piety and righteousness), which is the perfect form or degree of worship, is the result of the functions of all these four senses. The Shari'a feeds them so that they develop, equips them with the necessary material, and directs them to the ultimate purposes for the existence of each.[126]

O God! Help us to be able to mention You, thank You, and worship You properly!

O God! Favor us with a good end in all of our affairs, and save us from humiliation in the world and punishment in the Hereafter! Bestow Your blessings and peace upon the Key of creation and the whole created realm, and the Conveyor and Teacher of the Qur'an, and upon his good, upright, and pure Family and Companions altogether, so long as days and nights continue.

---

125 The respected author refers to the *hadith*, "Certainly you will see (have a vision of) your Lord (in Paradise), as you see this moon, and you will have no trouble in seeing Him." (*al-Bukhari*, "Tawhid" 24; *Muslim*, "Masajid" 211.) (Tr.)

126 Bediüzzaman Said Nursi, *Khutba-i Shamiya* ("The Sermon of Damascus"), the Second Part of the Second Addendum. (Tr.)

'AQL (REASON)

Literally meaning understanding, perception, sober-mindedness and prudence, as a term, *'aql* is a Divine light with which a person can perceive the things that cannot be comprehended with external senses. There have been some who view *'aql* as a faculty abstract of matter but which acts in collaboration with matter, or as the "speaking soul," or as the "self" that is identified with the ego. There are others who see it as an important aspect of the speaking soul or self, or a faculty dependent on the spirit. According to many others, *'aql* is a Divine immaterial substance or faculty that is separate from the speaking soul and which distinguishes truth from falsehood, good from evil, and what is beautiful from what is ugly.

Another approach is that *'aql* (reason), the soul, and the mind are the three denominations of the three functions of the same faculty. From the perspective of its being an immaterial, luminous substance, this faculty is called the *'aql*; it is known as the soul in respect of its activities, and as the mind with regard to its perceptions. Although all of these opinions are no more than speculations, it is doubtless that reason (*'aql*) is one of the most vital faculties of humanity. Even though it cannot be considered an authority—able to give the final judgment concerning good or evil, or what is beautiful or ugly—it nonetheless provides truthful evidence for judging these and similar matters. As it can distinguish between what is beneficial and what is harmful, in many cases, it can also perceive the difference between facts, premises, what is unquestionably true, and theoretical knowledge. So long as it does not remain under the influence of the carnal, evil-commanding soul, it can direct its owner toward reflection, contemplation, and deliberation under the guidance of the heart and spirit and give a push to his/her aspirations for the sublime. The people of God, or saints, tend to call such reason, "the reason of the final destination," or "the reason of the Hereafter," while they describe reason which is completely closed to the sublime as "the reason of the worldly life," or "worldly reason," or "metaphorical reason."

In addition to these denotations, "reason" has been called by different names according to its capacity for perception. They are as follows:

- Reason which understands speech and can distinguish to a certain extent between what is good and beneficial and what is evil and harmful has been called "natural reason." This reason, which is the language of the spirit and the translator of sight and hearing, is held accountable for religious responsibilities.
- Reason which is conscious of itself, perceives the instances of wisdom in and basic purposes for Divine injunctions and prohibitions, evaluating the past and present with their relationships to one another, and which is aware of where its worldly and otherworldly benefits lie has been called "reason of evidence." While "natural reason" is a simple radiance of the spirit, which is found in everyone, this level of the reason is its shining light, and only those who can deeply reflect and contemplate possess it.
- The people of God, or saints, have preferred to call reason which reads the Divine laws of creation and operation in the universe, perceives the essence of the religious sciences, and uninterruptedly advances toward accurate knowledge and knowledge of God by making analyses of all that it reads and reaching syntheses the "reason of experience." The other designations made for this level of reason such as "knowledge," "deliberation," "intellect," and "perception," can be the names given to its different functions.

On whatever level, as a light of Divine Knowledge, reason is a precious substance that is able to perceive—even though limitedly—both itself and all things and events. Furthermore, reason that is able to scan the horizon of the heart and the spirit's observation can benefit from and even share in the gifts that come to them. As for unenlightened reason, which is called "the reason of the worldly life" or "the worldly reason," and which, with its extremely dark horizon, is unaware of the life of the heart and spirit, it is an example of being unfortunate and engulfed in the lowest of the lows.

In turn, reason which has been freed from the influences of carnality and lust and which has gained a certain degree of transcendence is a companion of the heart from a few steps behind, and is favored with the gifts that come to the spiritual intellect. It is through such companionship that reason transcends the earth and the heavens, hastens toward the observation of the mysteries of the universe, and reaches the points where it can hear the breath of the inhabitants of the higher realms. While "worldly reason" sticks fast to the outward appearance of things, "reason of the final destination" or "reason of the Hereafter" travels in the depths of the fields of perception of all inner and outer faculties, getting into the inner dimension of existence and thoroughly studying the apparent causes, shuttling between causes and effects. By solving the cipher of the wisdom in and ultimate purposes for the existence of things and events, it tries to read the Divine purpose for both creation and its existence. It is so active in this endeavor that every day it rediscovers both itself and the whole universe and events, and experiences continuous renewal or revival.

So long as such reason, which has gained luminosity, continues to study the metaphysical realms through the windows of the heart and the spirit, it continuously develops and receives new radiance, and thus acts according to its level of development. As a result, the constant act of turning to the Ultimate Truth causes new doors to be opened unto it, and the gifts that come through these doors encourage it to turn to God more. This profitable trade and interaction on the way toward the Infinite continues ceaselessly.

Indeed, by its very nature, reason is open to the Creator, and it is on a continuous quest for Him. So long as it is not totally overcome by lusts or desires, reason pursues light—and once it has transcended worldliness, it changes into a store of knowledge of God, beginning to live in love and eagerness for Him, and to suck milk from the same breasts as those from which the heart nurses. In respect of the purposes for their creation, the spirit (*ruh*) is turned toward the Realm of the Transcendental Manifestation of Divine Commands (*Malakut*) and dreams of the Realm of the Transcendental Manifestation of Divine Attributes and Names (*Jabarut*); the spiritual intellect (*al-latifa ar-Rabbaniya*) has eyes turned toward the Realm of the Transcendental Manifestation of Divine Attributes and Names, and aims to be able to be like the secret (*sir*); and the secret (*sir*) exists in ecstasies enraptured by the perceptions of the intensity of Divine manifestations and Grandeur. As for reason accompanied by the heart, it is like an observer of the horizon of distinguishing between the reality and spiritual perceptions, which dreams, indeed, can conceive of the stations that are attainable by the spirit, the spiritual intellect, and the secret.

According to Muslim philosophers, reason is a faculty that, in respect of its essential nature, has a connection with the spirit, is open to the horizon of the heart, and diffuses its light by means of the mind. Humans hunt and perceive through it the things that they cannot perceive through the senses. They perceive through it the relationship between cause and effect, and between the one who does something and the thing done. They deduce from the voice the one who speaks; from the scent they detect the flower that produces it; from the footprint they perceive the being who has left it; from the system they decipher the one who has founded it; and from the order they understand the one who has established it. Also, in addition to reason being a faculty which thus perceives the things included in the field of the perception of the external senses, reason is an important element of the spirit that can originate different thoughts and considerations without needing the senses. It sees, reads, makes analyses and syntheses, divides and multiplies, and shuttles between the whole and parts and draws conclusions. Its journeying or making comparisons between two individual things or situations or processes and drawing conclusions is called "analogy"; its making a judgment about the whole based on the information about one or some of its parts, or using known facts to produce general rules, is called "induction." Most scientifically established facts have been concluded through this latter process of reason. There is also another process which is called "deduction," which involves making a judgment about a part based on general information or facts concerning the whole. This third process of reason is an important way to draw final conclusions concerning matters relating to both religious law and the facts of creation and the operation of the universe.

Having comprehended the principle of causality well, reason can collect from God's signs—the facts of the creation and operation of the universe—countless witnesses and proofs for His Existence, His Oneness, and the comprehensiveness of His Mercy by means of the processes mentioned. It can also obtain some clues about its position, responsibility, and final end. However, there are two ways by which reason can get results through these processes. One is that through which reason acts slowly and makes gradual advancement; this is the way of reflection, deliberation, and remembrance, which takes reason a certain period of time. Through the second way, which is called "intuition," reason does not need time and reaches the target in a single attempt. However, intuitive knowledge has also two kinds. One is that which is attained after studies and experiences—it is described as "the intuitive knowledge gained"; while the intuitive knowledge that is reached through the almost instantaneous development of human capacities and special Divine assistance is evaluated as the "product of the sacred power." Every human being is created with a potential for this kind of intuitive knowledge. Those most advanced in receiving the showers of intuition or inspiration are the Prophets, and after them come the ones with sound reason, sound, sincere hearts, and pure spirits.

We should also point out that reason is not always able to find the truth, and thus is exposed or prone to err. Nor is it the inventor of the conclusions it reaches through logic and comparison or the other processes mentioned above. It is an instrument which God Almighty employs as a veil before His acts and something which receives what is sent or given. It is a spiritual mechanism that has been created with the ability to understand Divine address. So long as it is conscious of its true position, reason always stands turned to the Master and never submits to any other than Him. It remains in an interactive relationship with Him and reads existence properly. Changing what it perceives and learns into knowledge of God, reason entrusts this information to the heart and it is always occupied with breathing in and out knowledge and love of God.

Knowledge of God is both a need for reason to satisfy and a source from which it must feed itself. Reason which finds this source can study the creation thoroughly from its simplest level to where it stands, which is regarded as one of the peaks of the highest level of created existence. It feels gratified with the favors reaching it and is jubilant with continuous thanks to God Almighty. When lust, desire, or fantasy and fantastical thoughts cloud its horizon unwillingly, it immediately takes refuge in the pure teachings of God's Messenger, upon him be the most perfect of peace and blessings, and tries to remain as the companion of the heart, following it from a few steps behind, never averting its eyes from the heart's horizon of the observation of the metaphysical realms.

According to the Sufis, as well as being one of the most precious faculties of human beings, reason is paradoxically an instrument which may cause their perdition. In one respect, reason causes humans to rise to an important level above animality and carnality; it whispers to them many things from the perceptions of the heart and spirit that are related to the realms beyond; it acts as both a receptor and transmitter of the most transcendent truths. In return, reason benefits from all the gifts that come to the horizon of the spirit in proportion to the value of the service it renders. Through this service, it becomes priceless and becomes as if the spirit or heart, and is now familiar with the horizon of "the secret." The counter-pole of this reason is stupidity, which has no value in God's sight; it is not worthy of His address. Quoting in his *Mathnawi* the saying of the Prophet, our master, upon him be peace and blessings, "Whoever is stupid, devoid of reason, is our enemy and a bandit waylaying us," Jalalu'd-Din ar-Rumi says, "A person of sound reason is our soul. The breeze blowing from it brings us the scent of sweet basil. Even though it becomes angry and curses me, I do not oppose it. But if a stupid one comes and puts halva in my mouth, I will catch fever from his halva and become ill." On another occasion, he says, "Reason is something luminous which is in search of the truth and desirous of goodness." Ar-Rumi praises reason enlightened with belief as follows: "Believing reason is like a just police officer. It is both the governor and guardian of the city of the heart." Jalalu'd-Din ar-Rumi, the prince of lovers of God, who thinks in this way about reason that has found its way through belief, integrity, straightforwardness, and justice, in turn equates reason which is not turned to God with poisonous insects or vermin, and says, "If your reason hinders you from God's way, it is not reason; it is a snake or scorpion." Sharing the same view, a famous sixteenth-century poet, Fuduli,[127] refers to such corrupt reason as follows:

I ask my reason for guidance;
But my reason shows me to misguidance.

Jalalu'd-Din ar-Rumi uses even harsher language for the misguiding type of reason, saying:

---

[127] Mehmed Fuduli (1490–1556). One of the greatest poets of Turkish classical literature. He lived in Iraq and wrote many works both in verse and in prose. His *Diwan* ("Collection of Poems") which he wrote both in Turkish, Persian, and Arabic is the most famous among his works. *Layla wu Majnun* ("Layla and Majnun"), *Tarjuma-i Hadith-i Arba'in* ("The Translation of the Forty Hadiths"), and *Hadiqatu's-Su'ada'* ("The Garden of the Holy Ones") are among his most famous works. (Tr.)

> Sell and get rid of that misguiding reason; in its place, buy astonishment and admiration. Such reason is the source of whims and suspicions. Admiration is a different viewpoint. Sacrifice reason for the Prophet Muhammad, upon him be peace and blessings; then say, "God is sufficient for me."

Thus he reproaches the misguiding reason, while welcoming the reason which has been sacrificed for the Prophet Muhammad, upon him be peace and blessings, and which is full of admiration for its Creator.

While some of the Sufis have put forward considerations similar to those of Heraclitus and Anaxagoras concerning the essence, nature, and functions of reason, other Sufis have viewed it as the Divine Being's manifestation at the rank of being known. According to them, it is this stage of creation which is also described as the rank of Divinity, wherein the Divine Attributes and Names have not yet been fully manifested, each according to Its own area of manifestation. This initial manifestation has also been called "the initial identification" or "the initial ability" or "the station of two-bows' length" or "the greatest passage" or "the supreme spirit" or "the initial shadow" or "the truth of Muhammad." Those Sufis have maintained that when, as required by His Essence, God Almighty manifested Himself with His Attributes of Glory from the realm of "the absolute identity," or the realm of "being unidentified and unknown," the "truth of Muhammad" emerged as the essence of the tree of the universe. Some have called this rank of manifestation "the universal intellect," or "the initial speech," or "the initial light." In the view of these Sufis, the whole of creation and all events are a comprehensive mirror formed of the manifestation and development or unfolding of this initial rank.

Some other Sufis, such as Sayyid Sharif,[128] opine that "the first intellect," or the "truth of Muhammad," comprises the truth

---

128 Sayyid Sharif al-Jurjani (1339–1413), was one of the leading theologians of the fifteenth century. He visited Istanbul in 1374, and, upon his return in 1377, he was given a teaching appointment in Shiraz. *Sharh al-Mawaqif* is his most famous work. (Tr.)

of the Divine glorious Names and also forms the essence or seed of the universal existence. Some have called it "the soul of unity" with respect to its being the essence or the initial substance of existence, while some others, who consider it from the perspective of its luminosity, describe it as "the first intellect." Nasimi sums up these considerations as follows:

> The universal intellect boiled up and the universe came into existence;
> The whole universe has been enraptured with the command, "Be!"

Some Sufis regard "the first intellect" as the "Tablet and Pen," which is free of matter and imperceptible. From the viewpoint of its being the first in creation, the essence or truth of Prophet Muhammad, upon him be peace and blessings, is a Pen, while it is a luminous tablet as the essence of the following identifications. Those who have put forward such opinions have tried to reinforce them by basing them on some narrations attributed to our master, upon him be peace and blessings. The Prophetic narrations such as, "The first thing God created was reason (or intellect),"[129] and "The first thing God created was the Pen,"[130] and "The first thing God created was my light,"[131] have been used by them as the foundations for such considerations.

There have been some who have called the first intellect "the brightest light." This designation seems to be completely proper as it is associated with the initial manifestation of existence from its purely unseen and unidentifiable stage in Knowledge, in the form of the initial identification, and as existence or all things and events are a book readable or an exhibition observable with the light that the first intellect or the essence of the Prophet Muhammad diffuses. Indeed, a book that is unreadable, an exhibition that is unobservable, and treasures that remain hidden cannot be regarded as having existence. So, existence was initially identified and mani-

---

129 ad-Daylami, *al-Musnad*, 1:13; Ibn Hajar, *Fathu'l-Bari*, 6:289.

130 *at-Tirmidhi*, "Qadar", 17; *Abu Dawud*, Sunna, 16.

131 al-'Ajluni, *Kashfu'l-Khafa'*, 1:311.

fested as that pure, brightest light, and after having passed through many stages of identification and manifestation, it emerged as an observable magnificent and perfectly orderly system, which is represented by the universe as the macrocosm and humanity as the microcosm. The light which the Prophet Muhammad, upon him be peace and blessings, brought made the universe a perfect book to be read and a perfect exhibition to be watched or observed.

Upon him be God's blessings and peace to the fullness of the heavens and the earth, and on his Family and Companions altogether.

NAFS (THE SOUL)

The soul (*an-nafs*) is a substance that is essentially free of matter but which is in close connection with it in its acts and functions; it is the origin or essence of something or its self. There have been those who have used it in the sense of the spirit or the heart or the body, or in the sense of lusts or the mechanism through which Satan penetrates humans, or even in the sense of reason. In religious terminology, *an-nafs,* or the soul, is the origin or center of certain states or faculties such as lusts, anger, ill will, grudge, hatred, and irritation, and it is a transformable, reformable, and refinable mechanism connected to human corporeality.

The soul has a constant, experienced connection between the body and the spirit. It is through this connection that humans receive, recognize, and distinguish their outer and inner sense-perceptions and go beyond the corporeal realm into metaphysical worlds. It is again through this connection that any state, experience or gift that occurs in the spirit leaves its imprint upon the body and provokes it to move in a certain direction. Just as every influence on the spirit makes itself felt on the body, so too every state of and effect on the body shows itself on the horizon of the spirit.

For example, thinking of something which is nauseating may produce an urge to vomit. Certain events which touch the spirit and rouse distress may cause physical ailments that we call psychosomatic illnesses. The reaction that the sense of taste shows at the mention of something sweet or sour or bitter is also this same sort of impression. In short, there is a continuous interactive relationship between the spirit and the body. Similarly, evil conceptions and disagreeable manners and actions impress not only the body but also the spirit, while agreeable thoughts and considerations, and the plans and projects that are undertaken to please God Almighty, and the mentioning of the Divine Being by the heart and tongue all produce expansion and exhilaration in the spirit. It frequently occurs that even if we are not aware of it, this state gains some sort of luminosity and surrounds the entire horizon of the spirit by means of the spiritual intellect. It rouses the "secret" and begins to manifest itself in the metaphysical depths of human existence in different modes. Also, whenever the body expresses its submission to the Ultimate Truth through the acts of worship and obedience and lives in accordance with the purpose of its existence, deepening in belief through worship or religious acts and crowning its worship with excellence and awareness of God's omnipresence, the breezes of great happiness and joy begin to blow in the spirit. Hope and expectation stir up eagerness for God, the Ultimate Truth, and the acts leading to consciousness and awe of God produce feelings of respect, self-possession, and wakefulness in the spirit. As a result, like the seas vaporizing to rise and form the clouds, and the clouds raining on the earth, and rains forming rivers and torrents that flow into the sea, there appear continuous currents between the body and the spirit.

Amidst such mutual influences between the spirit and the body, it is possible for humans either to fall into the lowest of the low as a result of being overcome by their corporeality, or to rise to human perfection and the highest of the high by God's help and permission, through acting around the orbit of Islamic thought, belief, and awareness. Thus, what we call "spiritual journeying" is one of the significant ways of advancing toward and reaching the Ultimate Truth, and being a perfect human being through this tide.

All these tides, continuous mutual influences and flows, and journeys occur on the steed or ship or spacecraft of the human soul. The compass of this apparently abased vessel is belief, the path or direction it must follow is Islam, and its captain or guide is the Prophet Muhammad, the Master of creation, upon him be peace and blessings, and the dynamics to advance along this path are provided by reflection and remembrance of God. However, there are some apparently harmful characteristics incorporated in the nature of this steed for certain purposes. If the soul has not been purified of these characteristics and refined, it is inevitable that the meanings, conceptions, pieces of information, knowledge of God, and remembrances, and reflections that travel between the spirit and the soul suffer from some turbulence and even serious falls along the way. Such turbulence and falls should not be viewed as occurrences independent of certain other factors that originate in humans themselves. Sometimes sins, heedlessness, and carelessness cause them; sometimes temporary "whirlpools of contraction"[132] or "spasms" interfere with the working of the rudder or the compass; sometimes direction is lost due to certain carnal amusements and relaxations; and sometimes they happen because of our unawareness that certain actions are contrary to the manner of traveling along the way, and our feeling proud of the good deeds done. If travelers view such things as viruses that can cause the demise of the spirit, and remain distant from them, and if they display serious endeavors to be purified of them under the shower of repentance, penitence, and contrition when accidentally exposed to them, then *God will replace their evil deeds with virtuous ones* (25: 70). That is, He will change their faculties which enable evil deeds into enablers of virtuous deeds.

Despite its satanic characteristics such as haughtiness, arrogance, egotism, jealousy, injustice, and enmity, all of which break the wings of the spirit, the soul has a fundamental potential so important and valuable that it raises it to companionship of the spirit. Provided it grasps that its essential function, as required by its position, is to become a unit of measurement to recognize God—thereby abandoning arrogance and the accompanying self-assertive,

---

132 In Sufi terminology, "contraction" (*qabd*) is used to mean that the link between an individual and the source of his or her spiritual gifts and radiance has been severed for a certain period. This causes distress and makes one suffer from spiritual obstruction and blockage. For further explanations, see *Emerald Hills of the Heart – Key Concepts in the Practice of Sufism,* The Light, NJ, 2004, vol. 1, pp. 167–170. (Tr.)

self-aggrandizing claims; so long as it turns to God in worship and prayer and seeks refuge in Him from the potential evils in its nature, following the heart and the spirit on the way to reaching God, then the soul can advance to the highest of the high on the way together with its companions, namely the heart and the spirit.

Indeed, the soul is also of great importance for humans to maintain a metaphysical tension. It (the soul) is like a mainspring allowing them to rise from being only potentially human to true humanity. This continuously keeps them busy, without allowing them to have a rest. It ceaselessly sharpens the resolution of people to struggle against its negative characteristics, and causes those who have brains to frequently beat their brains out. When, finally, human nature is matured to the degree intended for its creation, the soul becomes a slave of the king of human existence—the heart—and adopts an attitude that is capable of feeling the need to warn it from time to time, saying, "Do not be proud, O my king! There is God, Who is greater than you!" You can call the soul which has reached this point of maturity after having gone through the filters of purification "the soul refined and grown in purity," as stated in the following verses: *And (by) the human soul and that (All-Knowing, All-Powerful, and All-Wise One) Who has formed it to perfection; and Who has inspired it with the conscience of what is wrong and bad for it, and what is right and good for it. He is indeed prosperous who has grown it in purity* (91: 7-9).

Whatever you call it, the purified soul is the double of the spirit, continuously trying to keep away from evil, and always advancing toward good until it finally comes to a point where it abandons its basic mission—that is, being a powerful mechanism with negative aspects for human self-purification and perfection—to the nerves, extreme sensitivity, and other human temperaments. It begins to spend the remaining part of its life in the company and service of the spirit.

We have tried to explain in detail the stages of this journeying of the soul, which the Sufis experience in their spiritual journeying, under the titles of the Carnal, Evil-Commanding Soul, the Self-Condemning or Self-Accusing Soul, the Soul Receiving Inspiration, the Soul at Rest, the Soul Well-Pleased (with God, with however God treats it), the Soul Pleasing (to God), and the Perfected Soul, or the Purified or Innocent Soul.[133] As the soul passes through these stages upward, the veils of darkness that veil human nature are torn apart one after the other. According to the degree of each, the rays of spirituality begin to shine on all sides of a human being, and an initiate or traveler thinks that they are floating in the elevated horizons of the inner, immaterial dimensions of existence.

Each of the stages mentioned above has a gift, pleasure, horizon, manner of expressiveness, and perception particular to itself. Sometimes the guide tells initiates at which stage they are, and sometimes sensitive, self-supervising initiates who are aware of themselves and lend an ear to the voice of their spirits are informed of their stage in a special way.

Even though the soul is mainly characterized by always commanding evil, when it undergoes an effective process of purification and is directed to obedience to its Lord, it can be transformed into a source of bright light, like the full moon receiving light from the sun. If, on the other hand, it is not purified, the fog and smoke of the lusts invade its horizon, and it suffers corruption under the influence of carnal thoughts and considerations, becoming so blind as not to be able to see into the transcendent dimension of existence. Then, the soul cannot continue its companionship with the spirit and becomes a marsh of evil in human nature, in conformity with the aspects of its nature, which is open to evil. Making use of certain weak spots in its owner, the soul attacks him from many fronts, and—may God preserve us—can knock him down with a single blow. The continuous request for forgiveness from God and prayer are important defenses against such attacks; the disciplines which have an important place in the spiritual journeying are a petition pre-

133 See M. Fethullah Gülen, *Emerald Hills of the Heart – Key Concepts in the Practice of Sufism,* The Light, NJ, 2004, vol. 2, pp. 251–261. (Tr.)

sented for Divine protection, and following the way of God's Messenger, upon him be peace and blessings, strictly offers a reliable refuge. Further, restricting our consumption to absolutely essential human needs, silencing the soul by being content with legitimate pleasures, and incessantly warning the soul against illicit desires and appetites form another way of keeping it under strict control.

* * *

Basically, the soul is one of the faculties with which humans have been equipped. Provided that humans employ these faculties, which have been entrusted to them in their creation, in the direction established by their Creator, they greatly add to their value. For example, the eyes are windows for seeing things within their scope of sight; the ears are receptors and transmitters that receive and conduct sounds and voices at certain wavelengths to the brain; the tongue is an inspector of innumerable tastes, and the translator of thoughts and feelings. If the eyes are used to see things which are religiously permissible to observe, if the ears are kept closed to harmful, evil sounds and voices while transmitting the good ones, and if the tongue stirs up feelings of reflection on and thankfulness to the numberless bounties bestowed by God Almighty, and also acts in conformity with the Divine purpose for its creation as a means of speech—then individually and collectively these organs become wings for human beings to rise to human perfection. But if, on the contrary, the eyes busy themselves with those things that the Religion condemns as harmful or ugly, thus abandoning themselves to contamination; if the ears work like a telephone exchange for vices, receiving and transmitting that which is religiously forbidden; and if the tongue lives in attachment to the tastes it recognizes, in oblivion of its duty of inspection, and speaks without recognizing any criteria—then the wings of the heart are broken, and the spirit becomes as if nitric acid were poured into its eyes.

The soul is no different from the faculties mentioned above with respect to its duties and its fulfilling or not fulfilling them properly. If the soul is purified and preserved against working like a telephone exchange for Satan, then while being, by its primordial nature, a reptile-like creature crawling on the ground, it becomes like a dove flying over our heads, as if it has undergone a mysterious metamorphosis, and it is praised by the words of God Almighty: *I swear by the self-accusing soul* (75: 2). When it takes two steps further, it is honored with the breezes of appreciation: *O, you soul at rest! Return to your Lord, well-pleased (with Him and His treatment of you), and well-pleasing to Him* (89: 27-28), and establishes itself comfortably next to the spirit.

Thus, this hard-natured substance, more harmful than snakes and scorpions, which is described by the Divine statement as *Surely the carnal, evil-commanding soul always and insistently commands evil* (12: 53)—by asking God for forgiveness in awareness of its sins, by avoiding its faults due to repugnance, by trying to keep distant from unbelief, hypocrisy, vice, and transgression, by shuddering with fear that the favors coming when it is in an agreeable state may be a means of perdition, and, in a further attempt, by finding its true purification through always seeing itself as impure, this primordially hard-natured, evil-commanding substance can rise to great heights and approach the heavenly beings. The soul at this level, which philosophers call "the speaking self or soul," and which the Qur'an describes as "the soul at rest," has become such an earthly being able to rise to the horizon of the heart and the spirit and possessing angelic manners, that it begins to take pleasure in religious responsibilities, which previously it did not like and which were difficult for it to fulfill. The things which it found bitter up until this point have become sweet, and in parallel with its attaining this station, the cloud of dust and smoke over the spiritual intellect and the secret that was produced by corporeality has been completely removed. Things and events appear differently to its view, and time and again it experiences raptures with the call to Him it hears from every thing and event, thinking itself to be among the pure spirit beings in great joy.

A time comes when reason becomes like the heart, and its products take on the color of those of the spiritual intellect. An initiate with such a level of reason feels stunned by awe of God and advances full of the feeling of modesty; he sometimes becomes exhilarated with the showers of Divine gifts. The heart beats "God! God!", combining this with the breaths of reason that utter, "O the All-Forgiving! O the All-Veiling (of His servants' sins and shortcomings)!" The initiates at this level of reason hear the whole of creation mentioning God by His Names, and their breaths resound with Him. While, on the one hand, signals come to them from the horizon of the spiritual intellect, arousing them to the worlds beyond, on the other hand they feel great worry that the gifts may be interrupted and unexpected obstacles may come in between them and the Source of these gifts, causing them to turn to Him more frequently and more intimately, admitting that whatever good visits them is essentially from Him.

The zeal they feel is the zeal of the heart, and the sorrows they suffer are the sorrows of the sincerely penitent ones. While looking at their past with repugnance, they are revived and refreshed with the hope of a brighter future and the hope that they will be able to compensate for their past defects with future opportunities. They try to fill their past voids with heartfelt sighs and groans and with reflection and remembrance. While others are busy with a life of ease, thinking that they have already lived so before, they always try to do whatever they must on the way to God.

Such people always feel themselves to be in the presence of the Lord. They stand before Him in awe, bow before Him in utmost modesty, prostrate before Him with utmost humility, and sit before Him in self-supervision. They advance with utmost awe and care, and try to fulfill what is required by having reason in the company of the heart. They shudder with awe while thinking of Him, they breathe His mercy with reflection and remembrance of Him; they focus their observations on deepening their knowledge of Him with new discoveries, and their eyes twinkle with eagerness for reunion with the All-Beloved. They do not forget their defects, which are incompatible with servanthood to God, seeing them as precipices between them and their Lord; they entreat Him, saying, "Do not abandon me to myself, even for the blink of an eye!"

Now they have distanced themselves from Satan, but they also reinforce the barriers they have put before Satan's inlets into their heart and continue to erect new ones. Whenever they remember Satan, they feel as if they are in the valley of bandits, and they always seek refuge in God, saying, "*I seek refuge in You from the promptings and provocations of the satans; I seek refuge in You, my Lord, lest they be present with me*!" (23: 97–98).

They never rely on themselves, their labor, or their deeds; they do not approve of their acts, and treat them with disdain. They are always troubled and shake like a tree in a storm with the worry that hypocrisy and expectation of others' acceptance and appreciation have found, and do find, a way into even their best deeds. These considerations follow them ceaselessly along the way, until finally the soul is welcomed with the compliments, "*O you soul at rest! Return to your Lord, well-pleased (with Him and His treatment of you), and well-pleasing to Him! Enter, then, among My servants (fully content with servanthood to Me)! And enter My Paradise!*" (89: 27–30); while those who have dropped halfway groan with deep regrets, "*Would that I had forwarded (some good deeds) for my life (to come)*!" (89: 24). They are honored with surprising bounties of the Hereafter, and favored with many different gifts from the horizon of the heart.

They are treated thus because they have lived a life of austerity without being deceived by worldly pleasures, and they have advanced toward the horizon of the peace of the heart, spiritual contentment, and resignation to God's treatment of them. They felt obliged to advance so, conscious of their essential impotence and poverty and their absolute need of Him. They have advanced and been favored with His special wealth. They have heard many things which other ears could not hear, and seen many things which other eyes could not see; they have experienced how the most honored of creatures—humanity—was created from wet clay, how matter rose almost to the level of the spirit, and how the evil-commanding soul developed into the soul at rest. With the pleasure of watching the smiling face of their fate, they have proceeded beyond space within space and toward the All-Beloved within corporeality, to the point where the invisible becomes visible.

The exacting people of truth and wisdom have seen the soul as we have so far tried to explain. If the Master of all domains had willed it to be so, there is none who could have willed or done otherwise. If He has dressed non-existence in the array of existence, why then should we wonder at "nothing" being "everything"? If He wills, He can make a drop into a sea, a minute particle into the sun, manifest thousands of instances of existence in non-existence, and bestow kingdoms upon those who initially have no trace of one.

> *O my God! Surely I ask You for a soul content with You, believing in meeting You, resigned to Your decrees, and content with Your bounties. And bestow blessings and peace on the most perfect and complete of the spirits, who is our master Muhammad, and Your beloved, and on His Family and Companions, whom You love!*

KARAMA (WONDER)

Before explaining *karama*, since there is a close resemblance between it and miracles (*mu'jiza*) in respect to their occurrence, we will first briefly examine miracles.

Derived from the root verb *A-Ja-Za*, meaning "that which people cannot imitate," a *mu'jiza* (miracle) is the extraordinary state, event, word or attitude which God creates at the hands of a Prophet to show the truth of Prophethood, confirm the Religion, and generate conviction and contentment in the hearts of believers. It is beyond the power and ability of other people. A Prophet works a miracle according to God's will in order to demonstrate his Prophethood in an undeniable and indisputable way. The miracle is created by God, not the Prophet. The Qur'an, other Divine Scriptures, and the Prophetic Traditions all mention numerous miracles worked by the Prophets, and refer to the consequences of believing or not believing in them.

As for *karama* (wonder), this word is derived from *karam*, the root meaning of which is honor, munificence, and bounty. *Karama* is used to designate extraordinary states, words, acts, and effects displayed by saints through God's will and creation. To give a more detailed description, the extraordinary states displayed by the Prophets to demonstrate their Prophethood are "miracles," while such states exhibited by the saints who have succeeded in purifying their souls and refining their hearts in adherence to the true Religion are considered to be "wonders." Similar extraordinary states and acts can sometimes be witnessed in some people who have no belief in and adherence to the true Religion. But these states and acts are called "gradual perdition," as they usually cause particularly the unjust, dissolute and sinful people gradually to descend into perdition.

From another viewpoint, a wonder (*karama*) is an extra miracle-like gift of God with which He honors His servants who love and obey Him and whom He loves; it is God's unusual or exceptional treatment of these servants for following the Prophet. The beloved people of God have divided this treatment into the spiritual *karama* and the *karama* that is beyond the normal laws of life and creation:

1. The spiritual *karama* or wonder is the sum of perfect belief, good deeds, sound knowledge of God, heartfelt love for God, and perfect devotion to God, the Ultimate Truth. The people of God usually refer to this state, which is a gift from God, when they talk about *karama*. Profundity in knowledge and efforts to disseminate it, effectiveness in endeavors to guide others, the effort to love God and make others love Him, and the resolution and performance displayed to enable the Muhammadi spirit to blossom throughout the world can also be included as examples of this kind of Divine gift or *karama*.

2. As for the wonders that are beyond the normal laws of life and creation, they consist of certain extraordinary performances such as increasing a little food or drink without making any addition, being able to remain hungry for days without eating or drinking anything, covering great distances in a very short time, being present in many places at the same instant, walking on water without sinking, and moving some objects from afar. The devoted people of God have never considered such performances as a virtue, nor have they sought them; if God creates such things in their hands, they try to conceal them. Fearing that such extraordinary performances may be the cause of gradual perdition, the faithful servants at the door of God have turned to God with repentance, penitence, and contrition, scrutinized their sincerity, and renewed their devotion from the heart. Furthermore, some of them have likened such wonders to playthings of children and never attached any importance to them. The respected scholarly saint Ahmad ar-Rifai maintained that such wonders should be kept concealed, and he emphasized following the way of the Prophet, upon him be peace and blessings. Some others with the same approach have regarded wonders such as fly-

ing in the air and walking on water as the acts of some animals, and stressed that the main wonder is being able constantly to pursue God's good pleasure and approval while trying to remain distant from other kinds of extraordinariness. They have prayed, saying, "O my God! Favor my 'secret' with familiarity of Your Essence, and do not test me as one who is familiar with Your secrets!" They have preferred to remain shut off from all other kinds of extraordinariness than belief, knowledge of God, and love of God, and they have not even sought spiritual pleasures.

Nevertheless, there may be some sincere ones who view wonder-working as a gift from God and make it a means of praising and thanking Him. However, it is always possible for those who have not yet been able to purify their souls completely to fall into conceit and pride. For this reason, if such a gift and performance, which is regarded as a fruit of nearness to God Almighty, causes one to become distant from God instead, then it must be more prudent to keep one's heart distant from everything, including spiritual pleasures, other than His approval and good pleasure purely for His sake.

However, miracles are not like wonders. First of all, since miracles are displayed to confirm a Prophet in his Prophethood, to silence the opposing side, and reinforce the believers, they concern the spirit of the Divine Messengership, and a Messenger is obliged to display them when necessary. For Prophethood is one of the basic pillars of the Religion, and the most important support of religious life. Miracles are granted to draw attention to this pillar and support, and they are able to silence the opposition. Miracles have other benefits such as reinforcing the believers, offering a proof for the truth of the Divine Message to those who are sincere in their quest for the Straight Path, and depriving the obstinate unbelievers of their excuse for denial. It is for all these reasons that Prophets are obliged to display miracles.

Numerous books have been written concerning the meaning, content, sorts, and truth of miracles. The Nineteenth Letter, included in *The Letters* by Bediüzzaman Said Nursi, is one of them. Those who want more information about miracles, in particular the miracles of our Prophet, may refer to those books. Here we will be content with a quotation from Mawlana Shibli an-Nu'mani[134] about the spiritual life of our Master, upon him be peace and blessings:

> Just as the "natural" world has disciplines and laws of its own, manifested in whatever takes place in it, such as the alternation of the day and night, and the spring and the winter, and the opening of flowers in spring, the trees yielding fruits in summer, and the harmonious movement of some stars in the heavens, so too does the world of spirituality have laws and rules particular to it. In the same way that the sun, the moon, the stars, and the events that take place on the earth display continuity according to certain laws that have been appointed for each, guidance and deviance, mercy and punishment, the Divine Messengership and the realities relating to it occur in accordance with certain Divine laws. The Prophets are chosen by God and sent at the time which He wills. People either accept or reject them. Those who accept them and believe are saved, while the others, who reject them, suffer loss and punishment. As a dimension of the struggle between the Prophets and those who reject them, God Almighty creates certain wonders that are beyond our capacity at the hands of those perfect ones whom He chose and sent to us as His Messengers....
>
> However, just as we are unable to know completely how the flowers come into existence in spring or how the trees yield their fruits, of which we are in need, or how some stars move around their appointed orbits, or why the trees grow from seeds, or how the seeds are formed, or the exact nature of the mysterious relationship between our bodies and the sustenance we take, so too we cannot comprehend fully or exactly why the Prophets are chosen as Prophets and sent at different times. We can only know the fact that some persons are chosen and sent to certain people with the mission of Prophethood, and

134 Mawlana Allama Shibli an-Nu'mani (1857–1914) was a Muslim scholar from India. He founded the Shibli National College in 1883 and the *Daru'l-Mussanifin* in Azamgarh. Shibli was a versatile scholar, especially in the fields of history and literature. He was also a poet. His famous work is *Siratu'n-Nabiyy*.("The Life of the Prophet"). However, he only managed to write two volumes of it, and his disciple Sayyid Sulayman an-Nadwi made use of an-Nu'mani's material and his own and wrote the remaining five volumes of the work after the death of his teacher. (Tr.)

that they realize important revolutions, concentrating on such basic matters as belief and religious life.

In fact, it is a miracle that the Prophets emerge as Prophets, and all the states of their manners are silent proofs of their Prophethood. Those with open eyes immediately know and understand them without needing another sign; those who are not deaf know them from their messages; and those who are able to use their intellects confirm them. But there have always been others with a lower level of sight, hearing, and understanding. Therefore, in order not to deprive the latter of knowing the Prophets, God Almighty created miracles which would cause their guidance and silence the deniers. As a matter of fact, miracles were displayed to such people. Indeed no one among those who were fortunate enough to recognize the Prophets by virtue of their good conduct and character demanded miracles from the Prophets.

Distinguished personalities such as Aaron and Joshua, who were in the company of the Prophet Moses, and the Apostles around the Prophet Jesus, and "the first and foremost" to embrace Islam from among the Companions of our Master, upon him be peace and blessings, never demanded miracles. They unhesitatingly confirmed their Prophets, whom they knew by their absolute truthfulness, their trustworthiness, their dedication to their cause and communication of God's Message, their sinlessness, and unerring and undeceiving intelligence and prudence, their straightforwardness in their relationship with people, and their untainted altruism.

Those distinguished followers of the Prophets never demanded miracles; but if they witnessed some miracles of their Prophets, this increased their confidence in their way and urged them even more to follow it with greater zeal.

As for the others, such as the Nimrods, Pharaohs, and Abu Jahls,[135] they insistently demanded miracles from the Prophets; but when they witnessed the miracles, such as the fire being cool and peaceful for the Prophet Abraham, upon him be peace

---

135 Abu Jahl, 'Abr ibn Hisham (d. 624 CE) was the most obstinate and merciless one in opposition to the Prophet Muhammad in Makka. Abu Jahl, meaning the Father of Ignorance, was the name given to him by the Prophet, upon him be peace and blessings. He was killed at the Battle of Badr two years after the Prophet's emigration to Madina. (Tr.)

> (21:68–69), the Flood, in which the people of the Prophet Noah, upon him be peace, drowned (11:42; 54:12), the invasion of the residences of Pharaoh's clan by floods, locusts, vermin and frogs, and water turning into blood while the Prophet Moses, upon him be peace, was still in Egypt (7:133), and the moon being split into two by the Prophet Muhammad, upon him be peace and blessings, (54: 1), they described them as magic and continued in their obstinate denial. There were indeed those who came to belief from among those who witnessed these and similar other miracles, but the others who insisted in their denial did not abandon their way. Nevertheless, many among the believers increased in their belief, certainty, and conviction in the face of such unusual Divine acts.

After having assigned tens of pages to the meaning, content, and nature of the miracles, Shibli an-Nu'mani then gives answers to the objections raised by some concerning the miracles. He sums up his views as follows:

- A miracle is an extraordinary accomplishment created by God at the hands of a person who has been distinguished with Prophethood and who possesses its basic characteristics; it is not possible for us to perceive how it actually occurs.
- Although miracles are extraordinary, they are not impossible. Even though they are rare with respect to their occurrence, they are accomplishments which the infinitely Powerful One has created time and again.
- Such extraordinary events do not show continuity like what we perceive as ordinary "natural" events. However, it is only because of their continuity that we view those latter events as ordinary. Each of them is, in fact, a miracle; indeed, all events of creation, origination, giving life, and causing to die, as well as many others, are miracles. Since the miracles of the Prophets happen outside what we see as the "usual or normal laws of nature," we call them miracles. What we see as normal or usual laws of nature are, in fact, excuses for us to be able to observe and describe what we call "natural events" and continue our life. Such events have no creative effect at all in their own coming into existence.
- Belief is not always the result of an apparent effect or sense-perception. Seeing is something, while comprehen-

sion is another thing, and evaluating our sense-perceptions is completely different from both. As for belief, it is a spirit or meaning which Divine Will kindles in the consciences of those who can evaluate, free of any prejudice. No one can kindle it by means of apparent causes.

- The emergence of such a spirit or meaning in the heart or conscience partly depends on being open to believing in the Unseen. The haughty, obstinate ones, the unjust deniers, the distorting commentators, and those who crawl in the net of false imitations can in no wise attain belief unless extra Divine aid comes.
- If a conscience is open to the Unseen and ready to believe, its owner believes in both miracles and the message intended by them.[136]

* * *

The considerations of Elmalılı Hamdi Yazır concerning the subject are also worth quoting. After setting forth a powerful defense in his monumental Qur'anic commentary against the thinkers and philosophers who deny miracles, he gives invaluable explanations, which we can summarize as follows:

> We do not have substantiated or confirmed information about how the "law of causality," which we regard as responsible for the apparent continuity of "natural" events, works in nature. We have only partial and relative knowledge about this matter. For this reason, we have no right either to deny the forces originating in Divine acts and wisdom, and the substantial causes the Almighty creates and employs, or to regard the law of causality as an absolute principle responsible for everything that happens, thus attributing impotence to the Absolute Divine Power by claiming that "that thing is impossible." Leaving the existence of the spirit aside, simply, the speed in the shining and extinguishing or the appearance and disappearance of a light shows us the rapid events of creation and extinction that happen. But unfortunately, those with hardened hearts are blind to all these

136 an-Nu'mani, *Asr-ı Saadet* ("The Age of Happiness": Turkish translation of *Siratu'n-Nabiyy*), vol. 3, under the heading of "The Spiritual Life of Our Prophet." (Tr.)

> observable and similar occurrences and drown in despair in every matter which their narrow minds cannot grasp and with which they are entangled. More than that, among those are some who never accede to anything which does not suit their interests or taste, even if that thing is a truth, nor do they avoid committing any wrong to fight with it. Each of these is a pharaoh, and what they do is pharaohship (absolute despotism).[137]

Humankind has seen many pharaohs, ranging from those who claim divinity to those who deny everything beyond matter, from those who use humans like slaves and brutalize them to those who regard them as animals, from those who put a ban on the freedom of thought and speech to those who degrade and mock the Religion and religious life, and from those who ignore the events that are extraordinary in occurrence or spiritually to those who deny the limitlessness of the Power. Even though these pharaohs are not based on any right or substantiated truth in their claims and actions, they have been able to impose their wishes on the masses with brute force. Without needing to justify their plans even once, they have always applied brute force with the belief that "might is right." These are such rebellious spirits that they neither recognize God and the Prophet nor accept Messengership and the miracles. They are examples of those who have disrespect for both the creation and the Infinite Power Which creates. It is useless to spend time hoping whether they will reform their ways; what we should do concerning them is to avoid provoking them so that they do not bite people. Both miracles and wonders are manifestations of Divine favor for unprejudiced persons and acts of stirring up certain inherent tendencies. Even if thousands of such acts are displayed before those with deformed characters, they are not in the least affected by them.

Even though miracles and wonders resemble each other in appearance and occurrence, they are different in essence. Miracles are extraordinary states or events that confirm the truthfulness of the

---

[137] Yazır, *Hak Dini Kur'an Dili* ("The Qur'an, the Language of the Religion of Truth"), 2:2238. (Tr.)

Prophets in their claim of Prophethood. They are the means of coming to belief and salvation for some, while they cause the destruction of haughtily obstinate ones. As for wonders, they are special favors of God Almighty bestowed for adherence to Prophets.

Miracles are displayed to confirm the claim of Prophethood and silence the deniers, while wonders are and should be kept concealed as a mystery of God so long as there is not something that requires their exhibition.

Besides being a proof for Prophethood, miracles are such exceptional Divine gifts which awaken hearts to the Divine Message that they are binding on anyone who witnesses them or hears of them from a reliable source. As for wonders, they are God's gifts that are particular to those who have been favored with them and are binding on no one.

When a Prophet works a miracle, he can comfortably describe that extraordinary state, action, or word, which God Almighty has created in his hands as a miracle; indeed, he is obliged to display it. But at whatever level they are, saints cannot claim any similar extraordinary accomplishment when they are favored with a wonder. More than that, they shudder with fear that such an accomplishment may be the beginning of their gradual perdition, or that they are consuming here the fruits that will be given to them in the Hereafter for their good deeds.

A Prophet who works miracles proclaims his mission with a miracle, using it as grounds for conveying his Message and the fundamentals of the religious life he must communicate. As for the saintly people of God, they see whatever gift and effulgence they are favored with only as a reflection of the miracles of the Prophet they follow.

A miracle indicates the truth of the office of Prophethood, which is one of the essential pillars of Divine Religion, while wonders and other accomplishments or Divine gifts, such as the discovery of some realities that are hidden to common people, are evaluated as the fruits of following a Prophet.

Truthfulness, trustworthiness, freedom from sin and any mental or physical defect, intellect or perfect sagacity, and being a Prophet receiving Divine Revelation are the prerequisites for any unusual accomplishment or state to be accepted as a miracle. However, in addition to the fact that a saint favored with wonder-working can never be regarded, and indeed never is, as a Prophet, he or she is not necessarily expected to have perfected the other attributes mentioned as well.

As discussed before briefly, a Prophet displays extraordinary things by God's creation, and is doubtlessly certain that they are miracles—but saints feel doubt about the extraordinary things that originate from them whether purposely or unaware, because unless these are intended for guidance knowingly, they may be a test for them involving the risk of loss.

It is a fact that sometimes, because of some necessity or need, and sometimes with the intention of serving a religious purpose or under the unavoidable influence of the spiritual state they are in, some saintly people of God may display some extraordinary things within the limits of Divine permission. However, they should view this Divine gift as a reward for their adherence to the Prophet they are believing in and following, and never attempt to use it as a means of personal credit. Whether a saintly friend of God works it knowingly, or it appears purely as an unexpected Divine gift, a wonder resembles a miracle with respect to its occurrence. For example, miracle-like wonders, such as being unexpectedly offered some food or water in time of dire hunger or thirst, exhibiting extraordinary behavior in time of war, covering a great distance or extraordinarily performing many things in a very short time (shortening of distances or expansion of time, respectively), breathing temporary life by God's leave to someone who has just died, walking on water without sinking, and traveling in the air as if flying, like the Prophet Solomon, upon him be peace, have been frequently witnessed.

Both the Qur'an and the books of the reliably narrated sayings of our Prophet, upon him be peace and blessings, mention similar and other kinds of miracles worked by different Prophets.

We read about many extraordinary states, action, and words of respectful saints in the books that narrate their lives. Here we will be content with a few examples:

- We read in the Qur'an (2:49) that the Prophet Jesus, upon him be peace, revived the dead by God's leave. Similarly, it is narrated in reliable books that just like some saintly people of God, such as Abu Ubayd al-Busri,[138] Shaykh Ahdal,[139] and Abdu'l-Qadir al-Jilani, revived dead animals. When, during a war, Abu Ubayd beseeched God to revive his dead horse, God Almighty restored the horse to life. Shaykh Ahdal called to his cat that had just died, and the cat was revived by God's leave and approached him. Abdu'l-Qadir al-Jilani ordered the bones of a consumed chicken, "Rise up, by God's leave!" and the chicken came to life and stood up. These are only a few examples; many others can be found in relevant books.
- It is narrated in the same books that some saints, such as Abu Sa'id al-Harraz[140] and Abdu'l-Qadir al-Jilani, spoke with corpses.
- There are many other miracle-like wonders worked by saints, such as flowing water parting and opening a passage for the saints, some saints not dying even though they were poisoned many times, the shortening of distances, wild animals serving them, their prayers being instantly accepted, their being prevented from eating and drinking any forbidden thing, their observing events that occurred in distant places, and their being protected against their enemies. All these

138 Muhammad ibn Hasan Abu Ubayd al-Busri (d. 859) was a famous Syrian scholar and Sufi. He is regarded as one of the greatest saints. (Tr.)

139 Shaykh Abu'l-Hasan Ali al-Ahdal al-Husayni (d. 1604) was one of the saints from Yemen. The Sufi order of Ahdaliya is attributed to him. (Tr.)

140 Abu Sa'id Ahmad ibn 'Isa al-Harraz of Baghdad, a cobbler by trade. Author of several books including some which have survived, the date of his death is uncertain but probably occurred between 892 and 899. (Tr.)

> events demonstrate that wonder-working is undeniably real, and some saintly friends of God have been honored with it.

The extraordinary states and actions which proceeded from our Prophet, upon him be peace and blessings, from his birth until his Prophethood, are of the same nature as wonder-working. However, the wonders and gifts which are, in one respect, a means of honor for saints, are only of a primordial degree in proportion to the gifts and honors of the office of Prophethood, and they are regarded as drops that emerge from the atmosphere of the Prophet whom the saints follow. For this reason, the friends of God never think of using such Divine favors in promoting themselves, nor do they pursue them. Neither do they damage their relationship with God based on their servanthood by making use of them for personal credit. They try their best to keep the favors that come without demand concealed, and they even check their relationship with their Lord, fearing that these acts may be a test for them. They renew their devotion to Him and only pursue His approval and good pleasure. This is what is most suited to the faithful servants of God, the Ultimate Truth.

Those faithful servants of God turn to Him a few times a day with the petition of their awareness and admission of their innate impotence and poverty; they are enraptured with the joy of being the servants at His door and always move with thankfulness for being on His way. They are in turmoil with the hope of attaining His constant company. Consequently, they are shut off from anything—whether it is a spiritual discovery or wonder-working, or spiritual pleasures, or any other kind of favor—other than intense longing to meet with God. They consider themselves to be nothing within nothing, recognizing others as much more virtuous than themselves, always living as examples of utmost humility and the deepest sincerity toward God, and they are so compassionate and magnanimous toward people that they are willing to sacrifice themselves for their happiness; they abandon all desires and expectations for any Divine gifts that will come to them in the world, they pursue only God's approval and good pleasure at every instant of their lives.

These heroes are primarily distinguished with such qualities as equipping as many hearts as possible with belief, endeavoring that the Religion becomes the life of all humankind, illuminating all dark souls, trying to remove all the hardship and troubles that their community suffers, showing the same degree of sensitivity to preserving the honor of others that they show to preserving their own honor, asking for the good of all Muslims as much as or even more than they ask for their own good whenever they stretch out their hands to pray to God, praying every morning and evening for mercy toward and forgiveness of the Community of Muhammad, saying, "O my God! Have mercy on the Community of Muhammad! O my God! Forgive the Community of Muhammad!"; they act so magnanimously and tolerantly that they forgive those who have done them harm, embracing everyone with love, mercy, and generosity, showing the utmost care in adhering to the Religion down to its smallest detail, and following the Prophet, upon him be peace and blessings, step-by-step in their life. They try to fully represent the elevated morals and virtues that the Qur'an portrays and are resolved to remain distant from all evils and vices, such as resentment, vengeance, hatred, jealousy, suspicion, and enmity. Each of these qualities is a wonder to be sought and much more valuable than the other wonders that are manifested as some extraordinary actions or events, some examples of which we have mentioned above.

Indeed, the greatest wonder is living a life completely according to the precepts of the Qur'an, and those who are the nearest to God must be the representatives of this spirit.

> *O my God! Make us among Your servants who are sincere and who have been endowed with sincerity in faith and in the practice of the Religion, and who have achieved piety and righteousness, and abstinence from all forbidden things, big or small, and whom You have made near to You, and who are well-pleasing to You, and with whom You are well-pleased, and who love You and are loved by You, and who stand in awe of You, and whose character has been molded by the Qur'an! Amen! And bestow blessings and peace upon the Master of those who love You and are loved by You, and on his Family and Companions, whom You made near to You.*

NAZAR AND *TAWAJJUH* (ATTENTION AND REGARD)

Even though they appear to have the same meaning and, in fact, suggest certain common feelings and ideas, the concepts of *nazar* (attention)—which means looking (at), taking into consideration, and complimenting—and *tawajjuh* (regard)—used to mean turning to, feeling nearness to, and showing sympathy and regard for—are different in many respects.

Those two concepts express different meanings when they refer to the Divine Being and creatures. God Almighty's attention and regard manifest themselves as favoring, sending gifts, and having special mercy on certain things or persons, while when refer to His creation, they are the ability to receive and reflect the Almighty's special attention and regard.

God Almighty brings everything to existence and honors some of His creatures with special, extra capacities. Then, He treats them according to their extra capacities and exalts them with extra favors. In addition to His all-embracing protection, maintenance, mercy, favoring, and assistance as the universal, all-encompassing manifestation of His Names, He has special mercy, favoring, and regard for certain beings, which is known as His manifestation of Grace or the concentrated manifestation of His Names on individual creatures. At the same moment He looks, as He uninterruptedly does, at the whole of creation with His all-encompassing Sight, He also looks at each species and each individual creature according to its position, need, and capacity. He answers all their wishes, voiced verbally or in the language of disposition or necessity, and He leaves no creature deprived, except as required by His Wisdom.

The attention and regard of a Prophet manifest themselves as his turning to God Almighty with all his extraordinary capacity, pursuing His approval and good pleasure with all his strength and outer and inner senses and faculties, reading and interpreting correctly all His laws of life and commands which are included in the Religion and which concern the creation and operation of the universe, holding the rights of God above all else, educating his community in the light of the Divine Message so as to enable them to improve the world and gain eternal happiness, showing people to the horizon of true humanity, guiding his followers on the way to Paradise, and so on.

As mentioned before, God attends or shows attention for the universe and whatever is in it from the perspective of His Grace, Majesty, and Perfection, which demonstrates His absolute freedom from any defects or from having partners. This attention is called "the all-encompassing attention," and His bestowal of favors proceeding from this attention is designated as "the all-encompassing favoring." This all-encompassing attention is also described as "the manifestation of Unity"—the overall manifestation of His Names throughout the universe. God has another regard for, or view of, the realms of existence, species, things, and individual beings. This proceeds from His special mercy, wisdom, care, and justice. In addition to His universal and majestic attention and regard, manifested as preserving and maintaining everything with mercy, arranging, administering and controlling with wisdom, guarding and caring with compassion, giving everything its due and restoring rights with justice, and keeping the whole universe with all its parts down to the minutest ones in balance, and so on, He also has particular attention, regard and favoring for individuals with special capacities; this is particularly so for those who have a capacity, concern, and endeavor that enables them to represent the entire species, including primarily the Prophets and pure, saintly scholars and saints. This special consideration and favoring of His is known as "the manifestation of Oneness"—the concentrated manifestation of His Names on individual things or beings.

When the Absolute One of Favoring has such special regard for any of His servants, it is as if their corporeal existence, which is considered to be their unreal nature, completely disappears and is replaced by an ever-young, active existence, by means of which an initiate can reach in an attempt to rise to the horizon of those endowed with sincerity. This form of extra promotion is very different from the ranks and gifts that come or are conferred as the result of "the certainty of knowledge." The saintly people of God have called the special Divine regard and attention that bring this honor "the manifestation of knowledge." By means of this attention and regard that open the door to "the special knowledge from God's Presence" for an initiate, the nature of everything suddenly changes, with the result that a person becomes like an angel, the body takes on the quality of the spirit, fire changes into a cool, peaceful place, salty seas are transformed into rivers of Paradise, and poison becomes an antidote.

Initiates or travelers on the way to God who are awarded with such attention and regard reach the horizon of being heroes of the heart and spirit through the development of their inner faculties. They breathe heavenly air while on the earth and become a polished mirror where the Ultimate Truth manifests Himself with His Attributes. To express this special gift, a saintly friend of God said:

> When the Light of the Ultimate Truth is reflected,
> The home of the heart is filled with light;
> And this nest of the body changes
> Into a genuine, pure substance.

The continuity of this gift depends on constantly having one's eyes fixed on the Realm of the Divine Names and Attributes in utmost respect, and continuously turning to the Realm of Divinity with worship and devotion. Even though those who have felt love on the horizon of knowledge of God and sipped the spiritual pleasure at the peak of love and enthusiasm do not feel weariness in constantly turning to the Almighty at His door, the initiates who have not yet been able to have a share in knowledge of God to such an extent may show signs of slackening. For this reason, those who pursue God's good pleasure and love should continuously stand at His door, bent double, and never show signs of weariness or tedium. As God's noblest Messenger, upon him be peace and blessings, states, "So long as you show no signs of weariness, God will not abandon His consideration or cut off His gifts";[141] thus, the continuity of God's gifts and consideration depends on one's never turning one's eyes from His door. If we do not turn our eyes from His door, we will not be deprived of His breezes of regard, and our prayers and worship will not be left unrewarded.

Those who act erroneously in turning to Him are deprived of His consideration of mercy and compassion; those who have no resolution to get near to Him through worship suffer loss and deprivation. He says, "Whoever draws near to Me by a hand-span, I will draw near to him by a yard."[142]

Divine gifts come as the Divine considerations of mercy in response to complete, continuous turning to God Almighty. If the heart is not purified of attachment to everything else other than Him, so long as God's Mercy, Which surpasses His Sacred Wrath, does not manifest Itself with special favor—then the Divine attention and regard may not continue. Turning to Him continuously and maintaining constant self-supervision are important dynamics for reaching every destination pursued and surmounting every obstacle. Initiates or travelers on the way to God should refrain from acting erroneously by turning to God continuously and exercising self-supervision while they are trying to carry out their known religious responsibilities so that they are not left deprived of the breezes that come through faithfulness, loyalty, and steadfastness.

---

141 *al-Bukhari*, "Iman" 32; *Muslim*, "Musafirun" 215. (Tr.)

142 *al-Bukhari*, "Tawhid" 15; *Muslim*, "Dhikr" 20–22. (Tr.)

We are reminded above that God Almighty demonstrates both universal and particular attention and consideration or regard. However, just as He employs apparent means and causes as veils before His Dignity and Grandeur, so too He may employ either a Prophet, saint or teacher as a veil before His consideration and attention for certain servants, offering His gifts through their hands. This type of treatment may be a sign of the special honor He confers on that Prophet, saint or teacher, just as it may be a test for initiates or seekers as well. Therefore, even when His gifts come to us by means of one of His beloved servants, we must recognize that they are from Him absolutely; we must believe that it is He Who is the genuine source of all the gifts that come to us, and it is He Who sends them. If we want to kiss the hands of those whom He employs as means, we should kiss them with the conviction that they are only the means employed by the Almighty. Indeed, we should kiss those hands without being negligent of the True Source and Agent, because the respect shown for them is, in fact, respect for the knowledge, attention, and regard that come to us through them, and also, therefore, an acknowledgement of the True Origin or Source of all bounties and gifts.

There are many maxims circulating among people, such as, "Service from the initiate and breath from the guide!"; and "Please lend me a hand, O guide; render your efforts O child!"; and "Show attention so that you may be shown attention." All of these indicate the same reality that any attention or regard usually comes in return for the attention and regard that has been shown. So long as the apparent causes or means are viewed only as causes and means, and the Creator or the Original and True Cause of all causes is acknowledged as the origin and sender of all gifts, it is not harmful to feel and show respect for the Prophets, saints or teachers who are employed as causes or means. What is harmful is attributing creative effect to apparent causes or means and distributing the Divine acts—for example, creating, inventing, fashioning, giving life, causing to die, and providing—among animate or inanimate things or forces.

According to our belief in His Oneness, all changes, formations, and transformations from the microcosm (atoms) to the "normocosm," (humanity) and from there to the macrocosm (the universe) occur by His regard or turning to existence with His Attributes and Names; all instances of maintenance, sustenance, and rearing are through His all-embracing attention. All the uninterrupted and all-encompassing manifestations of His, and the continuous changes, alterations, transformations, forms, and colors that we observe in existence as a result of His manifestations are the imprints of His regard or consideration. Viewing things and events from this perspective is true guidance, while viewing them only on their own account, as being independent from Divine creation, administration, and control, is deviation from the right path. An insightful initiate whose eyes are fixed on the Almighty's works and whose heart is turned toward His acts, Names, Attributes, and even His Essence that are beyond these works—indeed, any initiate according to his or her level of knowledge and certainty—becomes occupied with praying, "O my God! I ask You to enable me to be resigned to Your judgment after whatever happens to me, and for a happy life after death, and the pleasure of observing Your Face!" They make every morning and evening of their journeying toward meeting God a moment of meeting with Him.

Whatever such initiates observe, they do not see it as something that is restricted to its corporeal existence but rather how it actually is with its nature and essence. On the contrary, those who are unable to turn to the Almighty as turning to Him requires and whose view of things is restricted to their materiality cannot view anything in its true nature or identity—for anyone deprived of a face turned toward the Almighty has no "eyes" to see with. Those who have no eyes to see with are unaware of the correct way to look or give attention, and those who are unaware of the correct way to look or give attention are not given attention or regard. It is only those who are able to look at everything, particularly at the human face, with insight who always gaze upon the Divine Names in these mirrors; it is only they who are absorbed in knowledge of the All-Holy One who is called by these Names; it is only they who advance toward the observation of His Attributes of Glory with the eyes of the spiritual intellect, entranced in astonishment; it is only they who boil up with the desire to watch the realms far beyond the horizon of observation of the secret; it is only they who travel between amazement, stupor, and passion.

There are two points to be noted concerning how the Prophets—particularly, the Prince of the Prophets—turn to God. On account of his mission and transcendent knowledge of God, the Prophet, upon him be the most perfect of blessings and peace, turns to and views God as the Lord of all time and space and the whole of creation, viewing and evaluating all things and events from this perspective. He is both a student and teacher of the book of the universe, the chief guide of the palace of the world, the exuberant herald of the exhibition of things and events, the most sincere representative of servanthood to God, and the never-deceiving leader on the way to the eternal happiness. Although these qualities are shared by all the Prophets, our master, the Prophet Muhammad, upon him be peace and blessings, has particular wishes and demands that arise from the particularities of his mission. These particular wishes and demands of his may be regarded as, in addition to the extra attention and consideration shown to him by God in return for his perfect response to God's attention and consideration, his request for God's particular, extra help and consideration for his Community.

In addition to turning to God in perfect response to God's consideration for him, the Prophet Muhammad, upon him be peace and blessings, demonstrates universal attention and consideration with mercy and kindness for all of creation; this is manifested as distributing what he receives and thus responding to God's treatment of him with his treatment of all creation. This kind of attention and consideration on the part of the Prophet can, by God's leave, change coal to diamonds, stones and earth to gold, and extremely hardened hearts to wax. More than this, with a few moments of his presence, the Prophet can elevate the consciences which have been blinded by arrogance, wrongdoing, erroneous and prejudiced viewpoints, and blind imitation of ancestry to the horizon of being the Companions. He can transform apparently living corpses that until this auspicious meeting have been crawling on the ground into doves that wing their way through the heaven of perfect humanity as if having experienced a rapid spiritual metamorphosis.

Since they are vicegerents of God and the successors of Prophet Muhammad, upon him be peace and blessings, the scholars who sincerely practice the Religion and the perfect saints are faultless and sincere in their turning to God and effective in their attention and consideration for their followers. They act as veils before the glorious actions of the Almighty in penetrating hearts, guiding spirits, and transforming some natures by God's leave. This is what is usually meant by the concept of "attention" in Sufism.

Those beloved servants of God look at the elevated realms not with their eyes but with their insight. One can see only this corporeal realm with one's eyes. But insight penetrates the corporeal realm and the immaterial one, the realms beyond, and the truth of everything. For it is the sight of the innermost heart, which is the meeting point of the outer and inner realms and the focus of God Almighty's sight, much like the spiritual intellect that is regarded as the first observatory of the inner realms of existence. A person can observe his or her own horizon only from this observatory; the showers of Divine gifts pour unto it; and the Eternal All-Observing One treats people according to its being prosperous or in ruin. For this reason, we should always have our eyes fixed on Him, keep our hearts turned to Him, and be in expectation of His gifts so that "coral" and "pearls" may pour unto that house of God from the realms beyond.

The Prophets and saints, whose attention and consideration function as explained above, are luminous means for Divine gifts to reach their communities or followers. Not only receiving their attention, but also shaking hands with them, remaining in their presence, listening to their sermons, and sharing their atmosphere are means of receiving Divine gifts. Although there is an important place given to the attention of spiritual guides in all the ways of Sufism, the Mevlevis and Malamites assign it special importance. There are some among the leaders of these two ways who regard attention as one of the essentials of spiritual journeying. According to them, an initiate or traveler can, by God's leave, rise to the horizon of feeling attraction and being attracted toward God through an instance of attention from the guide, and thus cover long distances that normally will be covered in long years of journeying in an instant. This attention is called "royal attention."

Among the Sufis are some who interpret *nazar* (attention) as initiates or travelers fixing their eyes on where they will step (noticing their steps) and remaining distant from anything or anyone that will separate them from the Almighty. This interpretation must be about those who have reached the horizon of *nazar-qadam* ("attention-step")[143] at the final point in spiritual journeying. The turning or attention to God which relates to all travelers is that they try to comprehend the Almighty's acts and practices, each according to their capacity and the horizon of their relationship with His Names and Attributes; that they perceive their innate helplessness and poverty, relying on Him and asking Him for help with an expression of looking for points of support and asking for help in their consciences; that they respond with thankfulness to the gifts coming to them in return for turning to Him, and zealously endeavor to be favored with more and more such gifts. This act of turning to God is open to everyone and safer because it is far from show and affectation.

> *O my God! Forgive us, have mercy on us, be pleased with us, accept our good deeds, admit us to Paradise, save us from the Fire, and improve all our acts and states. And bestow Your blessings and peace upon our Master, the Master of all the children of Adam, on his pure Family and Companions altogether.*

---

143 The horizon of *nazar-qadam* (attention-step) means that an initiate can place his feet where his sight reaches. It signifies the highest point from where they can see the created realms under their feet. (Tr.)

SUBUHAT-I WAJH
(THE FLOOD OF GOD'S FACIAL LIGHT)

The *subuhat-i Wajh* ("the flood of God's Facial Light") is the flood of light that God Almighty causes to pour out so that He may eliminate all else but Him from the hearts of the travelers who are on the way to Him, and make those pure hearts feel His all-transcending Existence. Since what is meant by the word *Wajh* ("the Face") is the Divine Essence, and this Light, which surrounds the horizon of all human sensations and feelings, contains or encompasses the lights of the Divine Names and Attributes of Glory, some have preferred to call this "the Light of the Essence." In the face of this all-encompassing Light, Which pours down without any veils, a traveler feels the reality that *Everything is perishable (and so perishing) except His "Face" (His eternal Self)* (28:88) is manifested in the horizon of their inner perceptions and everything other than Him, including even His Names, is wiped away. Fully surrounded by this Light, the travelers endowed with knowledge of God find themselves in different states of astonishment and even beyond astonishment.

According to the Sufis, all things and events (the truths of things) comprise the manifestations of the Divine Names. In addition to the Divine Names Which are the essence of existence, there are the Names that denote that the All-Majestic Divine Being is absolute free from having any defects or partners. These Names function as veils before the actions of the All-Majestic Divine Essence. The Sufis say, "There are seventy or seven hundred veils preventing us from observing the Divine Essence of Majesty. If these veils of Dignity and Grandeur were to be removed for an instant, everything would be wiped out by the manifestation of the Light of the Divine Essence, with the result that neither the earth nor the heavens would remain, nor would the names or any being that is called by a name other than His." This means that were the Divine Essence to manifest Him with His Uniqueness—some call this the manifestation of Divine Unity—both the existent beings and their individually identified existences would disappear completely.

Those who are absorbed in the manifestations of the Light of the Divine Essence perceive that all time and space is surrounded by that Light and, partly under the influence of their temperament and the spiritual path they are following, tend to express their impressions by saying, "There is no existent being save He," or "There is no being witnessed save He," and conclude that whatever exists apparently is a perishable shadow.

Indeed, the whole of existence originates from the Light of His Existence; all actions and happenings depend on His Names of Glory; all states, attributes, and features have their source in His Attributes of Glory, such as Knowledge, Will, and Power. To explain more clearly, all things and events comprise the manifestations of Divine Attributes and Names. Everyone absorbed in knowledge of God perceives on the "face" of the All-Beautiful Names the All-Holy One Who is called by these Names, tries to recognize Him properly by means of His Attributes of Glory, is surrounded by the Light of His Essence if they reach the point where they can inwardly experience this Light, travels or is taken from "astonishment" to "amazement," from "amazement" to "stupor," and from "stupor" to "passion," and consequently no longer feels any existent thing or being, including their own selves, other than the All-Holy Being. Even if they have the ability to be aware of other things, they never wish to be so, for they look from the horizon of their "secret," and their sight is controlled by their spiritual intellect. Do they act so out of their own volition or involuntarily, or is this state of theirs the consequence of their feeling attraction or being attracted toward Him? No one who has not experienced this state can answer these questions, and those who have experienced it have remained silent. In fact, the tongue has nothing to say at this point where reason and intellect are silent and remain a few steps behind. If reason knows its place, it must keep itself behind the heart and maintain itself in silent supervision.

Since this station is the station where the One of Absolute Grace and Perfection manifests His Existence with His Dignity and Grandeur, one of these two things happens: either all tongues cannot help but remain silent or concepts and words change into symbols, signs, and allusions under the influence of the Divine Grandeur and Majesty. Some of those symbols and allusions may cause confusion or wrong understanding, and can therefore become—and indeed have become—a means of trial for common people. However, the disappearance of things and events in our world of perceptions due to the intensity of the Divine Essence's manifestation and of His Grandeur and absolute Infinity is one thing, while their actual appearance is quite another.

Some exacting Sufi scholars describe the mental and spiritual state of those who are absorbed in knowledge of God, in which they are unaware of the existence of anything other than Him, with the concept of "*istılam*," which means the complete vanishing of a thing or obliteration. This cannot be considered to be incorrect from the viewpoint of relevant considerations. To explain a bit further, while experiencing and being intoxicated with compound amazement and stupor, surrounded by the manifestations of Divine Perfection in the horizon of Divine Grace and by the manifestations of Divine Grace at the peak of Divine Perfection, those endowed with knowledge of God come to their senses by means of special Divine help, which they call "the veils of special help," for a period when they can perform their religious obligations, perform them carefully and deeply as befits their level, and then they are lost again on the horizon where the Light of Divine Essence is manifested.

In the same way that apparent causes are created and placed as veils between the Divine acts or practices and things and events so that those of a superficial view do not criticize the Divine Wisdom, Will, and Power because of some apparently ugly, disagreeable, or insignificant incidents, "the veils of special help" function as special grace and favoring in order to return an initiate who has reached the final point in the spiritual journeying where they live absorbed, feeling that everything is lost in the manifestations of the Divine Essence's Dignity, Grandeur and absolute Infinity, to the horizon of Names and Attributes, and to remind them of the fact that the duties of servanthood or worship are never canceled. Furthermore, such grace and favoring also mean allowing initiates to take a breath and enabling them to experience distinguishing or differentiation in utter absorption. Therefore, while an initiate who is endowed with knowledge of God lives in a state of intoxication and even utter annihilation because of the overwhelming flood of Divine Facial Light, and is unaware of apparent existence, the duty of worship, and the necessity of remembrance due to being lost in the Light of the Absolute Existence, and the profundity of their relationship with the Absolutely Worshipped and the Absolutely Remembered One respectively, they are returned to the flow of worship through "the veils of special help," and breathe the air of "You alone do we worship and You alone do we ask for help," acting with the consciousness of being a servant.

Some travelers on the way to God who are not able to direct every step of theirs toward their destination in the light of Prophethood may utter some words incompatible with Islamic essentials under the influence of this state. Since they are sincere and sound in faith, and in adherence to Islam and the noble Prophet, upon him be peace and blessings, such utterances of theirs should be viewed as a consequence of being overcome by the state in which they find themselves. If, however, there are, and have been, some whose utterances actually originate in their belief and are intended to philosophize, we advise those from among them who are alive to follow the way of the Prophet, upon him be the most perfect of blessings and peace, and we refer to God the matter of those who have died.

It must also be for the preservation of the beloved friends of God that "the veils of special help" have been placed. The travelers on God's way believe and say, "He is the Lord, and I am a servant; He is the Creator, and I am one created; He is the All-Powerful, and I am innately impotent; He is the All-Wealthy, and I am poor and needy. I owe my existence to the Light of His Existence, and my life to the manifestation of His Life; I subsist because of the Self-Subsistent by Whom all subsist." Even if this differentiation or distinction fades in some states of self-obliteration or annihilation, their conviction is that which we have mentioned above.

In fact, even though those who continue their journey according to the strict observance of the religious essentials may sometimes see everything veiled under the flood of Divine Facial Light and experience complete amazement or astonishment, they try not to make any error in self-possession, and if they become aware that they have made such an error, they correct any of their words that might be liable to misconception or confusion. They do their utmost not to cause others to become exposed to danger.

In one his quatrains, Mawlana Jalalu'd-Din ar-Rumi says:

There are thousands of shining roses in the garden;
There are roses and violets smelling of musk;
There is water flowing abundantly in the streams;
These are all excuses; it is only He Who exists.

In another quatrain, which is so clear that it can correct any misunderstanding which the above quatrain may have caused, ar-Rumi expresses the same meaning as follows:

O human, you are such that both your existence and
non-existence are from Him;
It is He Who is the capital of both joy and grief.
But you have no eyes so that you can see His Power or works;
It is His Art and Power Which are observed in your existence.

The feeling of vanishing and disappearance experienced under the flood of Divine Facial Light has both positive and hazardous consequences. It is worth appreciation that one favored with such a level of advancement on the way to God because of continuous turning to Him sees everything as the result of Divine manifestations and feels the whole of existence surrounded by His Light, provided that he preserves the balance established by the Shari'a. However, uttering words incompatible with religious essentials and suggesting self-extolment, being unaware of the balance of the Shari'a, under the influence of the feeling of self-annihilation is risky, forbidden, and misleading. For this reason, the feeling of self-annihilation or intoxication may cause loss and perdition for those who have not been able to perfectly adopt or absorb the criteria of the Shari'a.

In addition to always feeling a deep connection with God and turning to Him with love and enthusiasm, a traveler on God's way must always pursue self-possession, attribute whatever exists to Him exclusively, not confuse the Eternal One with the created, and consider such false doctrines as Union, Incarnation, Pantheism, and Monism as deviation, heresy, and disrespect for the One Whom they love and worship. They must try always to act in self-possession, and breathe awe and respect.

Some Sufi scholars have considered reaching the horizon where the Light of the Essence is manifested, and the experience of self-annihilation and oblivion which emerges in the heart as the result of being favored with this manifestation, as the highest rank in the spiritual journeying toward the Almighty. As for the manifestations that are known as flashes or dawning or radiances or illuminations, these are names of almost the same thing which are used to designate the surprises that come to travelers as they rise, encouraging them upwards more and more. They also serve as gleams shining in the minds or hearts of the travelers as evidence from the outer and inner worlds, as a result of reflection, deliberation, and contemplation. These illuminate the path of the travelers, urging them to advance without stopping, and indicating the destination. However, the travelers cannot fully know the Ever-Sought One in their conscience. In fact, it is absolutely impossible to know His Essence, for His Essence is beyond the knowledge of any created being. A beloved friend of God said:

> How can it be possible to describe the Master?
> So it is incumbent on us to avoid describing Him.

The manifestation of the flood of Divine Facial Light is very different from the manifestations mentioned above. Travelers favored with this manifestation are unable to perceive anything, including themselves. They cannot even feel the light of the Divine Names and Attributes in the face of the continuous and encompassing rays of the concentrated manifestations of the Divine Names on them individually. Furthermore, some among those who are fully absorbed in the manifestation of the Divine Facial Light cannot feel the distinction or individual identification at the rank of Knowledge, and adding to the Prophetic Tradition, "There was God and nothing existed besides Him," the statement that expresses their state, "Now it is the same as it was then,"[144] they are unable to see the realities of things, and like Jami', maintain that everything is a mirage.

This state is continuous in some, and they see their state of self-annihilation and intoxication as the reality and all the existence we perceive with our senses as the product of our imagination and conception. However, some others, who temporarily experience the flood of Divine Facial Light, return to the world of distinction or discrimination. This temporary perception, or the temporary manifestation of Divine Facial Light to some, is called "the lightning of manifestation." They preserve their self-possession in adherence to and strict observance of the Shari'a, and always try to remain awake. While those who have not been able to adopt or absorb the spirit of the Shari'a so deeply as to make it their second nature, or whose subconscious is not under the control of the Religion, can expose themselves to the danger of considering the All-Holy Creator within their scope of perception. This means overstepping one's limits, attempting to restrict the

144 For the *hadith* and the addition, see notes 70 and 71. (Tr.)

Absolute Infinity, and regarding the All-Encompassing as both the all-encompassing and the encompassed at the same time. This is contrary to the fact that the Legislator of the Shari'a has restricted our scope of thought to the realms of Divine works, acts, and Names, and has forbidden us from thinking about the Divine Essence.

Whether it occurs as the manifestation of the all-encompassing Light of the Divine Essence, or "the lightning of manifestation," all these manifestations are a special consideration or favor of God Almighty for the heroes of the spiritual life. This is also a call to those who study and perceive what lies beyond the veil of things and events as taught by the Prophet Muhammad, Ahmad, Mahmud, Mustafa, upon him be as many blessings and as much peace as to fill the heavens and earth, and who avoid attachment to anything fleeting and mortal, to turn to the "Ka'ba of Lordship" or the Monarch Who has the Attributes of Existence, Eternality, Permanence, Oneness, Non-resemblance with creation, and Self-Subsistence, with all the inner and outer senses. This special consideration may also be either a kind favor for the travelers' turning to the Almighty or a special regard of God for some talented spirits. Looking at it from another aspect, it is a manifestation for those who have preserved their primordial nature and endeavored to develop it to awaken in them the zeal to progress toward the Divine Being; it is a special gift of spiritual knowledge to those who have attained knowledge of God.

In fact, whenever travelers or initiates, or those endowed with knowledge of God, are resolved to reach the point where they can perceive the manifestation of the Light of the Divine Essence, the All-Bestowing One awards them with surprising gifts, and enables them to adorn their inner world, thus purifying them. By equipping the inner and outer dimensions of their being with respect for and awe of Him, the All-Bestowing One prepares them for His special presence, and by making their spirit aware of the mysteries of His friendship, He shows them the direction to which they must turn. Also, by engendering seclusion within them, He sharpens the feeling in their spirit of turning to Him alone, and

He elevates them to the horizon of the life of the spirit and heart by causing them to undergo a series of inner transformations. By thus making them continuously travel in the shades of meeting with Him, and causing their faculties to feel the urge to meet with Him, the All-Bestowing One readies them for His intimacy. Then He enables their secret to feel the mysteries of His Essence, crowns their hearts with considerations of His Holy Presence, and realizes their dreams of meeting with Him through the manifestation of the flood of His Facial Light. In the end, travelers who have been completely distant from everything other than Him turn to Him with all their being, and the All-Holy Creator honors them through the Light of His Face with extra favors which neither eyes can see nor ears can hear.

How beautiful the following couplet by Şemseddin Sivasi[145] is in this respect:

No one can meet with the Ultimate Truth
without being distant from all else;
The Treasure is not opened in a heart
before the heart is filled with light.

O God! O, the One Whom eyes cannot see, nor thoughts can comprehend, nor those who attempt to describe Him can describe, nor events can change! Forgive us, have mercy on us, and guide us to the path most sound!

And bestow Your blessings and peace on the most honorable of Your creation, Muhammad, and on his Family and Companions altogether!

---

145 Ahmed Şemseddin Sivasi (1520–1597) was born in Tokat province in northeastern Turkey. He taught in the madrasa of the highest education in Istanbul for a short period. Then he returned to Tokat and a while later was invited to Sivas by the governor. He lived there as a spiritual guide for about fifty years until his death. (Tr.)

WARIDAT AND *MAWHIBA* (GIFTS AND FAVOR)

M*awhiba* (favor) literally means benevolence, kindness, and extra Divine bounties, while *waridat* (gifts) denotes what occurs to or emerges in one's heart as a Divine gift. The Sufis use them to signify God Almighty's special attention and consideration for those who travel toward Him, and His particular enlightenment and guidance, which can be described as "the lights of Divine Attributes" or "the lights of Divine Names." They are manifested in certain circumstances in the inner world of initiates so that they can see and evaluate everything correctly.

First and foremost, the Prophets and then all saints and pure, saintly scholars, including even minor saints, are favored with such gifts. However, the gifts that come to the Prophets, whether in the form of inspiration or Revelation, are certain to be from God, and it is impossible for Satan and the carnal soul to interfere with them. For this reason, they have a certainty and strength of evidence, and are therefore binding for believers. As for the gifts coming to saints or saintly scholars in the form of inspiration, since neither saints nor saintly scholars have absolute protection against Satan or the carnal soul, they are acceptable only in the case when they are in perfect accord with the Qur'an and the Prophet's Sunna, and are not binding for others.

Although there are differences between the literal meanings of "gifts" and "favor," and these terms are sometimes used to denote feelings of joy or sorrow, or exhilaration or distress, or expansion or contrition, appearing in the inner world of humans, the majority of Sufis tend to use them interchangeably and mean by both the sacred meanings that emerge in, or the breezes of inspiration that come to, the heart. Human free will has no part in their emergence or coming. Both the gifts and favor are Divine presents bestowed on the beloved servants of God without the means of either eyes or ears; they cannot be obtained through reason or logic.

Such a manifestation of Divine gifts sometimes occurs without the servant's turning to God or doing anything religious; sometimes it happens as a result of deep, serious reflective thought or concentration. In both cases, it is a special Divine radiance that is beyond the perception of senses or consciousness. However, a *hadith* the meaning of which is directly from God refers to human endeavor in receiving this manifestation and reminds us of how important human will, tendencies, and choices are in God's sight. It is as follows: "Whoever draws near to Me by a hand-span, I will draw near to him by a yard."[146] The maxim, "Endeavor is from the disciple and breath from the guide," is also good in expressing this reality; while the maxim, "The cessation of regular recitations causes the cessation of gifts," is a serious reminder which we should not neglect in our relationship with God, the Ultimate Truth. Indeed, just like the prayer for rain serves as a means for the rain to come, regular recitations and remembrance of God are regarded as among the most important means of obtaining the shower of gifts. Again, just like a baby who does not weep is not offered milk, the doors of the heaven are not opened to the one who neither sighs nor groans. It is true that it is a requirement of respect for God and sincerity in worshipping Him that we should not have any expectations in return for our turning to Him. However, if God has made His consideration and gifts dependent upon His servants' turning to Him, then the mysterious key to all the gifts and favors must be that we should turn to Him.

All such gifts and favors that come from God are always His extra bounties, which He grants in addition to His usual bounties. However, as stated in the couplet,

---

146 For the *hadith*, see note 141. (Tr.)

The effects of Divine effusions differ
according to the capacities of every being;
A pearl-oyster receives pearls from the rain of April,
but a snake, poison,

whether they come in the form of continuous breezes or in the form of lightning of manifestation, the gifts proceeding from the Divine Attribute of Speech manifest themselves differently according to people's capacities, sincerity, and purity of intention.

Gifts and favors sometimes suddenly emerge in the heart. They say whatever they will say, and then disappear. They sometimes appear as different signs or signals concerning a subject upon which the initiate has concentrated. In whatever way or form they come, any gift or occurrence in the heart which is in accordance with the Religion is a Divine repast, bounty, and guidance. Such a gift should be evaluated with self-possession and not be belittled.

Indeed, God Almighty sends warnings to His servants in different forms concerning whatever will happen to them, be it good or bad, agreeable or disagreeable, sweet or bitter, happy or sad, or exhilarating or distressing, and He calls on them to be aware. According to the position and responsibility of each, God sends signals to them concerning themselves or their environment, he awakens their hearts, shows them the ways of seeking refuge with His dispensation or forgiveness against His punishment, or arouses in them feelings of thankfulness by rewarding them with certain favors. Furthermore, God inspires in them some alternative ways to solve their personal or social problems, and to attain relief from the troubles they suffer. Thus, out of His compassion, He compels them toward the shores of salvation. Through such surprising gifts, God Almighty sometimes makes His valuable servants feel His continuous presence and suggests that He always cares for and protects them.

However, it sometimes happens that the suggestions of Satan or the carnal soul appear in the hearts of the travelers alongside the breezes of Divine inspiration. This is highly risky for those who are at the beginning of the journey and cannot distinguish between truth and falsehood. They may even take some thinly disguised suggestions from Satan for the "breaths" of the All-Merciful.

Since, in particular, those of "childish" nature who see human dignity and greatness in displaying extraordinary things and desire to be known as different from or greater than others, pursue unusual occurrences, Satan may deceive them by suggesting thousands of falsities, together with a few truths, which he uses as bait. The way to be able to remain free from such deception is to live in pursuit of God's approval and good pleasure in the footsteps of God's Messenger, upon him be peace and blessings, and to have, in return for servanthood to God, no expectations of extraordinariness such as wonder-working, or of spiritual pleasures.

Some maintain that the Divine gifts of inspiration and angelic evocations come together with some thrill or feeling of coldness, followed by a spiritual pleasure and contentment, while Satanic suggestions cause bewilderment, anxiety, and debasement. But it is difficult to say that this is always true. For this reason, what we should do is not to base our relationship with God on such favors or gifts, and we should not behave as creditors waiting for something in return for our worship; rather, we should act as one who is in debt, in deep awareness of our servanthood, regarding living in accordance with the Qur'an and the Sunna as His greatest gift and favor to us, and simply pursuing His approval and good pleasure instead of seeking extraordinary occurrences.

Any gift or favor that blows into us from the Divine Names and Attributes of Glory is both a special compliment and a warning to us; they are sent to strengthen our sincerity and faithfulness. Through such a compliment and warning, a traveler turns to God completely, desiring only Him and pursuing only His approval and good pleasure. Any gift of inspiration occurs in the heart unexpectedly, as if a manifestation of the Divine Name the All-Overwhelming, removing from the heart the desires for or tendencies toward fleeting things. Even though the spirit experiences intoxication during these moments, it usually finds itself in a wave of exhilaration and contentment. It is moved more with the desire of servanthood, and as a result of the ensuing virtuous cycle between the manners of servanthood and the flow of gifts, the traveler to God finds himself under a heavy shower of gifts.

Divine gifts sometimes manifest themselves in the form of "the lights of Divine Attributes." They sometimes illuminate the bodies of travelers along with their hearts, and take these illuminated travelers out of the narrow confines and corporeality to the height of the angels. Through the treasure of, "There is no power or strength save with God," the gifts make people powerful in their innate weakness and rich in their innate poverty, transforming them into polished mirrors reflecting God. These gifts are followed by new ones, with the result that God widens the horizon of knowledge and perception of such people, sharpens their resolution for worship and obeying God, equips them with an unshakeable resistance against sins, and increases in them endurance in the face of calamities by showing them their true nature and consequences. He also enables them to concentrate on their willpower against hastiness in their spirit, inspiring in them that there is an appointed term for any result to be obtained, and He directs their hearts to good, permanent deeds by showing them the true nature of transient things. The travelers favored with these gifts completely submit to the Will and commands of God, even if advancing to the observation of His "Face," and they are resigned to all His judgments concerning themselves while in the world, living each minute and second of their lives illuminated by the lights of His Attributes.

With their enlightened intellects, they read and interpret the corporeal realm correctly, and continuously advance toward Him; with their purified hearts, they observe the inner dimension of existence and keep pace with spiritual beings. With the horizon of their "secrets," they set out to transcend all existence and try to hunt the mysteries of Divinity, feeling as if they are hearing the speech of angels.

Those with enlightened hearts and intellects are not only perfect in their relationship with God Almighty but they are also, by

God's leave, able to solve all the problems they encounter. They easily penetrate the spirits of those who enter their atmosphere and can always move the hearts of those around them with knowledge and love of God.

It is by means of such lights of Divine Attributes and Essential Qualities that the hearts of the travelers to God favored with such gifts become a cataract of knowledge of God; the spirits of God's lovers overflow with Divine radiances, and the exacting sages, or people of wisdom, become translators of Divine mysteries. The horizons of the discovery and observation of Divine truths become clear to wakeful hearts, and the truths behind the Divine Names become manifest.

Some have viewed the light of these gifts as the rise or appearance of the Light of Prophethood in talented spirits, and all the favors to come as dependent on always turning to that source of light—and they have done their utmost to remain devoted to that source without suffering any eclipse. While they are so devoted to the Sun of the heaven of Messengership, upon him be peace and blessings, we ordinary people should be sensitive, respectful, and unbiased toward the saints and saintly scholars, who are like the moon in relation to the sun, so that we may be favored with such a light of gifts.

There is not another light more powerful and penetrating than this light which is regarded as being among the gifts of Prophethood. As for the Light of the Seal of Prophethood, it is the sole source of all the lights of Prophethood, and it has precedence over them all. As the Prophet Muhammad, upon him be peace and blessings, is the matchless pearl in the sight of God with respect to his mission, he is also peerless in human perfection. He is the seed of the tree of creation, and the ultimate cause for existence with respect to his mission. He is the most lovable to God and the most advanced in friendship with Him. He is the sole light that removes all the veils of darkness, and the dove that wings on the horizon of "the two-bow-length's nearness (to God) or even nearer." Eyes have been opened and the white and black distinguished through his guidance; the mysteries behind the veil of existence have been cleared through his messages, and the pains and anxieties of humanity have ceased, hearts have become calm through the glad tidings he gave.

All of us have recognized God Almighty with His absolute transcendence, holiness, and freedom from anything unsuitable for Him by means of the Prophet Muhammad, upon him be peace and blessings, and it is again by means of him that we have learned how to love the Creator and obtain His friendship. We had no knowledge of true love and friendship; it is by means of the light the Prophet Muhammad diffused that we have come to know what loving, being loved, making friends, and acting in friendship mean.

> *Upon him be the most perfect of blessings and most complete of salutations to the fullness of the earth of the heavens, and on his Family and Companions, who were the conveyors to all later generations of all the basic pillars, principles, and precepts of the Religion.*

KHULLA (SINCERE FRIENDSHIP)

Khulla means sincere friendship. It can also denote brother/sisterhood, or loyal friendship. Some have interpreted *khulla* as penetrating into the depth of something to change its nature, or enveloping it from all sides so that it gains a second nature. The Prophet Abraham, upon him be peace, who always lived in the horizon of contentment, realized his spiritual essence or reached the rank of sincere or intimate friendship with God by means of the extraordinary radiances from God Almighty, and by experiencing continuous inner revolutions; it was thus that he reached his horizon of perfection in feeling, thought, endeavor, and preaching. Finally, he became the voice of a different nature, proclaiming God, the Ultimate Truth, by whatever he did and wherever he was. In return, God chose him as His intimate friend and called him "My intimate friend."

Compared with sincere or intimate friendship's influence on and penetrability into the heart, love invades the "pupil of the heart," or the "seed of the heart," which is regarded as the core of the spiritual intellect, and gives it its own color, and makes it speak in its own language. In a heart which moves and groans with love of God, nothing remains of anything other than God, and all other interests than that felt in God vanish one after the other, with the result that it is only He Who is felt, thought of, and talked about.

Sincere friendship (with God) was entrusted to the Prophet Abraham's nature as a seed. It was an initial donation bestowed on Him in acknowledgement of his relationship with God Almighty and a gift given to him by the All-Merciful for his ingrained loyalty to Him. This initial gift or donation also symbolized that he would become an *imam* (leader) for those who would follow him. However, ignoring the gifts and favors particular to it, this intimate friendship with God manifested itself in the Lover and Beloved of God, upon him be peace and blessings, in the form of love as a special Divine regard or consideration for his transcending knowledge of God and intimacy with Him.

Sincere friendship is pure loyalty. As for love, it is passion, yearning, and consumption or burning. For this reason, sincere friendship is primarily marked by enthusiasm and thankfulness and then with sadness or sorrow. In other words, while it is enthusiasm and thankfulness that prevails most in people of sincere friendship, the people of love are known with remembrance, reflection, and continuous sorrow. How interesting it is that the Master of creation, upon him be peace and blessings, lived in continuous sorrow marked with hope, prayer, and entreaty.

God's Messenger was a loving and loved one whose sincere friendship was transformed into love and zeal or enthusiasm, and he was aware of being honored with such a favor. He knew that the Almighty loved him beyond all modalities of quality and quantity, and constantly breathed love beyond measure. He demanded no station, no rank, no rewards. He had perfect knowledge of the One Whom he worshipped and so he worshipped Him, deepened his faith with knowledge of Him, and ran in the tracks of more and more knowledge. As his knowledge increased, he loved Him more, from the bottom of his heart, without expecting any return and without taking reunion with Him into consideration, and with the most serious self-possession of worship and servanthood. It was God Almighty's extraordinary consideration for that Owner of the most powerful will among creation and a favor of His above all favors that the Prophet Muhammad was able to love and yearn for Him in a way befitting His Grandeur. He was the peerless hero of this highest rank. It was also he, upon him be blessings and peace to the fullness of the heavens and the earth, who gave sincere friendship the color of his sincerity and crowned that deep loyalty in human essence with love, yearning, and enthusiasm.

It is unquestionable that sincere friendship is a great rank and gift. All instances or breezes of familiarity, intimacy, inner peace and reassurance, and contentment that blow into the hearts of the faithful servants of God, the Ultimate Truth, are each an embroidery in the fabric of sincere friendship, or a spark from the love of or yearning for God. Moreover, the spiritual pleasures generated by this friendship, love, and yearning are a particular or universal manifestation of Divine consideration for turning toward that station, and breezes that blow on the slopes of the heart. As for love, it is the basic weft of that fabric, and it is the flame which produces that spark of sincere friendship. It is a fact that Divine acts are free from pursuing any ulterior motives, but we can say that the brightest wisdom in the creation of the universe is love. The series of creation appeared because of the Creator's sacred love for His Art and His will to see it, and He has given the one who loves and is loved by Him most its most important, greatest result.

Sincere or intimate friendship is a means of spiritual reconciliation, agreement, and harmony between creatures on account of its essential elements of mutual familiarity and accord. For this reason, the Prophet Abraham, the sincere Friend of the All-Merciful, upon him be peace, who is regarded as the hero of sincere friendship, was a comprehensive example and leader for those who were to come later; he was one who was able to concentrate all hearts upon a certain common point. The Qur'an describes this quality of the Prophet Abraham with the following expression of appreciation: "*Indeed I will make you an imam (leader) for all people*" (2: 124). Indeed, he is a leader for all who will succeed him in respect of the essence or spirit of the Religion. This spirit or essence is fully developed to its final borders by means of the noblest Leader or Guide of all, who is God's beloved and the greatest of the universal men, upon him be peace and blessings.

As clearly demonstrated by his blessed life, the noble Prophet Abraham, the sincere Friend of the All-Merciful, upon him be peace, was a pursuer of deeper and deeper contentment. As for the blessed, noblest Lover and Beloved of God, as stated in verse, "*In the assembly of honor, composed of the loyal and truthful, in the Presence of the One, All-Omnipotent, Sovereign*" (54: 55), he is the king seated on the throne of the greatest loyalty and truthfulness. He—the Prophet Muhammad, upon him be peace and blessings—was such a light-diffusing observed of Divine truths, setting his feet at the farthest point that his eyes reached, that he was not only at the unattainable peaks through his exceptional conceptions and observations, but also he is the most advanced of all, who "saw that which no other eyes have ever seen or will ever see, heard that which no other ears have ever heard or will ever hear, and witnessed that which no one else has ever conceived of or will ever conceive of."

Pursuing the utmost friendship and loyalty was God's special favor on God's blessed Friend, the Prophet Abraham, upon him be peace, while having an established position of friendship, loyalty, and love in God's Presence is the rank of the Master of creation, the Prophet Muhammad, upon him be peace and blessings. However, as stated in "*Follow, then, their guidance!*" (6: 90), the one who has an established position was ordered to follow, and indeed did follow, in one respect the one who was in constant pursuit of and realized God's special friendship. This was like a king following the principle, "The host's leadership in the Prayer is preferable," while visiting one of his subjects, and suggesting that the host should lead the Prayer.

In another sense, a sincere friend is one who is such a faithful companion that he shares the secret atmosphere of his friend and feels his love in the depths of his heart. It is an indubitable fact that few persons have ever been able to realize such a degree of loyalty and devotion. The Prophet Abraham, upon him be peace, is certainly the greatest hero of this realization, as he was particularly chosen for this special merit and had the mission of representing it in the best way. That sincere Friend of the All-Merciful is the brightest example of sincere friendship because he was perfectly loyal to his Friend, as stated in *"Abraham, who discharged his due, fulfilling all his duties to perfection"* (53: 37); and he was extremely sensitive in grasping the subtlety in obedience to God's every order. Also, having assigned all his faculties, including his heart, intellect, logic, and reasoning to the fulfillment of his duty, he called to the truth and proclaimed the Divine Oneness out loud wherever and in whatever circumstances he was, addressing all the outer and inner senses and faculties of his most stubborn audience, and endured all the hardships and evils he encountered with the utmost submission to and reliance on God. In addition, he entered the fire of Nimrod with a smile on his lips, and he spent his life migrating from one place to another for God's sake, leaving behind his beloved wife and little, beloved son in a completely desolate valley on God's order. Furthermore, as clearly stated in the verse, *"Then when both had submitted to God's will, and Abraham had laid him down on the side of his forehead...."* (37:103), he showed no hesitation in obeying God's order to sacrifice his son Ishmael, the fruit of his heart, the one who was a monument of forbearing and mildness and whom God had willed to be the start of a bright future.[147] He spent all his wealth in God's cause and the needy. In short, the Prophet Abraham, upon him be peace, was a perfect example in the human realm to represent the way of God. Having reached the horizon where he could be the pride of all other Prophets except the last and greatest one, he became the one whose prayer, *"And grant me a most true and virtuous renown among posterity"* (26: 84), was accepted. Accordingly, all the followers of the Divine Religion to come after him would remember and mention him with prayers and as an excellent memo-

[147] Here, the writer refers to the Prophet Abraham's attempt to sacrifice his elder son Ishmael on God's order. This was a great trial for both Abraham and Ishmael, upon them be peace, involving many instances of wisdom. By unhesitatingly obeying God's order, both Abraham and Ishmael, upon them both be peace, were greatly rewarded. God appointed Ishmael as a Prophet and made him the origin of a holy line which finally gave birth to the greatest of creation, the Prophet Muhammad, upon him be peace and blessings. (Tr.)

ry. Being one of the most distinguished, Abraham was a brilliant fruit of the Prophets who had preceded him and the luminous seed for his successors, including particularly the greatest of them, upon him be peace and blessings. When his Lord told him, *"Submit yourself wholly (to your Lord),"* he responded, *"I have submitted myself wholly to the Lord of the worlds"* (2:131). Such Prophetic submission was a spirit or seed in Abraham, upon him be peace, and it has become a blessed tree in the Pride of Humankind, upon him be peace and blessings, and a table in the Community of Muhammad as the fruit of adherence to him. The Qur'an indicates this fact as follows: *If they still remonstrate with you, say (to them, O Messenger): "I have submitted my whole being to God, and so have those who follow me"* (3:20).

When the basic elements of sincere friendship penetrate the outer and inner senses and faculties of heroes of nearness to God, they save such people from partial thoughts about things and events, causing them to reach the horizon of unity in all their sensations, impressions, perceptions, considerations, logical or rational comments, and evaluations. These heroes are raised, each according to their own capacity, to a comprehensive observation of things with their reason, mind, senses, consciousness, hearts, and secrets, and this causes them to observe through the telescope of their outer and inner senses indescribable scenes, multifarious but one within the other, and bearing the stamp of the same One Maker.

Every traveler who advances along the way of sincere friendship views existence from the horizon of the Prophet Abraham, upon him be peace, and travels around the axis of his sainthood, which is embedded in Abraham's Prophethood. In proportion to their ability to develop the spirit of sincere friendship, they are aware of existence as a whole, which they perceived as fragmentary or compartmentalized before. They are able to observe the drops as an ocean in one piece, and as if looking on everything from a point above, they feel that all things are interconnected with one another, all voice the same meaning, point to the same truth, and say, "God is the One, Unique," in the language of order, good composition, and harmony, and all are enraptured with the universal testimony.

The view and perception of such travelers display manifestations of Divine Attributes of Glory, and they see all existence with the view of the All-Merciful. They are sincerely compatible with the whole of creation. They know every thing to be a part of themselves, they embrace all affectionately, sensing all things as a sibling, and referring the intentions, thoughts, convictions, and comments of others to the judgment of the All-Knowing of all the unseen. They call everyone to their embrace and to the truth, like Mawlana Jalalu'd-Din ar-Rumi, and they tolerate every improper behavior toward themselves. For they are God's faithful vicegerents traveling in the horizon of sincere friendship vast in proportion to the comprehensiveness of mercy, and they are mirrors of God's Attributes of Glory held up against all existence. They reflect the Divine Names in their acts and manners, and they observe all things through the different windows of their faculties. Like two eyes seeing the same thing, such travelers see all things as if a single entity but with different depths.

Sainthood marked with sincere friendship of God is the best of sainthood. It is true that there is no limit to nearness to God because of His being infinite, but every individual human being has a limit of perfectibility according to his or her capacity, which marks the boundary of every traveler who is endowed with knowledge of God. For this reason, even when a traveler reaches the seventh heaven through the sainthood of God's sincere friendship, this forms a limit for them. If there is a single exception to this, it is the position of the one, namely the Prophet Muhammad, who is distinguished by having all human virtues to the highest degree and *al-Maqam al-Mahmud*.[148] The All-Bounteous Lord of the worlds honored the Prophet Muhammad with extra favors, and he

[148] Having *al-Maqam al-Mahmud*, which belongs to the Prophet Muhammad, upon him be peace and blessings, and literally means the position or station of being praised, is being one specially praised by God and the whole body of the believers, by virtue of which he will be honored with permission to intercede on behalf of all the people on the Place of Supreme Gathering. Humankind, who will have been gathered on the Place of Supreme Gathering after the Resurrection, will be allowed to advance toward the other realms of the Hereafter through his intercession. (Tr.)

reached a point where space ends in infinity, the body is identical with the soul, and all secrets are manifest. It is a point that is impossible for even the angels or other spirits ever to reach.

God Almighty distinguished each Prophet with a particular virtue in which he excelled above the others. For example, the Prophet Adam, upon him be peace, was distinguished with the utmost purity and called the Pure One; the Prophet Noah, upon him be peace, was God's Confidant; the Prophet Abraham, upon him be peace, excelled others in sincere friendship; the Prophet Moses, upon him be peace, was one to whom God spoke in a particular way from behind a veil, and called the Addressee of God; and the Prophet Jesus, upon him be peace, was a Spirit breathed by God. The most distinguishing mark or virtue particular to our Master, the Prophet Muhammad, upon him be peace and blessings, is love—and the title, the Beloved of God, is particular to him.

During his Ascension, God's last and greatest Messenger, the Prophet Muhammad, upon him be peace and blessings, found each Prophet in relationship with God Almighty at the level of the heaven which symbolized his particular position among the Prophets. For example, he visited the Prophet Moses, upon him be peace, at the sixth level of heaven, and the Prophet Abraham, upon him be peace, at the seventh. He advanced further and further until he reached the highest tower of the pure spirit beings amidst the welcoming voices of angels. He arrived at the point described as, "two-bow-length's nearness, or even nearer," and he was honored with a special Revelation revealed with no words or speech. Through the lenses of his fully developed faculties, he observed all that is invisible, heard all that is inaudible, and knew all that is unknowable, to others. Going beyond the Garden or Paradise of Refuge and Dwelling, he reached the *Sidrat al-Muntaha*,[149] marking the highest point of rise for a created being.

---

149 *Sidrat al-Muntaha* signifies the boundary between the realms of Divinity and creation, which marks the highest point of any created being's rise and nearness to God. (Tr.)

Our Master, upon him be peace and blessings, left the way he followed open to those who would succeed him and follow that way in the shade of his sainthood. He was perfectly generous so that anyone who would follow him could benefit from the favors to come from God along his way.

It is by virtue of the Prophet Muhammad's mission that all saints can feel sincere friendship with God according to the capacity and rank of each; believers feel brother/sisterhood and loyal friendship with each other; and thanks be to God, those serving the Qur'an follow the way and style of the Prophet Abraham, which was developed by our master, upon him be peace and blessings. Bediüzzaman deems such brother/sisterhood that arises from sincere friendship to be indispensable to the service of the Qur'an and to being a good Muslim, and he regards it as a character of belonging to the *Milla* (way and nation) of Abraham, which is characterized by purity of intention and absolute devotion to God's Oneness. He says:

> Our way is the closest friendship. Friendship requires being the closest, most self-sacrificing friend, the most appreciative companion, and the most magnanimous brother or sister. The very basis of this form of friendship is heartfelt sincerity. One who destroys this sincerity falls from the pinnacle of friendship. They may possibly fall to the bottom of a very deep pit. They cannot find anything in between to cling on to.[150]

According to Bediüzzaman Said Nursi, this fall is destructive deviation and means straying from the right path.

> *O my God! Equip my soul with righteousness and piety and purify it. You are the Best in purifying it, and You are its Guardian and Master.*
>
> *And bestow the best of blessings and the most perfect of salutations and the most excellent peace upon the Start of the Prophethood and its Seal, and on his Family and Companions, all valuable and faithful.*

---

150 Bediüzzaman Said Nursi, *Lemalar* ("The Gleams"), The Twenty-First Gleam, The Fourth Principle. (Tr.)

INDEX

A

B

C

D

E

F

G

I

J

Q

R

S

T

U

V

W

Y

Z